YUM

·······························

*plant-based recipes for
a gluten-free diet*

THERESA NICASSIO PhD

**SIMPLE RECIPES THE WHOLE
FAMILY WILL ENJOY**

"With her YUM 'philosophy' and accompanying recipes, Dr. Theresa Nicassio makes me think of the beautiful and bountiful way of life in Southern Italy, with its emphasis on food, family—and also fun. Her psychological background brings a much-needed dimension to the discussion of special diets and the role that food plays in the total picture that makes up our health."

ALESSIO FASANO MD, Director, Center for Celiac Research and Treatment, Massachusetts General Hospital, and author of *Gluten Freedom*

"Theresa Nicassio gives healthy eating the look and taste a gourmet cook would love. Armed with the recipes in this book, you'll find yourself head over heels in recipes that pack a nutritional punch as well as a hefty dose of deliciousness. Eating a low-fat, vegan diet is the best way to promote health, and Theresa has embraced this in her YUM philosophy. Pairing wholesome plant-based foods with her recipe-making talents, these easy-to-make meals will leave you feeling better than ever."

NEAL BARNARD MD, President of the Physicians Committee for Responsible Medicine, Adjunct Associate Professor at George Washington University School of Medicine and Health Sciences, and author of *Power Foods for the Brain* and *Dr. Neal Barnard's Program for Reversing Diabetes*

"Nicassio's *YUM* is a food lover's book for even the reluctant foodie. Her own journey to good health through food is chronicled throughout, drawing the reader in, as if holding her hand, to join her in a responsibly hedonistic relationship with food. Her encyclopedia of ingredients is one I know I'll refer to again and again and her recipes are irresistible. The photos are stunning, and as inviting as the text is ebullient. Nicassio somehow manages to infuse her sunny perspective on life into the soul of this book, thus inspiring the reader—no matter their dietary restriction—to press on and find joy in food again."

JULES SHEPARD, Founder of gfJules™ Gluten Free Flour and Baking Mixes and author of *Free for All Cooking, The First Year: Celiac Disease and Living Gluten-Free* and *Nearly Normal Cooking for Gluten-Free Eating*

"*YUM: plant-based recipes for a gluten-free diet* is a yummy read for anyone interested in adding more delicious, health-promoting plant foods to their diet. Author Theresa Nicassio has a wealth of information and shares it in a book that is beautiful to look at, easy to read and fun to use."

CHERIE SORIA, Founder and Director of the Living Light Culinary Institute and author of many books including *Angel Foods: Healthy Recipes for Heavenly Bodies* and *The Raw Food Revolution Diet*

"Just holding and looking at this fabulous book makes me want to eat every one of the recipes. Not just eat but prepare myself. So many new and innovative ingredients make the book stand out of the crowd of the usual fare. I have found Dr. Theresa's *YUM* creations feed well the body and the heart."

SAUL PILAR MD, Integrative Physician, Connect Health Centre for Integrative Medicine

"Delicious, nutritious and fun! My whole family loved preparing, admiring and eating these culinary delights."

DAVID R. BOYD PHD, environmental lawyer and author of *The Optimistic Environmentalist* and *Dodging the Toxic Bullet*

"Congratulations to Theresa Nicassio PhD for putting together such a well researched, well organized and easy-to-use cookbook. *YUM* is sure to encourage many people to try a gluten free diet—this book showcases such a plentiful and incredible variety of delicious food.

"*YUM* is a masterpiece in several ways. It is beautiful to look at and the photography brings the colours, textures and shapes of the foods and meals into a vibrant living experience. It reminds us that healthy foods are the art of nature. It is a masterpiece of healthy food combining, which will help those with gut problems and food sensitivities to not feel as deprived. It has cleverly excluded foods that are toxic or promote inflammation and replaced them with healing and delicious foods.

"Hippocrates taught doctors that good health begins in the digestive tract and that food should be our medicine. This beautiful recipe book embraces those eternal principles in a modern and exciting way. To feel well and energetic and to have a clear and happy mind, we need a healthy gut and liver. The gut-brain connection is huge. The gut-immune connection is just as huge.

"I highly recommend this book to everyone who loves eating living, healthful foods and especially those who love to cook."

SANDRA CABOT MD, author of the award-winning *The Liver Cleansing Diet* (www.liverdoctor.com)

"I love the hope-filled, joyful, luxurious approach that *YUM* brings to gluten-free, plant-based eating. Thank you, Theresa, for helping set people free from the 'tyranny of shoulds' with this delightful guide to delicious living."

SUSAN BIALI MD, wellness expert, *Psychology Today* blogger and author of *Live a Life You Love*

"Theresa has joyfully and elegantly presented a YUM Living philosophy of food that encompasses core values that are essential to healing and optimal wellness: mindful eating, self-compassion, non-judgement, personal empowerment, community and play! Her recipes are delicious and celebrate the beauty and intelligence of the plant world—each dish will 'speak to your DNA' with key information to turn on health promoting genes through 'nutrigenomics,' so that you can enjoy brilliant health and have fun while you're at it!"

DEVON CHRISTIE MD, CCFP, Functional Medicine Practitioner, Connect Health Centre for Integrative Medicine

"Besides making me wish I was Italian, Theresa represents love in action. Many talk the talk, but she's the real deal—her recipes are full of her generosity and spirit as well as deliciousness!"

SHARON HANNA, author of *The Book of Kale* and *The Book of Kale & Friends*

"Theresa's vision to make healthy food taste delicious inspires us to bring the JOY back to healthy eating and is a wonderful resource for patients who have celiac disease or multiple food sensitivities. Absolutely love this!"

JILL CARNAHAN MD, ABFM, ABIHM, IFMCP, Medical Director, functional medical expert at Flatiron Functional Medicine

"*YUM* is an exciting passport to a more vibrant and delicious life. A planet-friendly, palate-stimulating collection of plant-based culinary adventures, the pages ooze with amazing recipes, tantalizing photography and love."

SYNTE PEACOCK PHD, environmental scientist and author of *Earth on the Edge*

"It is time someone put together this awesome book of gluten-free recipes, healthy eating ideas and photographs to show the adventure of food. The photographs are masterpieces. You can just about eat the fruit and vegetables right off the page! Give me a spoon and I will have some of that ice-cream! The colours of the photographs are a delight and tantalizing to the tastebuds. I will certainly recommend this awesome book to my friends, family and business associates. It is a keeper."

MARGRIET DOGTEROM PHD, author of *Pollination with Mason Bees* and owner of Beediverse

"*YUM* is as eloquently written and informative as it is accessible. Enjoy this book in the kitchen or brew up a chai latte and take it in on the couch. *YUM* will be your friendly exploration guide to a myriad of wonderful tastes and healthy living we can all attain."

RUSH DHILLON PHD, Biomolecular Chemistry, University of Wisconsin

"Theresa came into my life like a splash of sunshine. Her glowing energy and desire to help others overwhelmed me as she intuitively understood what was needed by those around her. This book is a perfect example of that natural talent. It provides balanced, nutritious yet delicious recipes that can be prepared in any home. Theresa knew what was needed and has put her heart and soul into its creative, beautiful delivery. I'm sure you (and your tastebuds) will enjoy her work as much as I do."

KISANE APPLEBY (AKA ZANE), international raw food chef, author, holistic health educator and yogi (www.RealisticallyRawYou.com)

"I'm impressed with Theresa Nicassio's paradigm-shifting gift to the gluten-free world. If you are a foodie, a health enthusiast or simply looking to make a positive change in your life, *YUM* is that foundational text that arms you with all the resources, motivation and inspiration you will need to transform your life. Packed with recipes, complemented by stunning photography, you will never feel deprived when you indulge in the beautiful and nourishing meals that Theresa shares. If you feel like there's a better you waiting inside, the recipes in *YUM* can unleash the inner greatness."

VINNETTE THOMPSON, Executive Chef of the Raw Food Underground and Living Light Culinary Arts Gourmet Instructor

D&D
PUBLISHING

D&D Publishing

Vancouver, BC, Canada

Cataloguing data available from Library and Archives Canada

ISBN 978-0-9939156-0-4

COVER DESIGN: Bill Chung
INTERIOR DESIGN: Mauve Pagé
COPY EDITOR: Kilmeny Jane Denny
AUTHOR COVER PHOTOS: Alejandra Aguirre
FOOD COVER PHOTOS: Theresa Nicassio

Printed in China

DISCLAIMER

This book is designed as a resource and inspirational recipe book, made available to readers with the understanding that the author and publisher are not offering any professional or medical advice specific to any individual's needs or situations. The information provided is in no way a substitute for professional counsel, advice or treatment by a licensed healthcare professional.

Because some ingredients and other products may interact with certain health conditions or medications, or may result in allergic or other reactions, always check with your professional healthcare provider before incorporating new foods into your diet. If you have any known health conditions, you are advised to have your health monitored regularly by competent professionals who are familiar with your needs.

The author and publisher are not liable for any loss, injury or damage that might arise from using the information contained in this book or for any information that is not included in its pages or scope.

Please note that products and companies mentioned in this book are personal preferences of the author. Readers may have different products and companies that they prefer.

YUM is dedicated to my dad, who loved delicious food but didn't know how to let it be his medicine. My love for him lives in every page of this book, and I hope to help others like him enjoy a longer, easier and more pleasurable life while on this magnificent planet.

CONTENTS

THE PSYCHOLOGY OF EATING
THE CHALLENGE OF LIVING WITH DIETARY LIMITATIONS

EATING CONNECTS US. IT CONNECTS US WITH the food that we invite into our bodies. It connects us with the earth, plants, animals and the sky from which it is made. It also connects us with each other and, ultimately, connects us to ourselves. Whether we are aware of it or not, at a very primitive and even spiritual level, eating connects us with all that is, all that was and all that will ever be. Eating is a very big deal when we think about it.

Through understanding our relationship with food and the magnitude of its importance, we can increase our capacity for compassion when challenges arise concerning food, eating and weight. This need for heartfelt understanding when it comes to our relationship with food and our own bodies is something I have encountered frequently in my years as a practicing psychologist. In addition, when dietary challenges present themselves—whether it's diabetes, heart disease, cancer, obesity, lactose intolerance, celiac disease or other autoimmune problems, allergies, autism or attention deficit disorder (ADD)—there is invariably a sense of sadness and fear. These feelings can be directly linked to the forced changes to our familiar relationships with food itself, as well as the associated relationships with others and with ourselves. It is this level of consciousness I'd like to welcome to the table.

While it's important to know, learning that certain foods disagree with our unique physiology for any reason can be difficult news to accept. Such news challenges us to change our daily ways of living and to alter habits that we typically don't really want to change. What makes such information even more difficult to receive is that it also involves loss.

Whenever we are confronted with a loss of any sort in our lives, large or small, our understanding of the world and our place in it changes. We then have to figure out how to carry on living with new parameters that we're not happy about. We can resist the reality of the loss, we can get angry, we can get depressed, we can act out... we can do a lot of things. Ultimately, we also have an opportunity to surrender to the loss and accept the reality of change.

In the early moments of loss, our world can feel smaller, darker and lonelier. However, with an open mind, time and persistence, creative solutions for living can lighten the darkness. The tyranny of "shoulds" is replaced with excitement and with delicious possibilities that never would have been discovered had dietary limitations not been revealed. As you will discover, *YUM* is not just about recipes; it is also about empowerment and embracing life in an exciting new way. In *The YUM Story*, I share some of my personal journey of living with food limitations so you'll know you're not alone if you have found yourself facing similar challenges. I also want to share with you my joy and excitement at discovering the skills to live a richer, easier and more sustainable life.

Defying traditional beliefs about which ingredients are necessary to make food taste good, I invite you into a new paradigm of delicious living, where you can feel reconnected with the life-force and nourishment that food has to offer, along with all of the goodness of the sensual, social and emotional pleasures that can go with it.

Bon Appétit!
♥ Theresa

YUM LIVING

YUM LIVING IS A WAY OF LIFE. SIMPLY PUT, IT is about relishing the pleasures of daily living while nourishing our bodies and our lives at the same time. The philosophy of YUM Living is "responsible hedonism," a lifestyle reminiscent of the ethical hedonism espoused by the Greek philosopher Aristippus of Cyrene more than 2,000 years ago. Life is to be celebrated and cherished; to this end, responsiveness to others and service to the planet are as important as pleasure-seeking for one's self. So, while delicious and simple-to-prepare recipes are an important part of the YUM Living experience, they are just one means of enabling a joyful, mindful and respectful way of living.

In common with other species, we all share the need for food in order to survive. We also love pleasure and prefer to avoid pain and discomfort. Ideally, we desire all of these things with as little effort as possible!

YUM accepts, embraces and honours these inherent elements of human nature. Like Taoism, it acknowledges life as it is, instead of rejecting, judging or trying to control it (efforts that are typically futile and not sustainable anyway).

YUM Living invites us to enjoy the pleasures of living mindfully and to discover remarkable possibilities for deepening and transforming our daily existence.

YUM LIVING GENERAL PRINCIPLES

1. **INCLUSION AND COMMUNITY** Because YUM is about inclusivity, acceptance and love, anyone and everyone can be a part of the YUM Living community, regardless of what food you do or don't eat:
   » vegetarian/vegan (or not)
   » gluten-free (or not)
   » refined sugar-free (or not)
   » junk food (or not)
   » raw (or not)

2. **NO PERFECTIONISM** Because it separates us from ourselves, others and the natural way of the world, perfectionism is not part of YUM Living.

3. **NO "SHOULDS"** Expectations and judgements are not welcome, because they rob us of the experience of gratitude and joy.

4. **REAL FOOD CAN BE DELICIOUS** YUM rejects the belief that food needs to be unhealthy or difficult to prepare in order to be delicious.

5. **PERSONAL POWER IS CELEBRATED** YUM is about celebrating our personal power, creativity and uniqueness, leaving no room for self-flagellation, victimhood, guilt or shame.

6. **FREEDOM AND RESPONSIBILITY** YUM Living acknowledges and embraces the personal freedom we each possess, as well as the responsibility that is inherently linked with that freedom. Choices we make in our daily lives have an impact on others and on the environment that surrounds and serves us.

7. **PLANT-BASED FOOD IS LIFE-GIVING AND BEAUTIFUL** YUM Living is about increasing our plant-based food intake because we want to, knowing that our bodies like it and because it feels good to do something meaningful in the service of other beings and the planet itself.

8. **LIVE OUTSIDE THE BOX (IF THAT'S WHERE YOU FEEL AT HOME)** YUM Living is about unabashedly living freely and fully as the quirky being that you are. You can hug trees, sing with the birds, talk with the squirrels or do whatever your spirit moves you to do—all in celebration of the privilege of living.

9. **PLAY** Having fun is a core reward of YUM Living in and out of the kitchen. Go ahead: drink of the sweetness that touches your life. Life is here to be lived, so eat, love and live it fully—every delicious step of the way!

THE YUM STORY
HOW LIVING DELICIOUSLY CAN BECOME A WAY OF LIFE

WHO WOULD HAVE THOUGHT THAT AT AGE 50 I would be a chef writing a cookbook? Certainly not me! I started out as an animal-loving, artsy kid who loved to study math and science, and who grew up to become a psychologist, wife and mother. Working, raising my family, dabbling in the garden, dancing and doing crafts... I didn't have time to bother with cooking. Actually, I still don't, and that's precisely why I had to write this book! Once you read my story, you'll understand how *YUM* came to be.

In 1995, I married my long-time, beloved friend, Eric Mazzi. Together we were moving along in life with our dog and three cats, just like so many others. Then something unexpected happened that profoundly changed the trajectory of my life: I got pregnant! It wasn't that the pregnancy was unexpected—it had been planned for and hoped for, and was a wonderful blessing. What was unexpected were the consequences of my pregnancy: physical debilitation and a cascade of health problems that lasted for more than a decade after our daughter Alex's birth in 1997.

What the heck! I say this jokingly now, but—believe me—it was no joke. In fact, it was downright terrifying at times. My immune and respiratory systems began to fail, neurological problems and chronic pain reduced my mobility and general functioning, and my life became a battle against perpetual infection, inflammation, fatigue, weight gain and an endless list of food and environmental sensitivities. Medical appointments and visits to the hospital became a major focus of my existence, but all the while, I was still trying to be a good mom and contributing member of society in my professional capacity.

I knew this was not how I wanted to spend the rest of my life, but no matter how hard I tried, my condition only worsened. If it hadn't been for my meditation practice, my rebellious spirit of hope, my loving partner, our beautiful children and the gift of meaningful work, I don't know how I could have survived and functioned as well as I did.

My belief in the body's natural tendency and desire to heal itself was activated during this time and was a great blessing. A fire in my gut propelled me to fight against my condition; it felt like a force more powerful than I could have mustered alone, and I embraced it. I chose to fight for a cause. I chose to say "Yes" to life in all its forms and advocate for it, starting with the little world I was in—first my body, then my family, and then beyond.

This spirit resides in all of us, and I have been privileged to witness it on a regular basis in my work as a psychologist. However, I was still in awe—how could this spirit carry me through such difficult times, times of unrelenting pain, fatigue and weakness? Wow.

Somehow I was given the courage and tenacity to search for a way to transform myself and to emerge from this suffering. You name the treatment (even unmentionable ones I would never wish on anyone), I probably tried it! Most treatments, whether conventional or alternative, resulted in minimal or no benefit at best, and not-so-attractive side effects at worst. I'd enthusiastically complied with countless caring and competent professionals' advice, yet my health didn't improve and the chronic conditions and negative effects of some of my medications continued to worsen. I knew that something needed to change, but what? It was just one big mystery. I had met my Baba Yaga in a big way!

At a certain point, I realized that it was *I* who had to be the agent of change. The well-intentioned medical professionals at the time were unable to help, so I had to take responsibility for learning about my body

in a whole new way. While I didn't know where to start, my lifelong love of science became my best ally. It was time to pull out all the stops and become my own case study. I took every conventional and alternative course about health and healing that I could, and became immersed in a journey of discovery that has changed my world forever.

While in the midst of all this research and experimentation, I reconnected with my former colleague and friend from the University of British Columbia, Dr. Hal Gunn. Hal and I had shared a passion for honouring the mind-body-spirit connection and a belief in the body's innate capacity to heal itself. He had followed his dream as a physician by co-founding an innovative holistic and integrative cancer treatment centre in Vancouver, Inspire Health, with Dr. Roger Rodgers in 1997. During our visit, Hal gave me Inspire Health's comprehensive, research-based information package that contained resources to empower their patients living with cancer. One of the things that stood out most for me, as I later perused the centre's materials, was the section about foods that help to fight cancer. This excited me and launched my curiosity about how food could be used as medicine—and how healthy organic food, from naturally enriched soil, as fresh as

possible (ideally grown at or near your own home) can be even better medicine.

Another great discovery I made was the work of Functional Medicine pioneers who spoke about how the wrong food for an individual can result in an inner world of toxicity. I learned more about the role of environmental and food allergies and cross-allergens, as well as how food sensitivities contribute to inflammation. Reading and employing Dr. Natasha Turner's book, *The Hormone Diet*, was a pivotal point in my journey. Her book opened my eyes to the barrage of toxins I had been exposed to—in food, air and water—and how hard my body had been working to cope with these assaults. Natasha's book also introduced me to a simple elimination program to identify food sensitivities. Through this process, I discovered that when I completely eliminated gluten from my diet, the migraine headaches (from which I'd suffered all my life) disappeared. And the pain that filled every part of my body also lessened—all in less than a month! Holy cow—was that really possible? After all the treatments I had tried, this was the first clear improvement that I experienced. It did not resolve all of my symptoms by any stretch, but it made a significant dent.

Okay, I was hooked.

Also in 2010, Alex—then 12 years old—saw Alicia Silverstone (actor and author of *The Kind Diet*) on *The Oprah Winfrey Show*, talking about how farm animals are treated. After watching that program, Alex became a vegan in less than a week. Boom! How we ate as a family took another dramatic turn overnight.

Then there was the 2011 release of Dr. William Davis's *Wheat Belly*, a book that rocked the world. In it, Davis blew the whistle on wheat and demonstrated the connection between wheat and heart disease, diabetes, celiac disease, weight gain, the aging process and a host of neurological problems. Both Dr. David Perlmutter's in his book *Grain Brain* and Dr. Alessio Fasano in his book *Gluten Freedom* have subsequently brought more research findings about gluten and its potential health implications to light. For the first time since Drs. Colin and Thomas Campbell's 2005 book, *The China Study*, which linked diet with chronic illness and mortality, the public was whacked in the gut in a way that could no longer be ignored.

In an effort to care for the needs of all our family members, Alex and I started trying a huge range of plant-based, gluten-free and sugar-free foods in 2010. But we had a problem: most of them tasted terrible to us. So we started to read every recipe book we could get our hands on, as well as countless recipes from the internet, with only a few successes. We were able to find some products and recipes that were either vegan or gluten-free that we liked, but rarely any that were both. Those we did try were often filled with refined sugar, margarine and other ingredients that we prefer to avoid. After a year of major frustration, we realized that we had to create our own recipes if we wanted to enjoy food that met our standards for health and taste.

Ever so slowly, we were able to come up with delicious meals that reflected the high quality flavour, texture and appearance that we sought—and were also easy and quick to make, given our busy lives. Through the process of trial and error, we stumbled into food science, learning about ingredients that were new to us and dove headfirst into the amazing world of food behaviour. It was like being in the garage with my car completely dismantled, with pieces missing and no manual for how to rebuild it. I had to be creative to get it up and running again. To do this, I had to be willing to use new and unfamiliar tools.

The following year, three positive and supportive influences helped move our process forward. The first was the discovery of Connect Health Centre for Integrative and Functional Medicine in Vancouver, where I met nutritionist Haely Lindau (Haely's Hints). The second was Lovena Galyide and her Indigo Raw Food Café, also in Vancouver. The third important influence was Kris Carr (best-selling author of *Crazy Sexy Diet* and co-author with Chef Chad Sarno of *Crazy Sexy Kitchen*). All of these beautiful people demonstrated the possibility of delicious food while living with dietary restrictions and health challenges. By their example, we were energized and excited to continue our quest to create delicious, healthy recipes that were respectful of our bodies' unique needs and preferences. We felt propelled to accomplish all this,

despite the fact that we had no formal culinary or food science training or any clue about how to actually do it! We could choose to surrender to defeat or enthusiastically persist, with the belief that we could conquer this challenge. We chose the second option and are oh-so-glad we did.

It was amazing. When Alex and I decided to sink our teeth (so to speak) into taking on this challenge, it was impossible to stop us. Despite many culinary failures along the way, we were super excited when we had finally developed enough recipes to be able to once again invite friends over for meals—unapologetically. Yeah!

Then in 2013, Alex and I decided to go to the Living Light International Culinary Institute in California to learn even more. That year we became Associate Raw Food Chefs and Instructors. I went back in 2014 to complete the Gourmet Raw Food Chef program, and then later that same year, Alex and I returned for the Advanced Raw Food Nutrition Educator Certification program.

We've now become a resource for others, sharing our recipes with friends who have similar dietary challenges. We are not alone; it was mind-blowing to learn

how many folks live with food limitations! Along the way, I had started to photograph the dishes we created and type up the ingredients so that we could pass what we had made along to others. A special pleasure for me was creating and photographing the dishes I had made using fruits and vegetables from our organic garden. Taking pictures of the micro-world of nature and the beautiful creatures with whom we share our own garden was an added delight. That's how this book was born.

Knowing how many different opinions there are out there about food (such a controversial subject!) and having personally struggled with these conflicting messages, I really understand what a turn-off diet books can be. So I want to be clear: while this collection of recipes has been designed to be super-healthy, incorporating as much of the scientifically understood information about food-as-medicine as I could, this is *not* a diet book and it doesn't suggest any meal plans. Instead, *YUM* is about a change in attitude that involves creating an expanded world of possibilities that are outside conventional beliefs and practices.

Most people are tired of hearing about what they "need to," "ought to," "have to," or "should" be eating—or what they should be feeding their kids—because of health problems. I have found that such pressure not only results in very little sustainable behaviour change, but all too often also results in undue stress and guilt that serves no one. I want you to be able to shed any despair, frustration or self-blame, so that you are less likely to give up if you don't feel able to resist eating food that you know may be harmful to your body. When grace and love are invited in, shame and hopelessness fade. When this happens, like a seed inspired to sprout and thrive, you'll find yourself better able to make life-enhancing choices, almost effortlessly.

As a psychologist, I have absolutely no interest or desire in colluding with potentially harmful ways of thinking. Instead, I've created the recipes in this collection so that you can have fun eating what you want to eat, regardless of your dietary restrictions and preferences, with simple and often very fast recipes. Easy, healthy and delicious is a really great combination!

My passion runs deep, both personally and as a professional who has practiced psychotherapy for almost 30 years. So, while writing a cookbook is the last thing I ever imagined I might be doing, it is clearly what I have been called to do. And while an unlikely vehicle for my life path, this philosophically grounded project indisputably resonates with my heartfelt commitment to do what I can to help others suffer less.

This is a world I know extremely well: it was the inspirational guiding force that gave me the tenacity to develop this extensive collection of recipes. For years, I saw my beloved dad struggling with diabetes, heart disease, kidney failure and the associated circulation issues and neuropathy. Witnessing his struggles around food, which only worsened in his last years of life, was heart-wrenching. I'll never forget how he couldn't stop himself from eating the delicious cake at his granddaughter's birthday party, just days before the first of four amputation surgeries on both his legs. He died one year later, after living with unbearable pain every moment of that year.

I want to help prevent you and countless others from having to live through such agony, and at the same time make it possible for everyone to enjoy the pleasure of sharing celebrations with loved ones—including being able to savour every bite of delectable cake at your granddaughter's birthday, or graduation, or wedding. With the alarming increase in the rates of obesity and diabetes (especially for our youth), my longing to help turn the boat around couldn't be stronger. The great news is that delicious food doesn't have to wreak havoc on our bodies—it's time to shed that outmoded belief.

Go ahead, call me crazy, because I am—crazy about life, crazy about love and now, more than ever, crazy about delicious and non-toxic food that nourishes instead of harms my body and the planet. It hasn't been easy, but it fills my heart with indescribable joy to be able to transform my struggle and frustration into an opportunity to create something worthwhile for others, something that might help bring to your life, and the lives of others, a little more ease.

YUMMY PEOPLE

HAELY'S HINTS, BEV'S BITS AND BEE BITES

I'm very grateful to Nutritionist Haely Lindau, MSc, and Registered Dietitian Joanne Beverley Edwards-Miller, BASc, who contributed valuable nutritional information for this project. "Haely's Hints" and "Bev's Bits" help you understand some of the positive benefits and fun facts about many of the ingredients used in *YUM*. Their nutritional "food bites" can be found interspersed throughout the recipes.

HAELY LINDAU, MSc, NUTRITIONIST

Haely received her Masters of Nutritional Science from Hawthorne University. She is passionate about food and the great health benefits it provides. She not only works as a nutritionist in Vancouver, but has also recently launched her own healthy food company called Fresh Now (www.eatfreshnow.ca). Haely's approach of adding delicious, healthy food to her clients' diets has proven successful time and time again. She has a gentle, compassionate attitude and her love of great food and cooking is obvious and inspirational.

JOANNE BEVERLEY EDWARDS-MILLER, BASc, REGISTERED DIETITIAN

Bev received her Bachelor of Applied Science degree in Food and Nutrition from Ryerson University, with a Minor in Family Supports and Community Practice. More recently, Bev became an Associate Raw Food Chef and Instructor, certified by Living Light Culinary Arts Institute, and she is a Food for Life Instructor through the Physicians Committee for Responsible Medicine. She loves sharing with people the culinary delights and tremendous health benefits of plant-powered eating. Her blog can be found at www.theveggielicious dietitian.blogspot.ca.

BEES

Sprinkled throughout these pages, you will find photos and interesting tidbits of information I've picked up about these sweet little pollinators who make our lives possible. In many ways, they are the true superheroes of *YUM*: without bees to pollinate the blossoms, our fruit and vegetables would not come to fruition. They are crucial for the food chain.

TEST KITCHENS

At an earlier stage of this project, about 20 independent test kitchens in Canada and the US volunteered to test a sampling of the recipes from this collection and to provide feedback about their experiences. I took all this feedback very seriously, and it had a direct impact on how this book developed. Test kitchen feedback also made me determined to ensure that every recipe met my "12-year-old test"—so easy that a 12-year old (or the 12-year-old within) could succeed in creating the dishes, with minimal or no adult supervision.

MY FAMILY

A special feature of *YUM* is the hands-on involvement of my two beautiful daughters, Alex and Angeline, and my husband, Eric, in developing recipes for the whole family to enjoy. You'll discover just how much they've contributed as you read through the book. They have been a huge driving force behind the recipes' creation in countless ways.

ALEX NICASSIO, CAD (CERTIFIED AWESOME DAUGHTER)

Alex was my co-conspirator in the kitchen, helping with the creation of many of the recipes you'll find in these pages. Together, we became Raw Food Chefs and Raw Food Nutrition Educators—an amazing mother-daughter experience. A vegan since the age of 12, Alex has been an inspiration and teacher about the benefits of eating more plant-based food. Alex launched her blog, Cupcakes and Kale xoxo (www.cupcakesandkalexoxo.com), featuring delicious plant-based gluten-free recipes, when she was 17.

ANGELINE NICASSIO, CAD (CERTIFIED AWESOME DAUGHTER)

Angeline, 12 at the time of this writing, has been a cheerleader extraordinaire, offering honest feedback about the recipes from a kid's perspective. She knows what she likes and what she doesn't like, and makes no bones about it. Her input has been invaluable. Angeline was also my righthand helper and playmate in the garden. Her infectious laughter and excitement about learning how to garden, cook and create new recipes of her own brought unexpected surprises onto our table and into our home.

ERIC MAZZI PhD, RESOURCE AND ENVIRONMENTAL POLICY, AND MS, MECHANICAL ENGINEERING

An incredible father, husband and environmental scientist, Eric is also the ultimate one-pot cook. He says that this is so because he can't handle complexity, but everyone who knows his professional work knows that he is *all* about complexity and making it understandable! Over the years, Eric and I have had fun putting our minds together to co-create special recipes that can be made in a single pot or pan. His chili recipe has become a favourite in our home and community—he can whip it up in no time. Eric is also blessed and cursed to be my favourite taste-tester. He had no idea what he was getting into when I started this project! Eric is unbelievably patient, has been my beacon in the darkest of days and will always be a superstar in my heart.

PHOTOGRAPHY

AUTHOR & LIFESTYLE PHOTOGRAPHY

All of the author and most of the lifestyle photos in *YUM* were taken by my dear friend Alejandra Aguirre (www.photoali.com). Ali has been photographing people for 28 years. She has a passion and zest for life and a heartfelt interest in delicious healthy food, fitness and vibrant living.

FOOD & GARDEN PHOTOGRAPHY

All of the food photos in *YUM* were staged and shot by me in our own kitchen and garden after I had prepared the recipes. I also had the pleasure of communing with the beauty and wildlife in my garden, where the garden images were generously offered to me to share with you as part of *YUM*. Many of the produce photos were taken at the Mendocino Farmers' Market in California and at the Granville Island Market in Vancouver, BC.

USING THIS BOOK
HOW TO TRANSITION TO A DELICIOUS NEW WAY OF EATING

WELCOME TO THE WORLD OF YUM LIVING!
In the following pages you will be introduced to recipes, ingredients and tools that are new to you. This is one of the unique elements of *YUM*: no more doing the "same old, same old." YUM Living is a perspective shift, not a diet or edict of any sort. It is about living fully and embracing change—in the easiest and most pleasurable way possible!

As creatures of habit, we find change difficult. The truth is that few things we do are as habit-driven as food preparation routines and eating. Mindful eating alone requires disciplined practice, and then there's the challenge of preparing new dishes, sometimes using unfamiliar tools or ingredients.

If you are wanting to transition towards eating healthier food, *please* be patient with yourself. Ease in slowly and let the process be a fun evolution. YUM Living is about expanding your world of possibilities, not about obsessing over your restrictions or challenges (food or otherwise). There is no need to overhaul everything all at once! With *YUM: plant-based recipes for a gluten-free diet* as your resource, you will be equipped with everything you need for this new chapter of your unique health journey.

8 SIMPLE TIPS FOR EASING INTO DIETARY CHANGES

Here are some simple tips to help make your transition to YUM Living a stress-free, joyful adventure of discovery.

1. **FOCUS ON ADDING NEW COOL DISHES TO YOUR LIFE, RATHER THAN FEELING PRESSURED TO CLEAR OUT YOUR PANTRY AND REFRIGERATOR ALL AT ONCE** This is not one of those extreme makeover TV shows—this is simply your life in real time. As you gradually bring healthier ingredients into your kitchen and use up those that are less so, the transition will be easier on you *and* your bank account. Without too much effort, your home will soon be filled with more delicious and life-giving foods than you ever could have imagined. *YUM* gives you the knowledge of how to use these beautiful ingredients, and you may slowly notice changes in how your body feels and functions.

2. **ENJOY THE JOURNEY OF LEARNING ONE RECIPE AT A TIME** This is not a race: each new, healthy recipe that you love and feel confident creating is an empowering step. Every time you prepare that dish for yourself or others, you are gradually crowding out less healthy options and filling the cup of your life with more delicious food. One by one, learn, savour and master new recipes—it's much more fun and less stressful to play instead of work. Setting lofty goals is usually unrealistic anyway! Why work at it when you don't have to?

3. **START WITH RECIPES THAT USE INGREDIENTS AND TOOLS YOU ARE FAMILIAR WITH AND ALREADY HAVE ON HAND** Before venturing into completely new territories, experiment with recipes that are more familiar to you. This will give you the opportunity to build your confidence and will also fuel your excitement to explore new culinary landscapes when you feel ready.

4. **DISCOVER, AND THEN STICK WITH, WHAT YOU LOVE** You will like some dishes that you try more than others. That's great! Discover what appeals to your palate and your lifestyle and make those dishes. Forget the others and move on. Life is too short to fret about the small stuff. We all have different preferences. Just as in other areas of life, try new things, learn what works for you and then do more of that, letting go of the rest. This is all about the

pleasure principle. Remember, "shoulds" are no longer welcome guests at the table (or anywhere else, for that matter)!

5. **KEEP COSTS LOW** Some of the new ingredients can be extremely expensive in specialty food stores. When trying a new recipe requiring such ingredients for the first time, buy only a small quantity first, just to make sure that you like the recipe. Once you know that something is to your taste, you can begin to buy special products more affordably.

Ingredients like raw organic shredded coconut, nuts and seeds are available at a fraction of the cost when bought online, in bulk or through community co-ops or wholesale food clubs. If you let your friends know that you want to make an order, you can save money by buying larger quantities of products with them, as well as possibly saving on shipping costs. Farmers' markets are wonderful for a number of reasons, and also often offer ingredients at a lower price than in natural food stores. Ethnic markets often carry specialty items that are otherwise difficult to find in your neighbourhood, sometimes at very reasonable prices. These markets are where I first found unusual sea vegetables like agar agar, as well as certain types of gluten-free flour. You never know what gems you'll find in those little stores!

To make it easier for you to keep costs down, my website (www.yumfoodforliving.com) has an updated list of resources where you can buy ingredients and tools. Be sure to keep me posted by email (info@yumfoodforliving.com), message me on Facebook (AuthorTheresaNicassio) or comment on my blog about any additional great resources for ingredients you discover! Your feedback will help keep the list as comprehensive as possible for everyone in the YUM community.

6. **MAKE SUBSTITUTIONS TO SUIT YOUR PERSONAL PREFERENCES AND NEEDS** In many of the recipes, I've recommended ingredient substitutions and have made some ingredients optional. Please refer to the *Special Diet & Allergy Chart* on page 344 if you have food sensitivities or are on a special diet. This

table has been designed to make it easier to locate *YUM* recipes that are more likely to work for your unique dietary needs.

Feel free to experiment with omissions and substitutions based on your personal needs and those ingredients available to you; see what works, compensating for the adjustments as needed. The recommendations I've made are a mere sampling of possible alternatives you can try, plant-based or not.

7. **CONSULT WITH YOUR HEALTHCARE PROVIDER BEFORE MAKING ANY DIETARY OR LIFESTYLE CHANGES** YUM Living is an empowering and pleasurable philosophy and way of life. It is not a replacement

for treatment by a qualified health professional or health team. Every person's body is different and health requirements vary, sometimes in unexpected ways—it's called "bio-individuality." General nutrition information about foods is just that—general. Be sure to consult your family doctor or preferred healthcare provider before making any changes to your diet or lifestyle, especially if you have any health vulnerabilities or conditions.

8. **CONSIDER STARTING A JOURNAL TO RECORD YOUR MENTAL, EMOTIONAL AND PHYSICAL EXPERIENCES AS YOU TRAVEL ON YOUR YUM LIVING JOURNEY** At the beginning, have a check-up with your healthcare professional to get current information about and recommendations for your unique health needs, and include this in your journal. Separately, list your symptoms and any treatments you have been receiving. Put this list aside in a safe place, without looking at it for perhaps six to 12 months. While *YUM* is not designed to be a diet plan or magic health bullet, I believe it is valuable to take stock from time to time of our experiences—especially when adventuring into new lifestyle lands. Doing this is both informative and empowering. It can also be helpful in your future decision-making about how to best serve your body. If you do decide to keep a journal, it is important to remember that this is for information gathering and observation purposes only, and is *not* a goal-setting exercise!

The YUM badge highlights some of *YUM*'s signature dishes.

YUM

FUNKY INGREDIENTS
"TOTO, I'VE A FEELING WE'RE NOT IN KANSAS ANYMORE"
(THE WIZARD OF OZ)

As you enter these pages, you're being invited down a rabbit hole of possibilities into a pleasurable new way of living. Fortunately, this new way of life is delicious in every imaginable way for your body, mind and soul. Choosing to live in a new way is a decision that involves making a mental shift and becoming open to the unfamiliar. From personal experience, I can tell you that once you've made that decision and have begun to experience the joy and ultimate ease of living in this new manner, you'll never want to turn back—I feel more alive at 50 than I did at 35!

YUM Living is an exploration of an alternate philosophy that supports a culinary universe that is very different from the traditional mainstream diet. Instead, *YUM* is about being at a funfair with exciting new rides and attractions, with some of your familiar favourites also thrown in! You'll be exploring new cooking methods and learning about ingredients you may never have heard of. Hang in there through the initial stages of feeling out of your comfort zone—because soon enough, you'll be free-sailing like a pro.

In this chapter I will provide you with an overview of a variety of less common ingredients, plus give you some useful information about everyday ingredients that you may not know. I invite you to think of this section kind of like a tour in an art gallery—stroll through and first focus on the elements that seem most attractive to you, knowing that you can return at any time to reference other items. You can bet that I didn't start to use all of these ingredients overnight! It has taken me *years* to build up this repertoire. The same may be the case for you.

Developing the healthiest, easy-to-prepare, gluten-free, plant-based delicious recipes possible meant discovering and using the most nutritious ingredients available and preparing them in the least toxic way. I am also a stickler for flavour-balancing. These factors, combined with my knowledge about foods that inhibit or combat a variety of health conditions, resulted in recipes that make eating fruits and vegetables a sheer pleasure.

This task required a lot of creativity and resourcefulness. Our home became an experimental laboratory! For example, every healthy, low-glycemic sweetener we could find was tried on its own and in combination with others. We also experimented with different omega-3 oils and those with higher smoke points, to see which tasted and worked the best for the different recipes. Because some of these special ingredients were so unusual (and sometimes could only be ordered online), I considered omitting them from the book, not wanting to intimidate or overwhelm readers. But doctors, friends and family all encouraged me to include them in *YUM* as a way of introducing and educating readers to new possibilities that offer significant benefits, especially for those living with particular health conditions.

EATING CLEAN

> "Ninety percent of the diseases known to man are caused by cheap foodstuffs. You are what you eat."

This phrase was coined by nutritionist Victor Lindlahr and was the title of his important 1940 book, *You Are What You Eat: How to Win and Keep Health with Diet*. With additives, chemicals and GM foods, eating clean is even more important today than it was all those decades ago.

WATER

Tap water can have a lot of undesirable substances and chemicals, which can vary greatly depending on

Many local farmers who grow produce free of pesticides and genetic modifications have not gone through the process of organic certification for financial reasons. What's most important to know about the food you are buying is how the farmers grow it.

The Environmental Working Group (www.ewg.org) annually publishes The Dirty Dozen™ list, which highlights the fruits and vegetables that are most likely to be tainted with particularly dangerous pesticides. These are the foods where it's most important to buy organic produce. (They also publish a Clean Fifteen™ list that includes produce that is the least tainted with toxic chemicals.) As well, the EWG compiles an annual list of the most common genetically modified (GM) foods (eg vegetable oils, corn, soy, sugar, papaya, zucchini and yellow squash). In general, if you're consuming non-GM ingredients from their Clean Fifteen™ list, it is less critical to buy organic.

FUNKY FOODS

FRUITS & VEGETABLES

daikon

If you aren't familiar with daikon—a mild-flavoured radish from Asia—it is an incredibly healthy and delicious food. During the dozen or so years I was unable to eat onions and garlic (alliums are common cross-allergens with certain grasses I was allergic to), I discovered that daikon was an alternative that offered similar flavour dimensions to my dishes. It is rich in vitamin C and fibre and is one of the foods I first learned about from Inspire Health's information about beneficial foods for patients living with cancer.

goji berries

Increasingly popular in the mainstream, goji berries are certainly enjoying their moment in the sun! While delicious and lending a unique, earthy sweetness to recipes, goji berries belong to the nightshade family, which many individuals with autoimmune conditions are unable to enjoy. Also, if you are taking any medication, it is particularly advisable to confirm with your healthcare professional that it is okay to eat these

where you live. Eric is an environmental scientist who has spearheaded water sampling studies and he knows exactly what can be in our water. You can be certain that he ensures we only consume clean water in our home! "Generally, filtered water is preferred, particularly in older buildings," Eric explains. "However, you don't want to live on bottled water either, because of the energy and environmental impacts associated with drinking bottled water. So I recommend using filtered or purified water whenever possible."

ORGANIC, NON-GENETICALLY ALTERED FOOD

The health and ecological reasons for eating as much untainted food (free of pesticides and genetic alterations) as possible are far too many to explore in this book. Unlike most other things, I can't be *laissez-faire* about this issue, because of the seriousness of the implications. I recommend using organic, locally-grown ingredients whenever available and not cost-prohibitive. For recipes that call for vegetable or fruit peels, if you cannot find organic, it is better to omit the peel from the recipe than to use non-organic.

antioxidant-rich berries, since they can interact with some medicines.

golden berries (Inca berries)

This berry from South America is a beautiful fruit, fresh or dehydrated, and is called by many names, including "Cape gooseberries." Unlike other gooseberries, this particular variety is another member of the nightshade family, and so it may need to be approached with caution by those with autoimmune conditions. Preliminary research has led some to make claims of health benefits about this distinctive sour-sweet treasure. If proven, then this fruit will likely begin to appear on the mainstream radar.

jicama

A very thick-skinned root vegetable that can be enjoyed raw or cooked, jicama looks a bit like a strangely shaped potato and has a pear-like, crunchy texture and mild flavour. The best alternative to potato fries I've ever had, jicama can also be julienned or cubed and used raw in many salads to add a delightful crispiness. Depending on where you live, jicama may be more or less available.

juices (fruit and vegetable)

Whenever juice is an ingredient for a recipe, fresh-squeezed/pressed is best, both for nutrition and flavour. However, when that is not possible, the second-best juice option is frozen fresh juice, followed by bottled juice stored in the refrigerator.

kale

Did you know that kale is a good source of protein even though it is a vegetable? Just over 200 grams of kale contains more than 8.5 grams of protein, along with a host of other life-giving nutrients. Kale needs to be cut and prepared properly to bring out its beautiful flavour. Slice or chiffonade (cut into long, thin strips) the washed kale leaves and then massage them well with some lemon juice and a bit of oil for a couple of minutes. This breaks down the bitterness and coarseness of the leaves, making them more tender and much more delicious.

▲ FARMERS MARKETS
Farmers markets are not only a great resource for clean, locally grown food, they are also a wonderful slice of life and local culture. Here is "The Sprout Lady," Susie Jason, (www.mendocinosprouts.com) sharing her beloved sprouted treasures with her customers at the Mendocino Farmers' Market.

legumes

Antioxidant-, vitamin-, mineral- and fibre-rich, one serving of these beauties has about 7 grams of protein! Beans (kidney, red, black, pinto, etc) and lentils are a very important and inexpensive powerhouse of nutrition. This said, like everything else, not everyone is able to enjoy eating beans, which have become the target of some controversy that is beyond the scope of this book. Orthomolecular and Integrative Physician Dr. Saul Pilar at Connect Health explained to me that many people have difficulty digesting beans that have not been fully cooked, and canned beans are undercooked so that they will hold their shape when packaged. For this reason, he suggested that anytime canned beans are used, it is best if they are cooked before using, to make them more digestible.

lima beans (butter beans)

Like lentils, lima beans are quick to cook, low glycemic and full of great nutrients. Because they are difficult to find in canned form, they are infrequently prepared in most homes. Lima beans are full of soluble fibre, protein, vitamins (including folate, B1 and B6) and minerals (molybdenum, copper, iron, manganese, potassium and magnesium).

From a culinary perspective, lima beans are a cook's dream. I love the mild savoury flavour and creaminess they offer, and they can transform the mouth-feel and taste of dishes, without adding a lot of fat. For those sensitive to chickpeas and some other beans, these beans can offer an alternative in dip recipes like hummus. Anytime you'd like to add a little low-fat, nut-free and potato-free thickening or creaminess to a soup or other savoury dish, consider throwing in a few lima beans, mashed or puréed. They may become a favourite standby.

lovage

Lovage is a perennial herb in the carrot and parsley family, with leaves that look a lot like celery. Enjoyed since ancient Greek and Roman times, lovage has been used as an herbal remedy for a variety of conditions for centuries. Even though it is easy to grow in most climates, lovage is not currently familiar to most people in North America. With its super-distinctive taste, this herb is amazing in soups, stews and salads and contains quercetin, which is commonly thought to have anti-inflammatory properties. Lovage is not recommended if you are pregnant or have kidney disease.

okra

Most familiar to those in the southern United States, okra truly is a funky ingredient, with a unique mucilaginous (gooey) quality. Prepared properly, it is an amazing food, full of antioxidants, fibre and vitamin C, among other nutrients.

sorrel

Another perennial plant, sorrel has a spinach-like appearance and a slightly lemony or vinegar-like flavour. A great addition to soups, stews, sauces and salads when you want a touch of sourness to enhance your dish, sorrel is an easy and useful plant to consider growing in your garden. There are a number of sorrel varieties, some of which are becoming more available at local markets.

Bee Bite

Did you know about the declining population of bees? Scientists attribute what has been termed "colony collapse disorder" to the poisons the pollinators are exposed to by pesticide use. In 2013, the European Commission banned the use of neonicotinoid pesticides, which are suspected of being the leading cause of the population decline of bees and also that of the insectivorous bird population. Hopefully, other countries around the world will follow Europe's example.

Yet another reason to choose organic food whenever possible!

GRAINS

amaranth

Also known as "pigweed," amaranth is a wild plant with beautiful flowers and edible, spinach-like foliage. Its seeds are considered an extremely nutritious pseudograin. High in iron and protein (especially lysine), amaranth has a much stronger flavour than quinoa, making it less sought after by the mainstream population. While similar to quinoa in many ways, amaranth is a bit trickier to use in cooking. However, as you start to experiment with it, you will discover that amaranth can offer some really delicious flavour dimensions. People around the world grow this plentiful weed for its greens, which offer a high vitamin and mineral content.

buckwheat groats

Rich in beautiful things like flavonoids, manganese, magnesium, fibre, copper, phosphorus, iron and protein, buckwheat is an inexpensive superfood. Not only

is it full of healthy stuff, but the crunchy little groats are really delicious; they have become a favourite staple in our home.

Funnily, buckwheat has nothing to do with wheat, and isn't even in the grass family. These nutritious grains can be toasted or, like nuts and other seeds, soaked and dehydrated before using in recipes. Especially suitable for those unable to enjoy oats, soaked and dehydrated buckwheat groats are a terrific alternative grain base for granola. Because of their mucilaginous nature, soaking and dehydrating buckwheat is not quite as straightforward as with seeds and nuts, so for the recipes in this book, I recommend using toasted groats, which still produce delicious results. However, if you know how to soak and dehydrate them, please do so and use them instead!

quinoa

This protein-, vitamin- and mineral-rich ancient pseudograin has been enjoyed for thousands of years since the time of the Incas, who called it their "Mother Grain." In recent years, quinoa (a relative of beets and spinach) has grown in popularity because of these

nutrients and its unique grain-like qualities). Quinoa is a wonderful and hearty food and is a great option for those who want to eat more plant-based foods that offer quality sources of protein. Help to empower South American farmers in their efforts to grow organic quinoa by sourcing ethical suppliers, such as www.alterecofoods.com; alternatively, try domestically cultivated quinoa, such as offered by NorQuin (www.quinoa.com).

It is very important to rinse quinoa well to remove the soapy saponins. Saponins are bitter-tasting detergent-like substances that protect the grains from fungi, microbes and birds. Like a naturally occurring pesticide, if left on the grains, the saponins make them harder to digest and less tasty. Most quinoa, however, is pre-rinsed well before packaging.

Though tough on the gut, there are rumblings in the scientific community about the potential health benefits of saponins, which will be interesting to follow over time. Some people in other cultures use plant saponins as a healing agent (because of the antifungal and antibiotic properties) or as an environmentally-friendly cleaning agent.

PASTAS

Most of us grew up with wheat-based pastas, but there are now countless other alternatives available on the market. While this is not an all-inclusive list, here are some of my family's favourites.

bean pastas

These are my favourite conventional type of pasta. I went a little crazy when I discovered them a couple of years ago. They not only have a terrific and authentic pasta mouth-feel and cook in 3-5 minutes in boiling water (or can be soaked in water in the fridge for a day or so for those who prefer less heat-dependent food preparation), but they also have an amazing nutrient profile. Crazy, right? Alex teased me, saying that this type of pasta was my newest BFF. A variety of these organic bean pastas are now readily available: mung bean fettuccini, black bean spaghetti, adzuki bean spaghetti, soy spaghetti and red lentil penne, and the list is rapidly growing. If you are able to enjoy legumes, life doesn't get much better than these awesome noodles!

bean thread noodles

These translucent noodles (also called Chinese vermicelli, cellophane noodles or glass noodles) are usually made from the starch of mung beans. However, if you are sensitive to potatoes or other root vegetables (like I am), you need to be aware that some are made from yams or potatoes, cassava/manioc or other roots. For years I didn't understand why these seemingly benign noodles sometimes made my tummy get so upset, until I later learned about the occasional potato connection. Now I understand!

kelp noodles

A super-low-calorie, low-carb noodle option, kelp noodles are made from seaweed and are a favourite in the raw food community. Most people who eat kelp noodles prefer the clear (versus the green) variety, since the clear ones have less of a "seaweedy" taste. Kelp noodles have a rubbery texture, are more crunchy than regular pasta and have virtually no nutrients, carbohydrates, protein, and very little fibre and sodium. They do contain some iodine, which individuals with thyroid challenges might appreciate, while others may be advised to avoid (bio-individuality at work). Like shirataki noodles, they are considered by many to be a "free food," and can add an unusual textural component to dishes.

raw pasta noodles

This is a very exciting contribution from the Raw Food Movement, which has found some really cool ways to create pastas using fresh vegetables (who would've thought!). Raw noodles are surprisingly delicious and are easy to prepare— you don't even need to boil water!

The most popular raw pasta is zucchini pasta, but you can make these wonderful noodles from lots of other vegetables as well. Living Light Institute Chef Vinnette Thompson's favourite is kohlrabi, but I've even made noodles from such unlikely root vegetables as large carrots! Because they tend to have a higher water content than regular noodles, it is best to prepare

raw pasta noodles shortly before serving, so that they don't break down and become too soft. The invention of the inexpensive and readily available spiralizer (see page 34) has made making this form of pasta a breeze. Kids love preparing them and often want to eat the raw vegetable noodles right out of the contraption, making this tool truly priceless!

shirataki noodles

Another great option for those avoiding grains, shirataki noodles are traditionally made from elephant or konjac yams, with some now being made using soy. These noodles are extremely high in fibre and have very few calories, so many people consider them a "free food." Before rinsing and heating, you will notice that these noodles have a strong fishy odour. Properly preparing them reduces this smell, which is easily camouflaged by strongly flavoured sauces.

other gluten-free pastas

There are many other traditionally styled gluten-free pastas, made from ingredients such as rice, corn, quinoa, yams and buckwheat. As with any other food, if you have sensitivities, it is a good idea to always check

the label for other ingredients. However, as more and more folks are discovering they are unable to enjoy gluten, the options for gluten-free pastas are rapidly increasing.

SEEDS & NUTS

You know you are living in a new world when you find yourself discovering cool and nutritious omega-3-rich seeds! Some of the best sources of plant-based omega-3 fat (ALA) and full of protein, these seeds are an important part of the new era of health, especially brain health. However, omega-3-rich seeds tend to be unstable (see the section on Oils) and so are best enjoyed raw or heated at very low temperatures only.

For the recipes in *YUM*, I recommend using nuts and seeds that are raw or soaked and dehydrated, unless otherwise indicated. This is especially important for most of the raw food recipes, which must have raw nuts or seeds to turn out properly. Roasting nuts and seeds can release volatile oils, resulting in potentially negative health implications.

Mother Nature gave nuts and seeds enzyme inhibitors, a special chemical form of protection. They also help prevent them from prematurely sprouting. Unfortunately, these enzyme inhibitors also protect seeds and nuts from our digestive enzymes! Because of this, some people may notice digestive challenges when they eat raw food if the seeds and nuts have not been properly soaked and rinsed; our poor gut isn't happy with the little war going on inside when the enzyme inhibitors are still intact. When this happens, our body also loses out on a lot of the incredible nutrients that are locked inside these beautiful seeds of life!

This issue can be easily remedied by simply soaking and rinsing the nuts and the larger seeds to release and wash away these enzyme inhibitors (it is too difficult to do this with smaller seeds). The length of soaking varies, depending on the type of nut or seed, with the larger and harder nuts requiring longer soak times (eg walnuts, almonds and Brazil nuts can be soaked overnight, but soft nuts like cashews are best if only soaked for 2–4 hours). Freshly soaked nuts and seeds can be used immediately after soaking or can be dehydrated at

low temperatures (to maximize the nutrient content) for later use. When I soaked and dehydrated nuts for the first time, I was amazed by how much more delicious they were and how some of them puffed up and became much larger as well. For example, walnuts treated in this way become about 30 percent larger than those that are left untreated.

OILS

The smoke point of an oil refers to the temperature at which volatile components in the oil are released, creating a visible haze. Heating oils beyond their smoke points can have carcinogenic effects. Whenever cooking with high heat, I recommend oils that have a high smoke point. The data about smoke points is very confusing, though: different sources report varying estimated smoke points for different oils. I am not an oil-smoke-point scientist, but have done my best to share general principles that I've learned, incorporating them into the *YUM* recipes so you don't need to fuss about it—just enjoy the healthy goodness!

In general, refined oils tend to have higher smoke points than virgin, unrefined oils. If you replace any of the recommended oils in the cooked-food recipes, please do your homework to ensure you choose an oil with the appropriate smoke point. Refined peanut and sesame oils have relatively high smoke points (around 450°F) and refined coconut oil does pretty well at around 400°F. Macadamia, pecan, Brazil nut and almond oils smoke at temperatures above 400°F, but are more costly and may not be readily available. I typically avoid using canola, corn, safflower and sunflower oils because they are often made from GM crops, even though they have relatively high smoke points. While some people like grapeseed oil (which also has a smoke point above 400°F), I don't use it because I don't like its taste.

avocado oil

My absolute favourite oil to use for my higher-temperature cooking is refined avocado oil. Its 500°F smoke point is one of the highest! The good news is that avocado oil is becoming more common in stores, especially establishments that are responding to the growing number of consumers who want to eat healthier food. I was delighted to learn last year that it is even available at Costco!

camelina oil

A new discovery for me, this amazing oil is organically grown, harvested and produced by Three Farmers in Saskatoon (www.threefarmers.ca). Camelina oil is made from the seeds of brassica plants and can be used both for salads and for cooking, with lovely nutritive values, including a high vitamin E content. Even though it is omega-3-rich, it has a relatively high smoke point of 475°F, making it a great alternative to avocado oil. I think we'll soon be hearing a lot more about this gently nut-flavoured oil.

coconut oil & coconut butter

For decades I was unable to enjoy coconut products after being diagnosed with an allergy to it, but now I am so happy to discover that I can eat this incredibly versatile fruit again. It is important not to confuse coconut oil with coconut butter—*they are not the same!*

Coconut butter has more fibre and has a firmer texture and different mouth-feel than coconut oil. This product is also much more expensive and difficult to buy, since it is not available at many local stores, but is readily available on the internet (see resources at www.yumfoodforliving.com). For special treats, this ingredient is incredible and well worth the effort and expense, making it possible to enjoy creamy, decadent delights without using butter or powdered sugar.

Coconut butter is a very hard butter that tends to separate; because of its texture, it can be difficult to mix. I prefer to remove the separated oil from the top (reserving it for recipes calling for coconut oil) and just use the hard butter below. This step is necessary for a number of my sweet recipes calling for coconut butter.

Coconut oil, on the other hand, is easy to find in most stores and is easy on the pocketbook. In warmer temperatures, coconut oil will be liquid, while in cooler temperatures it will be firm. You will need to take this into account, and either refrigerate or warm gently as needed. We like to keep a little sealed glass jar

of coconut oil in a warm place in the kitchen (like on top of the dehydrator or refrigerator) for ready melted coconut oil. If you want to cook with coconut oil at higher heats, be sure to use refined (not virgin) oil and do so with care, keeping temperatures below 400°F.

olive oil

Unless otherwise specified, whenever recipes call for olive oil, extra virgin olive oil is recommended. When cooking or baking with olive oil, I suggest a 315°F oven, instead of the more conventional 350°F or higher. This is because the standard estimation for extra virgin olive oil's smoke point is 320-325°F. Some reports assert higher smoke point temperatures for olive oil, but I prefer to err on the conservative side for this one.

seed oils (flax, hemp & chia)

Oils with a high omega-3 (ALA) content are very unstable fats, which are extremely heat sensitive and can become rancid easily. The most notable of these are flax, hemp and chia oil. While soaking flax or chia seeds works as a great egg alternative for binding and has become popular in many vegan baked recipes, you will notice that none of the recipes in *YUM* involve heating these seeds or oils to high temperatures. Other

alternatives have been used for this purpose to maximize the health benefits and minimize the potential detrimental effects of such cooking practices.

CONDIMENTS

coconut aminos

The sap from coconut trees is surprisingly filled with minerals, vitamins and amino acids. Naturally aged by either slow evaporation or fermentation, this nutrient-dense sap, combined with sea salt, makes a wonderful alternative to soy sauce or tamari. This is fantastic, especially for anyone who is unable (or prefers not) to eat soy.

Himalayan salt

While not everyone agrees about the potential health benefits of Himalayan salt (some claiming it heals just about everything under the sun), from a culinary perspective the taste is far superior to any other salt I've ever tasted. With it now so widely available and inexpensive, it's easier to enjoy this unique ingredient. In our modern diet, salt is significantly overused, which can have serious health implications. While I've never been a big fan of salt and like to use as little as possible, the flavour-enhancing benefits of using it judiciously are indisputable.

In the *YUM* recipes, I specify either a recommended amount of salt (for optimal flavour) or a range. I encourage you to start with the lesser amount of salt, then adjust to your taste. Be daring and try some recipes with even less salt than indicated and see what happens! The worst thing that can happen (except in baked recipes like cakes) is that you may have to add more later—no big deal! Many people find that when they bring more flavourful, raw and herb-infused clean food into their bodies, their cravings for the familiar salty and sugary foods begins to fade. Who knows, that might happen for you too!

mesquite powder

I have only recently begun experimenting with this unfamiliar ingredient. When I first heard about it, I assumed it would have a savoury, barbeque flavour and was surprised to discover that it is actually a mild sweetening agent of sorts. The powder has a caramel-like colour and is high in protein and fibre.

miso (soy or chickpea)

Miso is a protein- and nutrient-rich flavour enhancer and a terrific base for many soups. Because most miso is made from soy, not everyone can enjoy it. Also, you need to know that the fermentation process to create it may involve rice or barley. Chickpea miso is a wonderful, soy-free alternative to the traditional version. It has been around in the Middle East for centuries and is typically fermented with rice, so may be a safer option for many people. If you can't find chickpea miso in your local stores, this beautiful food is available online. It is not very expensive and a little goes a long way, keeping for months in the fridge. Apparently, there are now other forms of miso being made from ingredients such as corn, adzuki beans, amaranth and quinoa.

nutritional yeast

This deactivated form of yeast has a creamy, nutty, cheese-like flavour and is a crazy-delicious ingredient. Nutritional yeast is a plant-based source of nutrients and protein that is also low in fat and sodium, and is totally free of sugar, dairy and gluten. My favourite

brand of this wonderful culinary ingredient is made by Premier Research Labs and contains protein from a wide range of amino acids. This ingredient is a real gift, and you'll find that I use it in many of the recipes in this book.

vanilla

Most people are familiar with and use vanilla extract, but this option is not feasible for those sensitive to the alcohol found in such preparations. The most common alternative, vanilla beans, are yummy but extremely expensive. Less well known is vanilla powder, which is the whole dried bean pulverized. The pure raw form has no additives; unfortunately some vanilla powder products also contain alcohol or other ingredients you may want to avoid. While it may sound crazy, I sometimes like to throw a whole vanilla bean into some of my pulverized recipes: no measuring, no cutting, no scraping—just toss in the whole pod!

SWEETENERS

Some medical experts suggest the total elimination of all foods from one's diet that have any sweetening agents, especially if trying to reduce cravings. While there is tremendous wisdom and healing offered by this perspective for some, this approach may not work for or be of interest to others. Given human nature, most people don't want to go "cold turkey" and eliminate sweets from their diet. That is why in this book I'm offering delicious, lower glycemic index (GI) alternatives for desserts and other sweets that minimize the negative effects of traditionally prepared dishes. GI is a measure, on a scale of 0–100, of how rapidly blood sugar rises after eating different foods. These numbers are not precise, and different studies show variable index ranges, but general trends offer useful information. However, learning that there are sweet foods with lower (some significantly lower) measures on this index than others is a really exciting and wonderful discovery! For recipes that use sweet ingredients, I've developed a new culinary method that reduces their glycemic load without sacrificing taste. I do this by strategically combining very low glycemic sweeteners (like *Chicory Root Inulin with Stevia*, page 324) with a reduced amount of higher glycemic sweeteners (such as dates and maple syrup). This technique is one of the most exciting innovations YUM has to offer. I hope that this contribution to culinary science makes it easier for people to be better able to manage their blood sugar levels (even those whose bodies find it particularly difficult to do so), while still allowing them the freedom to enjoy delectable treats, guilt-free.

Because people experience the taste of food differently, flavour adjustments in recipes using alternative sweet ingredients may be necessary. As with salt, you may want to experiment with using lower amounts of sweetening agents in your recipes and replacing higher GI sweeteners with lower GI alternatives. The recipes have been designed to be in keeping with the taste preferences of most people, helping to make the transition to eating healthier food easier. However, I have offered a variety of alternative sweetening options, allowing people to make adjustments according to their own taste and the availability of ingredients.

Here are various alternatives to sugar. Whatever sweetness path you choose to follow, I think that down deep we're all really sweet anyway. ☺

agave nectar

Previously touted as a wonderful, versatile and low GI raw sweetener, recent press about agave nectar has been negative because of the discovery that some unscrupulous suppliers were cutting this natural sweetener with high fructose corn syrup (HFCS), causing sensitive individuals to experience blood-sugar spikes. When processed properly, agave nectar can be safe to use. Wanting to reduce any unnecessary potential risks for users of this book, however, I have not recommended it in any of my recipes.

amazake

I've never tried this traditional Japanese yogurt-like beverage that is also used by some as a sweetener. It is made from fermented brown rice and has a reported GI somewhere between that of coconut nectar and maple syrup. If this is a familiar and favourite sweetener that you use, it might be wonderful to try as an alternative in some of the recipes in this book.

blackstrap molasses

Super-rich in alkalizing minerals like iron, calcium, copper and zinc, this rich syrup is made from the stuff removed from regular refined sugar. Like maple syrup, its GI is around 55 (slightly less than that of regular refined sugar). Because its flavour is so distinctive, a little goes a long way and it can deepen and enhance the flavour of foods when used carefully. Use only organic varieties.

brown rice syrup (rice malt syrup)

With the mixed information about this syrup, which may have a low GI yet reportedly can still rapidly spike blood sugar levels, this product may primarily be an option for individuals sensitive or allergic to other sweeteners. It also has a light yet distinctive flavour that appeals to some people.

chicory root inulin powder

This powdered ingredient is a soluble fibre that is full of fructo-oligosaccharides (FOS) extracted from chicory plants and has a somewhat sweet taste. I use this inulin powder, with stevia added, as the basic low-GI sweetener in many of the recipes in this book. See the *Chicory Root Inulin with Stevia* recipe on page 324.

coconut nectar

This syrup has received a lot of attention recently as an alternative to controversial agave nectar. Extracted from the sap of coconut blossoms, coconut nectar has a reported GI of around 35 (about half that of regular refined sugar, honey and maple syrup). I have found that different varieties of coconut nectar can have markedly different tastes, with some more fruity than others; you might need to try a few different brands to find one that suits your taste. While not as neutral as agave nectar, this syrup has a lightness that makes it a nice alternative in some recipes.

coconut sugar

Coconut sugar is a granular sugar that has a look and flavour that reminds me a lot of coarse brown sugar. Like coconut nectar, coconut sugar comes from the sap of coconut blossoms, but has been dehydrated into crystals. Similar to the nectar, it is estimated to have a GI of about half that of regular refined sugar. While not quite as sweet, coconut sugar is a fantastic alternative to regular sugar and can be used in a relatively similar manner. It's important to note that the brown colour can change the appearance of the dishes you create.

dates

A favourite sweetening option in the raw food movement, the GI of different types of dates varies widely, from medium to high (Medjool dates having the highest index). Like maple syrup, when strategically paired with *Chicory Root Inulin with Stevia* (page 324), the characteristic flavour and sweetness of this delectable fruit can be enjoyed with a lower net GI. Anyone with diabetes or other blood sugar sensitivities will want to consider this when carefully selecting sweetening options.

erythrytol

Erythrytol is a relatively accessible sugar alcohol, but is also controversial because it is derived from corn. Erythrytol is a favourite sweetener for some people (especially the sugar-sensitive) because it has few calories and a really low GI. Because it is fermented, this sweetener is said to be easier to digest than other sugar alcohols.

Erythrytol is naturally present in foods such as fruits and vegetables and has a crystalline consistency very similar to regular refined sugar. Like other sugar alcohols, it does not contribute to tooth decay. However, it is important to know the source of the corn used to make the erythrytol, and ensure that it is only made from non-GM crops.

fructose

In its natural form in fruits and vegetables, fructose offers a wonderful sweetness to foods. However, the highly-processed fructose sweeteners being sold are controversial. While many of the recipes use fruit (which naturally contain fructose), no recipes in this volume use the refined form of fructose, even though it is thought to have a low GI.

honey

Considered a superfood by many, honey is full of amazing healing qualities, minerals and other nutrients. In this book, however, none of the recipes call for honey. This was a conscious decision because honey is not a plant-based food and because of the inhumane harvesting practices of some bee product suppliers.

Because of my deep love of bees and concern about the decline in their population in recent years, *YUM* offers other alternatives to this sweet and delicious food created by our beautiful life-giving friends, who are currently in serious need of our protection.

Lakanto

Lakanto is a sweetening product you may have heard of because it has become popular in some circles and is relatively accessible. While I was at the Living Light Culinary Institute, they were exploring using it as a sweetening option. Lakanto is made by combining luo han guo (below) with a non-GM-derived form of erythrytol.

luo han guo

Luo han guo is a fruit that has an extremely low GI similar to that of stevia (zero) and reportedly offers

> **Bee Bite** 🐝
>
> **Did you know that bee stings may have some health benefits?**
>
> In different parts of the world, some health practitioners use the venom from bees to treat a variety of conditions, including rheumatoid arthritis, multiple sclerosis, tendonitis, allergies and fibromyalgia.

other health benefits as well. I've not yet explored this ingredient in cooking, but understand that when used on its own, it has negative flavour issues and so is usually combined with other sweeteners.

lucuma powder

While it is a stranger to most (except to those in the raw food community), lucuma powder has been used for thousands of years and is a very low-GI sweetener (similar to yacon syrup). It is touted to have antioxidant qualities, a vast array of nutrients and healing qualities as well. Lucuma is a commonly enjoyed fruit in Peru and other subtropical areas of South America. The powder comes from the dehydrated pulp of the fruit (which looks a lot like an avocado) and has a delightful, mild caramelly, maple-like flavour. It tastes terrific, but unfortunately is a sweetener to which I am very allergic. Because of this, you will not find lucuma used in any of the recipes in *YUM*.

maple syrup

Maple syrup is a common ingredient in most households, with a GI of around 55. It has some other nutritious elements and, when used in moderation in combination with lower GI sweeteners to reduce the overall glycemic load (GL), offers a wonderful flavour dimension to dishes.

stevia

I know what many of you are thinking, "Ew, not stevia. I've tried it before and it has a weird taste." You're right, it sure can—I've had the same experience! Let me be the first to let you know that not all stevia products on the market are created equal. Additionally, I have developed the art of combining the flavour dimensions of stevia with other sweeteners to create an incredible taste that is reflected in the recipes, and that also keeps the GI as low as possible. Like luo han guo, stevia is thought to have a GI of zero. Making flavour adjustments in this way was one of the most challenging and exciting aspects of my recipe development. With the growing global incidence of diabetes, as well as my personal experience of witnessing my dad and other loved ones suffering from it, there was no stopping me in my quest to create lower GI alternatives. I was committed to creating yummy treats that as many people as possible could enjoy.

Stevia is derived from the leaves of an herb that has been grown in South America for centuries as a natural sweetener. Traditionally thought to be good for individuals with blood sugar challenges, its sweetness is super-concentrated, estimated to be over one hundred times sweeter than sugar, with a bitter aftertaste when taken in concentrated form. Because of its bitterness, manufacturers cut it with other products. It is important to read the ingredients carefully to know what is in these products. Some (like my favourite, New Roots Herbal Stevia Spoonable) are mixed with only inulin (similar to my *Chicory Root Inulin with Stevia* recipe on page 324). This is my favourite combination, offering a sweetness when used in recipes that is very similar to sugar, but with a lower net GI. However, some brands may use other ingredients, such as erythrytol or "natural flavours." You need to really be careful of what you choose to buy when it comes to stevia!

xylitol

This highly processed sugar alcohol is reported to have a very low GI of about 7, making it a wonderful alternative for those with diabetes. Since it also lends itself nicely to baking, I decided to include xylitol as an ingredient in some of the recipes. I really enjoy using this product and think it is great for replicating the look and general feel of regular sugar. Because of its touted antibacterial qualities for the ears, nose and throat, many dentists recommend xylitol to their patients. Sometimes (but not always) I have found that xylitol and coconut sugar can be used in similar recipes.

Xylitol is another controversial sweetener. The controversy exists because some individuals experience digestive irritation when using it, and also because many manufacturers produce it using GM corn, instead of making it from birch (the preferred, safer source). I like to use Xyla brand xylitol, which is produced in North America by Xylitol Canada/Xylitol USA and is made from birch.

yacon syrup

Like stevia and luo han guo, yacon syrup is one of the safest natural sweeteners around for diabetics. This syrup has a molasses-like flavour and an extremely low GI, estimated around 7. It has been used in South America for hundreds of years as a folk medicine for individuals who struggle with blood sugar management, as well as for kidney and digestive challenges. It is also high in fibre and fructo-oligosaccharides (FOS). While it has been touted as a potential weight-loss aid, the research around this is too limited to be conclusive.

Unfortunately, yacon syrup is extremely expensive, so may not be a viable option for many to enjoy. However, it is wonderful to know that such a delicious syrup exists and might be a treat that you can enjoy for very special occasions when you want to keep the GI of your foods as low as possible.

FLOURS

gluten-free flour

All-purpose gluten-free flour is pretty widely accessible; however, the truth is these flours are not all the same, nor necessarily low GI. Most gluten-free flour blends have a combination of a starch (typically potato or tapioca) and some milled gluten-free grains (such as sorghum or rice), milled seeds (such as buckwheat, quinoa or amaranth) and/or bean flour (such

as chickpea or fava). Most also have a bit of xanthan gum or guar gum as a binding agent.

Bob's All-Purpose seems to be the most readily available gluten-free flour in stores in North America, and we like how it behaves and tastes in the little bit of baking that we do. Because of this, I standardized my recipes using only this flour. However, if you are very sensitive to potatoes, the potato starch in Bob's blend could pose a problem for you. I have heard great things about gfJules™ All Purpose Gluten Free Flour (www.gfJules.com) but haven't yet tried it myself. Because some of the ingredients in available gluten-free flours may not agree with your body, you may elect to make your own. There are lots of recipes out there to make your own all-purpose flour blends, and Jules Shepard has a number of great ones you can check out!

If you want to avoid xanthan gum as the binding agent in your recipe, you might be able to swap it out with another ingredient, such as a little psyllium husk powder. Because they are omega-3-based, I don't recommend using flax or chia seeds in baking because of the negative effects of the heat exposure on the vulnerable oils (see the Oils section). However, they certainly also can do the trick to help with binding and are popular with many bakers. Because of the gelatinous behaviour of buckwheat, some gluten-free bakers find that using buckwheat in the recipe addresses the binding issue. This is not a strategy that I have personally tried.

You can use whatever flour that is available to you, but know that you might need to make some recipe adjustments when you do (maybe a little more or a little less flour). You might also need to make adjustments around the liquids in recipes, since some of the flour mixtures vary in terms of how readily they absorb fluid. If you eat only vegan food, be sure to check the labels on flour blends, because some do contain animal products.

almond meal, almond flour & almond pulp
The terms "almond meal" and "almond flour" are used interchangeably for the same ingredient and refer to the granular, flour-like meal made from almonds. Some are made from nuts with the skins removed, resulting in a cream-coloured meal, while others are made from whole almonds, which have dark specks throughout the flour. The recipes in this book were designed using the cream-coloured meal. While they may work fine with the speckled almond meal, I cannot guarantee the results.

Almond pulp is not the same as almond meal: it is the fibre that remains after making almond milk. It doesn't have the same fat content and other elements as almond meal, but its qualities make it a useful ingredient, particularly in raw food cuisine.

baking powder
Only use gluten-free and aluminum-free baking powder. It is readily available, either in stores or online.

agar agar
While it's the weirdest stuff, agar agar makes a fantastic gelling agent. When I was able to create a perfect pumpkin pie custard without any eggs, I could hardly contain myself. For the magical gelling agent of this ingredient to work, it must be boiled for a few minutes. Agar agar powder acts more rapidly and does not need to be cooked as long, but I recommend using flaked agar agar, since it's easier to find. If you can find the powder, it will save you cooking time, but be sure to reduce the amount of the powder used to about one-third the recommended amount of agar agar flakes.

Liquids with a high acid or enzyme content (such as those found in raw fruits like papaya, mango, lemon and pineapple) can prevent agar agar from gelling properly. Experimenting with cooking times and quantity can result in successful dishes using these juices, but if you are a beginner I recommend avoiding them. If you are already an experienced cook or feel ready to explore in the new land of agar agar, it can be a really fun ingredient to play with that makes unexpected treasures possible!

cacao
No, this is not a spelling error (as I had thought for years): it is actually the name of raw chocolate seeds. If you are able to eat chocolate, it is exciting to learn about cacao, which is the pure, raw form of chocolate, full of antioxidants and magnesium, among many other nutrients. For all of the great press about chocolate, there is some controversy about whether or not cacao is as healthy as some folks suggest, but that discussion cannot be covered properly in *YUM*.

Cacao powder is the raw form of cocoa powder and can pretty much be used interchangeably with cocoa powder in recipes. While cacao has more fibre and a higher nutrient value than cocoa powder, you might choose to use conventional cocoa for reasons of price and availability.

Cacao nibs are just raw cacao beans chopped into little pieces, and are not typically sold in a cooked version. The nibs offer a wonderful crunchy chocolate chip-like quality, but remember that because they are unsweetened, they are very bitter. Raw cacao bars and pieces made without regular refined sugar are available, but are typically quite expensive, so feel free to replace this ingredient with the best quality dark chocolate you can find.

Whatever you do, be sure that any chocolate products you buy come from an ethical source. The majority of chocolate currently on the market, unfortunately, comes from sources that are not fair-trade and often involve child labour, taking much of the joy out of this beautiful food.

carob

Many think of carob (the edible seeds from an evergreen flowering shrub) as a replacement for chocolate. I am not one of those people. The taste of these little edible seeds is not at all like chocolate! That said, it is a terrific and nutritious ingredient in its own right, considered to have a range of health benefits. With its slightly sweet, caramel-like flavour, carob powder can brighten up recipes and add an unexpected dimension to the taste. If you do want to experiment with using carob in lieu of chocolate, keep in mind that the taste will not be the same and that the recipe will likely require other flavour adjustments in order to work.

coconut cream

Coconut cream is a tricky one, since the products on the market vary a great deal in terms of quality and creaminess. When young Thai coconuts are used, the cream is far superior to those made from older coconuts. It took me a while to find a premium, organic, full-fat coconut milk that works best in recipes requiring wonderful creaminess. You may have a similar problem. As I discovered in culinary school, even when making coconut cream from fresh coconut meat, the variation in quality can be huge, depending on the age and type of coconuts used.

To get coconut cream from a can (the method used in *YUM* for reasons of practicality), chill can(s) of full-fat premium organic coconut milk in the refrigerator for a few hours or overnight. When you remove the tin from the refrigerator, be sure not to shake it. Open the tin carefully, then spoon out the thick cream from the top of the can and place it in a bowl. Save the coconut liquid below to use in smoothies or other recipes. Using a premium variety is particularly important in the whipped cream, frostings and other creamy dessert recipes in this book. For use in soups, it is less critical to use premium coconut milk.

nori paper

Nori paper is an edible form of red seaweed that has been dried into very thin, paper-like sheets. Most commonly used to make sushi wraps, these sheets can also serve as a delicious, plant-based alternative flavour enhancer. In particular, I like to use a little nori in recipes that would otherwise call for fish sauce. These sheets can be purchased in raw or roasted form. To retain its characteristic texture, nori needs to be stored in an airtight container or zipper bag.

prebiotics

Prebiotics are food for the beneficial probiotics (the friendly microbacteria and fungi organisms) in the body, especially associated with gut microflora. They are most commonly fructo-oligosaccharides (FOS), but there are other forms, such as xylo-oligosaccharides (XOS), galacto-oligosaccharides (GOS) and poly-dextrose, among others. Prebiotics sold in supplement form are commonly derived from chicory root inulin. One of the great qualities of a fibre-rich, plant-based diet is that prebiotics from the non-digestible fibre in

fruits and vegetables are super-yummy to the probiotics. Foods that are particularly rich in prebiotics are chicory root, beans, garlic, onions, jicama, Jerusalem artichokes, dandelion greens, asparagus, yacon and bananas. Another cool fact about prebiotics is that heat does not destroy their value as a food to the probiotics! While there is some very exciting research about the potential health benefits of prebiotics, due to bio-individuality this wonderful form of fibre may not be suitable for every person's body.

probiotics

Probiotics come in many forms, but all of them are simply friendly bacteria or yeasts that reside in our intestines, fight unfriendly organisms and support our immune functioning. When we make probiotic foods such as yogurt, kimchee and the like, we are able to grow these wonderful organisms and can enjoy them directly from the food we eat. However, you can also purchase probiotic powder, such as acidophilus, either loose or in capsules. The best of these are those that require refrigeration to preserve the live organisms. Used in the kitchen, this powder can provide a cheese-like flavour to some dishes.

Recent preliminary medical research findings in controlled studies are suggesting that probiotics may be involved in our health in more ways than was previously suspected. In particular, studies are strongly pointing to a relationship between the presence of probiotics in the digestive system and improved health in unexpected areas, including respiratory and bone health.

Particularly intriguing is research that demonstrates the important connection between our gut and our brain. Neurologist and nutrition expert Dr. David Perlmutter has been increasing our awareness of the relationship between intestinal flora and brain functioning, including neurodegenerative conditions. There is reason to believe that probiotics may play a role in reducing depression, anxiety-related symptoms and other indicators of brain health, although research in this field is still in its infancy.

It will be very interesting to follow the unfolding discoveries about how probiotics might influence health. In the meantime, it sure does get me excited about experimenting with more beautiful, probiotic-rich fermented foods in our kitchen!

psyllium husk powder

Usually used as a digestive aid, this powder is a fabulous binding agent as well. It is an egg alternative to flax or chia gel and can be baked without the negative effects of heating the omega-3 oils found in those seeds.

tempeh

Like tofu, tempeh is a traditional soy product. However, unlike tofu, it is fermented and is higher in protein, fibre and vitamins than tofu, with a protein content comparable to meat. The fermentation process that breaks down some of the protein into amino acids makes tempeh easier for the body to digest than animal products. And because the whole bean is used in its creation, tempeh has a meatier consistency than tofu. As with all soy products, be sure to only use organic tempeh.

Vitamineral Earth

The company Health Force (www.healthforce.com) has created this amazing product that is full of beautiful herbs, spices and other nutritious goodness. In addition to the health benefits, I like to use it as a flavour-enhancer for soups and on salads. While it is pricey, a very small amount goes a long way and just 2 tablespoons have 4.8 grams of fibre and 2.4 grams of protein!

TERRIFIC TOOLS

COOKWARE

I recommend using glass, ceramic and stainless steel cookware, even though some believe that there is no conclusive scientific basis for avoiding aluminium exposure through the use of cookware. While there remains controversy over whether it can contribute to Alzheimer's, cancer, infertility or other health conditions, it is my preference to avoid this metal whenever possible. Parchment paper and wax paper are wonderful alternatives to aluminium foil and can be used to line aluminium bakeware. (It's also useful to know that aluminium is found in many brands of baking powder and the majority of antiperspirants.)

KNIVES

Having and knowing how to use good quality knives is extremely important. I have come to appreciate the value of sharp knives that are easy to cut with and how much safer they are to use.

MICROPLANE

This is an inexpensive, fine-toothed grater that looks like a woodworking tool. It makes grating nuts, ginger and garlic ultra-finely a cinch.

NUT MILK BAGS

Nut milk bags are fine mesh bags ideal for making non-dairy milks, green (or other) juices and for straining vegetables for a clear broth. They are a very cheap alternative to fancy juicing machines. Another use for these bags is to sprout seeds, since the seeds are easy to rinse in the bags, which can be hung to allow the seeds to breathe as they sprout. However, you don't need to buy special bags (even though they are available and convenient to use) unless you are wanting to use them for sprouting. For creating many types of non-dairy milk or juices from pureed vegetables and fruits, you can just use a vegetable mesh bag or a painter's bag, or even just a worn dish towel.

JUICERS

If you are serious about doing a lot of juicing, you might find it worthwhile to invest in a juicer. They are typically not only easier to use (especially when juicing a large amount of produce), but also result in less oxidation. Juicers vary greatly in terms of their efficiency and the level of oxidation that occurs in the juice. The most common types of juicers are electric (or hand-cranked) single-auger juicers, double-auger electric juicers and centrifugal juicers. While the centrifugal juicers are very fast and are typically less expensive, they do result in more oxidation than augered juicers and are not as efficient in extracting juice from the produce.

Juicers are expensive, but can frequently be bought second-hand and barely used. Before deciding to purchase one, you might want to spend time with someone who has a juicer; try it out first to make sure that it will suit you, since they do take a bit of space in the kitchen and require careful cleaning after each use. Augered juicers that come with a blank plate have an extra, bonus function: you can make instant raw ice cream by just pressing frozen fruit through them—great with bananas, peaches and berries.

HIGH-SPEED BLENDERS

Now we're getting to one of the big kahunas—the high-speed blender! Oh my goodness, this was one tool that I was determined *not* to buy. It seemed crazy to spend that much on a blender, of all things. I was able to make many of the recipes that called for a fancy blender, but some dishes just wouldn't turn out quite right. Then the motor on my lesser blenders would start to burn up. Once I finally agreed to get a fancy blender (after being prodded to do so for a couple of years by Alex), my only regret was that I hadn't done so sooner! The creamier textures that I could achieve, the ease of blending without pulling my hair out, and the increased possibilities for culinary creations were far more than I imagined possible.

But these blenders do cost a lot! The good news is that there are more choices on the market that have higher motor power, at lower and lower prices. You can now get a pretty good model in the $100 range. While not the top of the line and not resulting in quite the same textural fineness, these new machines enable more people to enjoy creating wonderful recipes that aren't possible without one of these devices. Some of the bigger companies also offer refurbished models, with the same warranty period as new models (five to seven years).

If you don't yet have one of these blenders, don't fret. Focus on the recipes that don't call for one, or use your regular blender to make the recipes that have more liquid ingredients, which will likely turn out just fine.

FOOD PROCESSORS

Like high-speed blenders, high-quality food processors can be very expensive. However, my experience has been that sometimes the less fancy, more affordable models of the quality brands can be just as good— and sometimes even easier to use and clean. My biggest issue with these machines is that some can have plastic parts that break easily, rendering the whole machine useless. I am hopeful that the price for quality food processors will continue to become more affordable and the design more robust.

DEHYDRATORS

It took me years to realize the value and huge range of possibilities of using a dehydrator. When used properly, dehydrators can enhance the nutritive and

antioxidant value of foods, since the low heat does not destroy many of the phytochemicals.

It's important to purchase a model that offers variable temperature options that go as low as 105°F. You will also want to be sure to get both silicone and mesh sheets. I strongly recommend choosing a model with a fan in the back, with the sheets lying flat in front of it, for a more even distribution of heat and drying (we love the Excalibur dehydrator). Without such a design, there is a greater risk for improper air movement and an increased possibility that uninvited organisms may choose to join your dehydrating party. Unfortunately, I didn't know these things when I purchased my first dehydrator and learned my lessons the hard way!

SPIRALIZERS

This ultra-simple hand-cranked device brings a grin to every face in the kitchen—turning vegetables into noodles in seconds! They only cost around $20 and are fantastic. Seriously, there's nothing like watching your 11-year-old walk into the kitchen, wash a zucchini or cucumber, cut it in half and then a minute later happily sit down to a dish of raw "pasta." After a long day, it's a great tool to help whip up a quick meal; just wash, cut and spiralize some vegetables, throw a sauce on top, or use for a salad and boom—dinner's served!

OFFSET SPATULA

Before going to culinary school, I had never heard of this tool and you may not have either. These cool little flat metal blades with round ends are super-useful for evenly spreading just about anything. In raw food cuisine, offset spatulas are a must when making wraps, crackers and crusts. Pastry chefs also love using these tools for frosting cakes and cupcakes. They come in different sizes and shapes to accommodate a variety of applications. Fortunately they are not very expensive, because once you see how much easier spreading becomes, your kitchen won't feel properly equipped without one!

POUR ME A STIFF ONE
HOT & COLD BEVERAGES

Angeline's Favourite Hot Chocolate · 38

Alex's Chai Latte · 40

Dandelion Tea · 40

Mint & Lavender Tea · 41

Carrot Blossom Tea · 45

Berry Punch Slushy · 46

Lemonade · 48

Classic Raw Green Juice · 49

Milks · 50
Raw Nut Milk
Raw Hemp Seed Milk
Raw Flax Seed Milk
Raw Coconut Milk
Quinoa Milk

Smoothies · 55
Peach Banana Green Smoothie
Pineapple Banana Hemp Smoothie
Orange Banana Green Smoothie
Chocolate Banana Smoothie
Strawberry Cheesecake Smoothie
Sunrise Sensation Omega Smoothie

ANGELINE'S FAVOURITE HOT CHOCOLATE

INGREDIENTS

1 cup favourite non-dairy milk

1 tbsp cacao or cocoa powder, plus a little for garnish

½–1 tsp *Chicory Root Inulin with Stevia* (page 324) or favourite sweetener, to taste

¼ tsp vanilla powder (optional)

If you knew our daughter Angeline, you would know how particular she is about her food—especially chocolate... her favourite! She fell in love with this unbelievably healthy recipe and began to make it herself on a regular basis when she was 11. I've named the recipe after her, in her honour. *Makes 1 cup*

DIRECTIONS

Blend all the ingredients, then heat to the desired temperature. Garnish with a sprinkling of cacao powder.

Theresa's Tip 🍃

This beverage is perfect for chilly winter nights, snuggling with a good book or loved one, or for those lazy weekend mornings when you'd love to have some special time enjoying your little ones. It's great to have a quick and yummy hot chocolate that your kids can take leadership in preparing if they want, making those precious moments even more special. This recipe was the first that Angeline learned to read and use. It helped her to understand about fractions, as well as multiplying and dividing, when adjusting the quantities. As the youngest in the family, being able to prepare something for all of us made her excited and really happy.

ALEX'S CHAI LATTE

While we were at Living Light Culinary Institute, we had a delicious chai tea that inspired Alex to make her own version. Shortly after we returned home, she created the most decadent chai latte on the planet! She posted it on her blog, Cupcakes and Kale xoxo, and later suggested that I include it in *YUM*. Loving her deliciously simple recipe, I took it and made a few tweaks, and here it is for you to enjoy! *Makes about 2 cups*

INGREDIENTS

1¼ cups boiling water

1 chai tea bag (caffeine-free rooibos or regular chai tea)

1 cup water

⅓ cup raw cashews, macadamia nuts or Brazil nuts

2–5 dates, pitted

DIRECTIONS

In a 2-cup glass or ceramic vessel, steep the tea bag in the boiling water for 5 minutes. While the tea is steeping, blend the nuts, dates and water in a high-speed blender until smooth. Add the steeped tea to the blender and process to combine. Serve immediately.

DANDELION TEA

Dandelion plants are often seen as a nasty weed in the garden. However, the health benefits of these prolific plants are pretty mind-blowing. They are full of vitamins and minerals and even have surprisingly high protein content. Recent research suggests that dandelion root tea may also be effective in killing blood-related cancer cells. Like the plants themselves, this simple recipe keeps giving and giving—even after several days! Originally, I hadn't considered including this recipe, but when I saw how much guests enjoyed it, their enthusiasm made the decision for me. I just know that when I drink this tea, my body really likes it, and that keeps me returning for more too, just like my friends. *Makes quarts to gallons of tea*

INGREDIENTS

2–6 dandelion plants (roots, shoots, leaves, flowers and all), washed well

water

DIRECTIONS

Place the washed dandelion plants in a slow cooker and fill the pot to the top with water. Cook on low overnight or even for a few days, topping up with more water after you enjoy a few cups. This is a wonderful alternative hot beverage to wake up to, and great throughout the day.

> **Bev's Bit**
> Did you know that dandelions—sometimes called Swine's Snout—can be used as a mild laxative to relieve constipation? Drink up and stay "regular!"

MINT & LAVENDER TEA

Mint and lavender are two of the easiest perennial herbs to grow in the garden. However, one important thing to be aware of when growing mint: if it's not in a contained area, it can really spread. Even though it thrives best in full sun, mint is so vigorous that I've been successful at growing it in partly shady places. Sunny spots are at such a premium in small gardens like ours that it's great to find plants that can tolerate some shade. I love to combine peppermint leaves with the lemon balm variety for a brighter, yet still soothing flavour. Angeline likes a touch of *Chicory Root Inulin with Stevia* added for sweetness. When I experimented with giving traditional mint tea a new twist by adding lavender, the result was an immediate family favourite. *Makes 4 cups*

INGREDIENTS

¼–½ cup fresh mint leaves (peppermint, lemon balm, spearmint—whatever you have), packed

2 lavender flowers or a few lavender leaves

4 cups boiling water

Chicory Root Inulin with Stevia (page 324) or favourite sweetener, to taste (optional)

DIRECTIONS

Wash the mint leaves and lavender flowers or leaves, then put in a teapot and cover with the boiling water. Leave the tea to steep for at least 5 minutes. Strain before serving either hot or chilled.

CARROT BLOSSOM TEA

Everything about the discovery of this unusual tea was a delightful surprise. After growing several varieties of heirloom carrots one year and failing to harvest all of them by the end of the season, our family enjoyed observing Nature's journey. We watched in amazement as the carrot plants grew to be six-feet-tall, with decorative foliage and unique flowers that were straight from Dr. Seuss. Our beloved bees were crazy about them! Walking past them one day, I noticed their incredible, sweet, floral fragrance and I thought of using these flowers for a beverage. After doing some research to ensure that they were safe to eat, I made this most delicious tea for myself and a friend who was visiting at the time. The tea's colour reflects the colours of the flower blossoms themselves: the pink blossoms produce a pink tea, while the white blossoms result in a clear tea. This is a special seasonal treat for anyone privileged to have access to carrot blossoms—and is another great reason to let some of these plants go to seed! *Makes 4 cups*

INGREDIENTS

¼–½ cup fresh carrot blossoms, packed

4 cups boiling water

DIRECTIONS

Place the washed, fragrant carrot blossoms from the garden in a teapot and cover with the boiling water. Allow the blossoms to steep for at least 5 minutes. To serve, strain and pour into teacups and enjoy like any other hot herbal tea. Alternatively, serve chilled or over ice.

Bee Bite

In the last decade, the world has experienced a catastrophic loss of honey bees. Known as "colony collapse disorder," this phenomenon means that worker bees suddenly and mysteriously disappear from hives, or whole bee communities entirely disappear.

BERRY PUNCH SLUSHY

INGREDIENTS

½ small lemon

1 cup strawberries, fresh
or frozen

¼ cup cranberries or
raspberries, fresh or frozen

*Chicory Root Inulin with
Stevia* (page 324) or favourite
sweetener, to taste

ice and water, to desired
consistency

There's nothing more satisfying on a hot summer's day than a fresh and fruity slushy. Strawberry and lemon are delicious together, but the addition of tart cranberries or raspberries turns this guilt-free frosty delight into a flavour explosion. Depending on whether you use fresh or frozen fruit and also how Slurpee-like you want the consistency, adjust the water and ice amounts accordingly. Because the sweetness and tartness of fruits can also vary, start with less sweetener than you think you'll need and add more to adjust. This drink is always a hit when the kids have friends over for playdates and parties, and other parents love you for not sugar-loading their kids! *Makes about 3 cups*

DIRECTIONS

Remove the seeds from the lemon half and chop roughly (peel, pulp and all). Since the relative thickness of the peel and pulp varies from lemon to lemon, you may need to adjust how much you include, according to your taste. Process all the ingredients in a high-speed blender or food processor until the slushy reaches a smooth, frosty consistency, tamping or scraping the sides of the container as necessary. Serve immediately.

Theresa's Tip 🌢

If you have a very small and/or mostly shady garden, you might still be able to grow raspberry or blueberry plants. They are easy to grow and bring a lot of joy once they start to produce fruit. Not only will you and your loved ones enjoy nibbling the sweet berries, but you will also be making the bees super happy—they are crazy about the blossoms!

LEMONADE

INGREDIENTS

2–3 lemons

1–1½ quarts water

Chicory Root Inulin with Stevia (page 324) or favourite sweetener, to taste

This is another recipe that I just took for granted, but the feedback and excitement of others when they tasted it convinced me to include it in this book: it is so simple and delicious, with a very low glycemic index. Everyone has individual taste and preferences, and lemons vary in terms of juiciness, sweetness and sourness. Because of this, providing specific amounts is nearly impossible—it depends on your personal taste. A staple in our home and a winner with kids, this sweet alternative to sugar-filled beverages is perfect for birthday parties. Angeline loves to squeeze the lemons and feels empowered to be able to make it whenever she wants. As an added bonus, she stays nicely hydrated as she drinks it all summer long. It is great to have a treat like this to teach kids that it really is possible to enjoy such simple indulgences without any sugar. *Makes 4–6 cups*

DIRECTIONS

Halve, de-seed and juice the lemons, but do not discard the pulp and peel. Put the lemon juice and water in a tall jug, add the sweetener and whisk or shake together well. If you want, you can also add the peel halves and the pulp (pith and all!) of the lemons and stir or shake the jug to combine. Serve chilled or over ice—the perfect summer refreshment.

Bev's Bit
Lemons help to purify your blood, and they're great for improving the health of your hair and skin!

CLASSIC RAW GREEN JUICE

Green juice is an excellent way to get all the nutritional benefits of a lot of beautiful produce into one little glass! Removing the fibre allows the juice to pass through your digestive system quickly and with minimal effort, so there is little drain on your energy level. It is important to know that, just as most of the vitamins, minerals, chlorophyll and enzymes go directly to your bloodstream, so too does the natural sugar content of the produce. Because of this, some people might like to be mindful of how much sweet fruit they add to the juice. Alex loves to make this recipe, which is a wonderful way to use up vegetable stems and the cucumber harvest! There's a double benefit to using kale stems in this juice: firstly, it reduces waste; and secondly, kale stems have a higher water content than kale leaves, making them ideal for juicing. I also like to add celery and a little parsley or cilantro to this refreshing beverage. Farmers' markets, here we come! *Serves 1–2*

INGREDIENTS

1½ cucumbers, thinly sliced, peels left on

3 lemons, peeled

1 large handful kale stems

1 broccoli stem

1–3 apples, cored

1 inch fresh ginger root

1 celery stalk, chopped (optional)

½ cup parsley and/or cilantro (optional)

DIRECTIONS

JUICER METHOD Run all ingredients through a juicer and enjoy!

FINE MESH STRAINER METHOD Blend the cucumbers with the lemons in a high-speed blender using the tamper. Then add the rest of the ingredients and blend again, using the tamper. Strain in 2–3 batches through a nut milk bag (see *Terrific Tools*, page 34) or through a thin dish towel into a large bowl, squeezing and wringing it to get as much juice out as possible. For easy serving, either return the juice to the rinsed-out blender or pour it into a tall jug. Serve as soon as possible; do not store for longer than 3 days in the refrigerator.

Theresa's Tip 💧

This juice loses some nutrients if stored in the refrigerator for hours or days, so if you know you won't be drinking it soon, I recommend freezing it. It's also great to make some extra juice to freeze at the end of the harvest season, so that you can enjoy it during the colder months. I've found it to be especially good to have some available to boost my antioxidant intake at vulnerable times, before or after a medical procedure, or when I might be on the verge of a cold or flu.

Haely's Hint ❋

Both parsley and cilantro are great for detoxification, while celery is a good blood builder.

MILKS

You won't believe how easy it is to make your own non-dairy milk!

RAW NUT MILK

Once you try this classic raw milk recipe, you'll never want to buy processed nut milk at the store again! *Makes about 4 cups milk or 2 cups cream*

DIRECTIONS

Soak the raw nuts for 8 hours or overnight (with a dash of salt). Rinse the nuts well, then blend thoroughly with the water and dates (if using). Use the Fine Mesh Strainer Method (page 49) to extract the milk.

INGREDIENTS

1 cup raw almonds or other nuts

4 cups water (2 cups water for a thick cream)

1–2 dates (optional)

tiny dash Himalayan salt (optional)

Haely's Hint ❁

All nuts contain phytates, which are Mother Nature's way of protecting them from insects. Phytates are poisonous to many bugs and irritating to human digestive systems. Soaking nuts will help break down and remove the phytates, and salt enhances this process. Rinse the nuts at least twice during the soaking process.

Theresa's Tip 🍃

Whenever you make this recipe, be sure to save the remaining pulp. See *Sustainable Kitchen Tips 101* (page 330) for ways to use this pulp. You can significantly change the flavour of the milk by using other nuts; try Brazil nuts, pecans, macadamia nuts, pine nuts or any combination desired. Equal parts Brazil nuts and almonds make an amazing classic milk or cream. For an irresistible raw ice cream and for other cream-based desserts, my favourite combination for creaminess and flavour is equal parts Brazil nuts, almonds and pecans.

RAW HEMP SEED MILK

INGREDIENTS

1 cup hemp seeds or other seeds

4 cups water (2 cups water for a thick cream)

1–4 dates (optional)

tiny dash Himalayan salt (optional)

While slightly more bitter in taste, this is a great alternative milk for anyone sensitive to nuts or just wanting the additional health benefits of these high protein, nutrient-rich treasures. Because of its high fat content, hemp seed milk can offer a similar creaminess as the nut milk and can be used interchangeably with nut milk in recipes that do not involve heating (because of their omega-3 content), see Oils in *Funky Ingredients*, page 22. *Makes about 4 cups milk or 2 cups cream*

DIRECTIONS

Blend all the ingredients thoroughly, then strain using the Fine Mesh Strainer Method (page 49) to extract the milk.

Theresa's Tip 💧

TEA-INFUSED MILK: For a very simple, lightly flavoured *Nut* or *Hemp Seed Milk*, replace some of the water used with tea. You can use green tea, *Carrot-Blossom Tea, Mint & Lavender Tea* or any other tea you like. With the wide range of herbal and regular teas, the sky really is the limit! The amount of tea you choose to use is a matter of preference. If you want to impress your friends without any effort, make an herb-infused cream and make an exotic ice cream with it!

RAW FLAX SEED MILK

INGREDIENTS

1 cup raw flax seeds

4 cups water

Theresa's Tip 💧

The remaining seed pulp from these seed milks can be added to low-temperature granola, cracker or chip recipes for additional fibre and nutrients.

This is the most brain-boosting milk on the planet! With an over-the-top amount of omega-3 fatty acids, this drink is phenomenal for the mind and body. Because of its very high oil content and unique binding quality, it also offers an extremely thick milk that has a gooey consistency. It has a characteristic taste that straight-up will not appeal to everyone. While this is not a milk that I recommend for general drinking, it can be a terrific addition to other milk or cream recipes when you want a creamier and richer flavour, such as with the *Quinoa Milk* (right) or rice milk. Apparently, you can make incredible ice cream with this thick milk as well. That will be a future recipe I want to create one day! Because of its omega-3 content, do not heat this milk. *Makes about 4 cups milk*

DIRECTIONS

Blend all the ingredients thoroughly, then strain using the Fine Mesh Strainer Method (page 49) to extract the milk.

RAW COCONUT MILK

Easy, delicious and empowering! *Makes about 4 cups*

DIRECTIONS

Heat the water to a fairly warm temperature (but not too hot or boiling). Blend all the ingredients really well for 1–2 minutes, then use the Fine Mesh Strainer Method (page 49) to extract the milk. If the milk is too hot to strain in this way, allow to cool a few minutes until you can handle the nut milk bag comfortably. Chill and enjoy.

(page 49)

INGREDIENTS

2 cups raw unsweetened shredded coconut

4 cups water

tiny dash Himalayan salt (optional)

QUINOA MILK

I was so happy to create this easy, protein-rich milk recipe for anyone who is allergic or sensitive to nuts, seeds and coconut. It does not have the same creamy quality that the other milks have, but it is still an alternative to consider for those who are sensitive to the other options. It is similar in consistency to rice milk and has a brownish colour. *Makes about 5 ½ cups*

DIRECTIONS

Blend all the ingredients thoroughly, then strain using the Fine Mesh Strainer Method (page 49). Use in recipes calling for milk, but not for recipes requiring a creamy milk.

(page 49)

INGREDIENTS

2 cups cooked quinoa

4 cups water

1–4 dates (optional)

tiny dash Himalayan salt (optional)

Theresa's Tip 💧
If you have a powerful high-speed blender that processes finely enough, you may not need to strain this milk through a nut milk bag.

Bev's Bit 🌱
Quinoa is one of only a few plant foods considered to be a complete protein.

Sweet Milk Variations

Once you know how to make your own creamy non-dairy milk, the possibilities for sweet milk variations are endless. Here are some of our favourites:

Vanilla Milk
Add 3–5 pitted dates or favourite sweetener, plus ½–1 tsp vanilla extract or powder, before blending any unsweetened, creamy non-dairy milk.

Chocolate Milk
Add ½ cup cacao powder to vanilla milk and blend.

Strawberry Milk
Blend vanilla milk with 1 cup fresh or frozen strawberries.

Caramel Milk
Add some *Caramel Sauce* (see page 328) to any of the creamy milks.

SMOOTHIES

Delicious fruit and vegetable smoothies feel like a treat while packing a major nutritional punch.

PEACH BANANA GREEN SMOOTHIE

In our tiny garden, we have fresh kale year-round—it even grows in the cracks of the cement pavement! As much as we love kale, we are always looking for new ways to use it. Once Alex put this number together, there was no turning back—we could not believe how crazy-delicious green could be! *Makes about 3–4 cups*

DIRECTIONS

Blend until creamy and serve.

> **Haely's Hint** ✿
> Kale is a true superfood—high in calcium and, surprisingly, a decent source of protein

INGREDIENTS

1 banana

2 peaches or 1½ cups frozen peach pieces

1 cup baby or de-stemmed kale, packed

ice and water, to desired consistency

PINEAPPLE BANANA HEMP SMOOTHIE

In addition to the omega-3-rich hemp seeds and potassium-rich bananas, pineapple makes this smoothie feel like you're enjoying a treat from a tropical resort. The bromelain in pineapples has potent anti-inflammatory benefits and is most concentrated in the core and stem, just below the fronds, so be sure to add the core if using fresh pineapple to make this creamy and delicious beverage. *Makes about 4 cups*

DIRECTIONS

Blend until creamy and serve.

> **Haely's Hint** ✿
> In addition to being a good source of omega-3s, hemp is high in protein and will help reduce the glycemic index of this delicious smoothie.

INGREDIENTS

2 cups pineapple, fresh or frozen

1 cup almond milk or favourite non-dairy milk

1 banana

½ cup hemp seeds

juice of ½ lemon

1 tsp lemon zest (optional)

3 dates, pitted (optional)

⅛ tsp Himalayan salt

vanilla extract or powder, to taste

ice and water, to desired consistency

ORANGE BANANA GREEN SMOOTHIE

INGREDIENTS

2 bananas

2 oranges

2–3 cups romaine hearts

3–10 dates, pitted (optional)

ice and water, to desired consistency

This is another easy way to enjoy more plant-based, nutritious raw food. What makes the transition easier for a lot of people is to start with smoothies that are sweetened with more fruit, before moving on to more vegetable-based ones. It is wonderful to find ways to try new things that are so delicious. *Makes about 6 cups*

DIRECTIONS

Blend until creamy and serve.

> **Theresa's Tip**
>
> A fun, plant-growing activity to do with kids is to put the cut base of a Romaine lettuce head in water, set it on a windowsill and then watch as new roots grow and little lettuce leaves begin to sprout. Children (and adults too) love how how quickly those little sprouts start to poke up and how fast they grow.

CHOCOLATE BANANA SMOOTHIE

INGREDIENTS

2 cups almond milk or favourite non-dairy milk

2 ice cubes

1½–2 frozen bananas

½ cup raw walnuts

1–2 raw Brazil nuts

¼ cup cacao powder

2–3 tsp *Chicory Root Inulin with Stevia* (page 324) or favourite sweetener, to taste

2 tsp cacao nibs

1 tsp carob powder

¼ tsp Himalayan salt

When Angeline was particularly challenging to feed, I began to make her irresistible chocolate banana smoothies with nuts, which she happily devoured. This treasure has become a mainstay for her (and the rest of us) ever since. Later, we began to slip a little flax oil into the mix and she still loves it. This yummy smoothie makes a delicious frozen dessert for the kids: just freeze in Popsicle trays and they won't realize how good this super treat is for them! *Makes 4–5 cups*

DIRECTIONS

Blend until creamy and serve.

> **Theresa's Tip**
>
> If you are looking for creative ways to get more green veggies into your children, this delicious smoothie that kids love may be the answer to your prayers. Start with adding just a very small quantity of spinach or kale, and the taste will still be fantastic. Be careful not to add too much too fast, though, because kids will notice the flavour difference and your efforts will be in vain. Increase the quantity very slowly and cautiously, and they are less likely to reject it. Believe me, I learned this one the hard way!

STRAWBERRY CHEESECAKE SMOOTHIE

A delicious, probiotic and nutrient-dense dessert beverage you can enjoy in a snap. Brazil nuts not only provide an additional dose of creaminess, but are also a rich, natural food source of the antioxidant selenium. Because berries are such an easy fruit to freeze, this smoothie can be enjoyed any time of year. Like the *Chocolate Banana Smoothie*, this recipe also makes a deliciously creamy, frozen treat—probiotics and all!
Makes about 3 cups

DIRECTIONS

Blend until creamy and serve.

> **Haely's Hint** ✻
> Probiotics support the good bacteria in your digestive system.

INGREDIENTS

1–1½ cups strawberries, fresh or frozen

⅔ cup raw cashews

6 raw Brazil nuts

1–1½ tsp *Chicory Root Inulin with Stevia* (page 324) or favourite sweetener

¼ tsp probiotic powder (or the contents of 4 probiotic capsules)

Himalayan salt, to taste

ice and water, to desired consistency

SUNRISE SENSATION OMEGA SMOOTHIE

This naturally sweet and refreshing drink is rich in antioxidants, anti-inflammatory bromelain and omega-3 fatty acids that can easily double as a summer treat on a hot day. *Makes about 4 cups*

DIRECTIONS

Blend until creamy and serve.

INGREDIENTS

½ cup almond milk or favourite non-dairy milk

1 cup pineapple, fresh or frozen

½ banana

¼ cup hemp seeds

½–1 orange (optional)

1 cup strawberries, fresh or frozen

15–20 raspberries, fresh or frozen

1 tsp vanilla extract or powder

ice and water, to desired consistency

MORNING GRUB

FLAX & CHIA RAW POWER BREAKFAST

For a delicious and convenient on-the-go healthy breakfast, make each serving in a resealable glass jar and add the walnuts, buckwheat groats, fresh fruit and cinnamon before heading out for your day. Our friend Lynda Hydamaka and her family premixed a large quantity of the dry ingredients and brought them along on an off-the-grid kayak trip with some boxes of coconut milk and enjoyed it as an easy breakfast cereal during their holiday. Feel free to omit or substitute ingredients based on your own unique dietary needs and what you have on hand. Be creative! *Serves 1*

INGREDIENTS

1 small or ½ large banana, mashed with a fork

1 tsp lemon juice (optional)

1 tsp goji berries or dehydrated blueberries

1 tsp raisins

1 tsp finely diced dates

1 tsp cacao nibs (optional)

2 tsp ground flax seeds

2 tsp chia seeds

2 tsp hemp seeds

1 cup favourite non-dairy milk

3–5 walnuts, pecans, almonds or Brazil nuts, crumbled (optional)

1 tsp toasted buckwheat groats (optional)

fresh seasonal fruits and/or berries

sprinkle cinnamon

DIRECTIONS

In a breakfast bowl, mix the banana, lemon juice, goji berries, raisins, dates, cacao nibs and all of the seeds. For a lower GI variation, omit the dried fruit. Cover with milk to about 1 inch above the cereal, stir and leave overnight in the fridge. To serve, add the nuts, buckwheat groats, fresh fruit and cinnamon, and more chilled milk if desired. Stir and enjoy!

Haely's Hint ✿

Our bodies can't digest whole flax seeds, so it is best if they are ground. Once flax is ground, it needs to be kept in an airtight container in the fridge or freezer. I grind a bunch at once and keep it in jars in the freezer. It stays powdered and doesn't clump, so is easy to use right from the freezer.

SUPERFOOD RAW BREAKFAST CEREAL

INGREDIENTS

3 cups toasted
buckwheat groats

2 cups almonds

½ cup Brazil nuts

1⅔ cups chia seeds

1⅓ cup hemp seeds

⅔ cup raisins (optional)

⅓ cup goji berries or other
dried fruit (optional)

1 tsp vanilla powder

1 tsp *Chicory Root Inulin
with Stevia* (page 324) or
favourite sweetener

This simple recipe was inspired by Nature's Path Qia Cereal.
Makes 8–9 cups

DIRECTIONS

Pulse the almonds and Brazil nuts in a food processor until broken into coarse pieces (do not over process). Place all ingredients in a large glass jar or bag and shake up until well mixed. Store in an airtight container for up to 1 month. For a lower GI version, omit the raisins and goji berries/other dried fruit.

SERVING OPTIONS For a cold cereal, add non-dairy milk and wait about 5 minutes before eating. For a hot cereal, heat ⅓–⅔ cup non-dairy milk in a saucepan, then remove from the heat. Stir in ⅓–½ cup of the cereal and allow the mixture to thicken. If desired, add a little of your favourite sweetener or some fresh fruits and berries, and serve, with or without some chilled non-dairy milk.

> **Theresa's Tip** 🖊
> This cereal has a multitude of uses. We love to sprinkle it on top of our salads for a quick superfood boost and it is a terrific, easy and versatile travel food. You can also add it to cookie and bread recipes for delicious and healthy variations.

> **Haely's Hint** ✿
> Despite the word "wheat" in the name, buckwheat groats are gluten-free!

APPLE CINNAMON GRANOLA

If no other recipe in this book transforms your life, this delectable granola will! Once dehydrated and cooled, it can be stored in an airtight container for several weeks—if it lasts that long. Enjoy it as an instant breakfast cereal, a travel snack or as a topper for ice cream or other desserts. You can even pour a little boiling water or warmed non-dairy milk on top for a quick hot cereal that your kids (and everyone else) will love. Our good friend and long-time cook, Michelle Stewart, loves this recipe, both dehydrated and freshly prepared as a delectable muesli... me too! Like yummy cookie dough, the final yield will mysteriously be reduced if you don't keep an eye on it!
Makes 6 cups

INGREDIENTS

4 cups gluten-free rolled oats

2 cups finely diced apples, firmly packed

1 cup unsweetened shredded (or ribbon) coconut

1 cup crumbled nuts (eg walnuts, pecans, almonds or Brazil nuts)

½ cup coconut oil

½ cup coconut sugar or favourite dry sweetener, or to taste

¼ cup maple syrup or favourite liquid sweetener

1 tbsp ground cinnamon

½ cup apple pulp* (optional)

DIRECTIONS

Stir together all ingredients until well combined and spread out on 2–3 dehydrator trays or cookie sheets (if drying in the oven). Set the dehydrator to 105°F and allow the granola to dry for 24–48 hours, or until completely crisp. For the oven method, place the cookie sheets in an oven set to the lowest temperature (usually around 150–170°F) and dry the granola for 2–4 hours, or until completely crisp.

Feel free to experiment with adding to and switching the ingredients in this delicious cereal. Try using not only different nuts and/or seeds, but also different fresh and dried fruit. If you'd like to create a completely raw variation, you can also replace the maple syrup with mashed bananas or puréed mango or persimmons to naturally sweeten and also gently bind the granola together nicely.

*Good way to use the pulp left over after juicing. Chop finely if it is not already pulverized.

Haely's Hint ❁
Cinnamon is great for blood sugar control.

Theresa's Tip 🌢
This is another great recipe for even very young children to make. It can give them a sense of confidence and pride in being able to contribute something that is really delicious for the whole family.

MANGO BANANA GRANOLA

INGREDIENTS

2 cups diced mango

2 bananas

¼ cup maple syrup or favourite liquid sweetener

4 cups gluten-free rolled oats

1 cup unsweetened shredded coconut

1 cup chopped walnuts, pecans, almonds and/or favourite nut(s)

½ cup coconut oil

⅔–1 cup coconut sugar or favourite dry sweetener, to taste

1 tbsp ground cinnamon

1 tsp orange zest (optional)

While not as high in pectin as apples, both bananas and mangoes are excellent sources of this magical type of soluble fibre, which reportedly has a range of benefits, including cholesterol-balancing properties. Oh, and they are also very yummy! *Makes about 6 cups*

DIRECTIONS

Purée the mangos, bananas and maple syrup until smooth and pour them into a large bowl. Add the remaining ingredients and stir until everything is well combined, with the moisture evenly distributed throughout. Follow the dehydrator or oven method, as for the *Apple Cinnamon Granola* (page 63). Cool completely, and store in an airtight container for up to 1 month.

Granola Bars

To make a sweet, healthy treat, divide the raw granola mixture into 2 equal-sized balls and put each ball on a separate teflex dehydrator tray or on a parchment-covered cookie sheet. Then press the balls into flat squares or rectangles, about ¼ inch thick, ensuring that the granola is pressed firmly together. With a dull knife, long straight scraper or long offset spatula, score the granola into bar-sized rectangles (about 1–1½ inches wide by 3–4 inches long. They won't reduce much in size when dried.

Use either a dehydrator or the Oven Dehydration Method (page 233) to dry. If using a dehydrator, turn them over halfway through the drying time onto a mesh dehydrator sheet. Let cool, then break into bars and store in an airtight container. *Makes 24–36 bars*

Bev's Bit 🥭

Keep macular degeneration at bay and help protect your eyesight with the antioxidant zeaxanthin found in mangoes.

KILMENY'S FRUITY ORANGE BREAKFAST QUINOA

One of the unexpected pleasures of creating this volume has been the sense of community it naturally created. Those touched by the project have generously offered to share favourite recipe creations. This recipe is a great example, contributed by my wonderful editor, Kilmeny Jane Denny. It's one of her favourite hot breakfasts, which sustains her through the morning. When I tried it, I also loved it. While I've kept the integrity of Kilmeny's basic recipe, I have made a few minor adjustments that I hope you will love too. You can experiment with using different dried fruits, nuts and seeds to switch it up and take the flavour into whole new directions. *Serves 2–3*

DIRECTIONS

Place all ingredients except the pumpkin and sunflower seeds in a medium-sized saucepan over high heat and bring to a full boil. Cover, reduce the heat to low and cook until all of the liquid has been absorbed and the quinoa is tender (about 20 minutes). It is important to watch carefully towards the end, because this burns easily. Remove from the heat, stir in the seeds and serve immediately.

INGREDIENTS

1 cup water

1 cup orange juice (or 1 peeled orange, pulverized in a blender, made up to 1 cup with water if necessary)

1 cup quinoa

1 tsp finely grated orange zest

3–4 tbsp raisins and/or dried cranberries, or to taste

1/8 tsp cinnamon (optional)

1 tbsp pumpkin seeds

1–2 tbsp sunflower seeds

Bee Bite

Did you know that bees are not only extremely sensual beings, but are also all-star dancers?

In 1973, Karl von Frisch won the Nobel Prize in Physiology or Medicine for his research about the European honey bee. Among other interesting facts, he discovered that bees have special sensitivities to smell, sight, orientation and timekeeping. Perhaps the most famous of his discoveries was what great dancers these little foragers are! The foraging bees' Round Dance communicates information about the presence of feeding places within 50–100 metres of a beehive, including the type of food available.

RISE & SHINE INSTANT HOT BREAKFAST CEREAL

There's nothing like a classic hot breakfast cereal with berries freshly picked from the garden or foraged from the forest. Feel free to omit or replace any ingredients to which you are sensitive or according to your taste preferences. Have fun being creative with other ingredients—try different dried or fresh fruits, nuts, seeds, etc. For this recipe, you simply create an instant breakfast mix. This is another easy travel food that makes it possible to enjoy a healthy, hot breakfast in your hotel room. *Makes 8–9 cups*

DIRECTIONS

Place all ingredients in a large glass jar or bag and shake up until well mixed. Store in an airtight container for up to one month.

To make one serving, pour ⅔ cup of the breakfast mix into a bowl, stir in ½ cup heated water or non-dairy milk and allow to set for 1–3 minutes. If desired, add more chilled milk, fresh berries and/or seasonal fruit. Enjoy!

Bev's Bit
Combat inflammation in your body with the plentiful amount of vitamin E found in sunflower seeds.

INGREDIENTS

3 cups gluten-free rolled oats

3 cups toasted buckwheat groats

¼ cup sunflower seeds

¼ cup pumpkin seeds

1½–2 cups chopped and/or whole nuts (eg walnuts, pecans, almonds or Brazil nuts)

2 tbsp ground flax seeds

2 tbsp hemp seeds

2 tbsp chia seeds

⅔ cup goji berries or other dried fruit

⅔ cup raisins

1 tbsp cinnamon (optional)

SAVOURY ONION HERB PANCAKES

I love it when recipe development doesn't work as planned, but sets the stage for a new creation. This unique recipe came about after one of my onion ring recipe attempts failed, and I decided to play with what resulted. Voilà! This discovery is reminiscent of potato latkes. Delish! *Makes 6–8 4–inch pancakes*

DRY INGREDIENTS

½ cup Bob's Red Mill or favourite gluten-free all-purpose flour

½ tsp baking powder

¼ tsp Himalayan salt

¼ tsp dried thyme

¼ tsp dried oregano

¼ tsp dried rosemary

½ tsp *Chicory Root Inulin with Stevia* (page 324) (omit if using syrup or nectar as below)

WET INGREDIENTS

¼ cup non-dairy milk

2 tbsp extra virgin olive oil

1 tsp coconut nectar or favourite sweetener (omit if using stevia as above)

¼ tsp apple cider vinegar or lemon juice

¼ cup onions, finely chopped

favourite cooking oil, for oiling the skillet

OPTIONAL GARNISHES

applesauce, syrup, blueberries, raspberries, strawberries, nuts or seeds, plus chopped savoury fresh herbs such as basil or oregano

DIRECTIONS

In a medium-sized bowl, stir together the dry ingredients and set aside. In a small bowl, whisk together the milk, oil, nectar and cider vinegar. Add them to the dry mixture and mix until just combined. Fold in the onions. Spoon or pour the batter into a heated and lightly oiled skillet over medium-low heat. Flip the pancakes when the bottom is golden brown and cook the other side. Serve hot on their own or with garnishes.

> **Bev's Bit** 🌱
> Along with making you cry, eating onions on a daily basis may also help keep your bones strong.

OLD-FASHIONED PANCAKES

DRY INGREDIENTS

1¾ cups Bob's Red Mill
or favourite gluten-free
all-purpose flour

2 tsp baking powder

½ tsp *Chicory Root Inulin with
Stevia* (page 324) (omit if using
syrup or nectar as below)

½ tsp Himalayan salt

WET INGREDIENTS

1 cup mashed banana

2 tbsp maple syrup, coconut
nectar or favourite syrup (omit
if using stevia as above)

1¼–1½ cups non-dairy milk,
water or juice (if using juice,
omit either the syrup or stevia)

½ tsp vanilla extract,
or to taste

favourite cooking oil, for oiling
the skillet

OPTIONAL GARNISHES

applesauce, syrup, jam,
blueberries, raspberries,
strawberries, nuts or seeds,
chocolate chips

I couldn't even begin to estimate how many recipe-development renditions of old-fashioned pancakes we went through before Alex and I finally perfected this simple recipe. They had to have just the right texture, taste, fluffiness and sweetness. I think the walls of the whole house released a big sigh of relief when we were finally successful! *Makes 8–10 4-inch pancakes*

DIRECTIONS

In a medium bowl, stir together the dry ingredients. In a separate bowl, whisk together the wet ingredients. Add the wet mixture to the dry and mix together until just combined. Over medium-low heat, heat the oil in a skillet until it becomes more liquid, then spoon about 2 tbsp of the batter per pancake into the pan. Flip when the bottoms are golden brown and cook the other side. Optional garnishes can be added during cooking or when served.

Theresa's Tip

Add ¼ cup shredded carrots or a few
tablespoons of apple pulp for an even
more plant-infused breakfast treat.

JANE'S KOREAN ZUCCHINI PANCAKES

This recipe holds a very special place in my heart, even though I've never met Jane, who is the mother of my friend and first editor, Mari Kim. At the end of her two-day visit from Seattle, Mari wanted to cook something for me and my family. She quickly whipped up these traditional Korean pancakes from her childhood, experimenting with our gluten-free flour and using zucchini from our garden. It was such a priceless moment and memory. When I asked if she would like me to include the recipe in this cookbook and name it after her mom, Mari was thrilled. Thank you, Jane! I think we probably need to meet now... *Makes 6–8 4-inch pancakes*

DIRECTIONS

Mix the flour and water together until smooth, then stir in the zucchini. Over medium-low heat, heat the oil in a skillet until it becomes more liquid, then spoon about 2 tbsp of the batter per pancake into the pan. Spread the batter thinly. Flip when the outsides of the pancake appear to be cooking through about an inch towards the centre of the pancake. Then cook the other side until the pancake is cooked through and a little crispy. Remove from the pan and serve with a very light sprinkling of salt or a little of the simple sauce.

Haely's Hint ❋
If you are looking for a gluten- and soy-free seasoning, coconut aminos is a good choice.

PANCAKE INGREDIENTS

⅔ cup quinoa flour, rice flour or Bob's Red Mill or favourite gluten-free all-purpose flour

⅔ cup water

½ cup grated zucchini, packed

sesame oil or favourite cooking oil, for oiling the skillet

Himalayan salt, to taste (optional)

SIMPLE SAUCE INGREDIENTS

2 tbsp tamari or coconut aminos

2 tbsp rice or white vinegar

pinch crushed hot red pepper flakes (optional)

HERB-INFUSED BREAKFAST SAUSAGE

Other than pancakes in the skillet, nothing can bring up memories of waking up on a lazy Sunday morning like the smell and taste of a rich breakfast sausage. *Makes 12*

DIRECTIONS

Blend all the ingredients together and massage well to mix. Use about 2 slightly heaping tablespoons for each sausage: form into balls, then flatten to about 1/3–1/2 inch thick and place on a silicone baking mat or on a parchment-covered baking sheet for the oven method, or on a teflex dehydrator sheet for the raw version.

BAKED VERSION Bake in a preheated 350°F oven for about 35–45 minutes, turning the sausages after 25–30 minutes.

RAW VERSION Dehydrate at 105°F on a teflex dehydrator sheet for 8 hours, turning the sausages after 5–6 hours.

Serve hot directly from the oven or dehydrator.

Bee Bite

Did you know about the sad plight of male honey bees?

These drones have only one purpose in life—to offer their sperm to a queen bee (usually a queen in another hive) and they take their job very seriously. They don't work like the other bees and don't even have a stinger. When food is scarce in the winter, drones are sometimes kicked out of the hive by the other bees. Karl von Frisch discovered that the matriarchal queen bee and her daughters are like the alluring sirens from Greek mythology. They attract the drones by emitting distinctive pheromones that are irresistible to the males. The drones are compelled to mate with the queen, as early as one week after being born. However, once they've made their sperm offering, they die. Such a tragic destiny!

INGREDIENTS

1 recipe *Best No-Meat Meat* (page 166, shitake mushroom variation), uncooked

1 tsp lemon juice

3/8 tsp dried ground sage

1/4 tsp dried thyme

1/4 tsp rosemary

1/4 tsp rice vinegar

1/4 tsp tamari or coconut aminos

1/2 tsp coconut sugar

1/8 tsp garlic powder

1/8 tsp Himalayan salt

1/8 tsp paprika

1/8 tsp crushed hot red pepper flakes (optional)

light sprinkle nutmeg

BREAKFAST SCRAMBLE

When my husband Eric and I created this dish after one of our morning walks in the forest, we ran out and picked most of the ingredients straight from our garden—I love that! *Serves 3–4*

INGREDIENTS

12 oz firm silken tofu

favourite cooking oil
for sautéing

1½ cups chopped onion

½ cup chopped leek or
1 green onion, chopped

2 garlic cloves, minced
or microplaned

1 cup sliced mushrooms
(shitake and/or crimini)

1–2 tbsp chopped jalapeño
pepper (optional)

¼–½ red bell pepper,
thinly sliced

2 cups chopped fresh kale

Himalayan salt and black
pepper, to taste

1 cup grated Daiya cheddar
or favourite vegan cheese

GARNISHES

fresh chopped cilantro and
cherry tomatoes cut in half,
avocado slices, fresh basil
and red bell pepper slices

DIRECTIONS

Put the tofu in a bowl and break it up with a fork so it resembles scrambled eggs, then set aside. Heat your favourite cooking oil in a large saucepan over medium heat, and sauté the onions, leeks or green onions, garlic, mushrooms, jalapeño pepper and red bell pepper until the onions begin to soften. Stir in the tofu and continue sautéing for another 1–2 minutes. Stir in the kale, salt and pepper and cook for about a minute, until the kale is just slightly wilted. Spread the mixture evenly over the pan and sprinkle the cheese on top. Remove the pan from the heat, cover and let the cheese melt for about 2–3 minutes. Garnish as desired.

Haely's Hint ❀
Soy is a common genetically modified (GM) crop so it's important to always buy organic tofu— organic food cannot be GM.

PEACH RHUBARB COMPOTE

In our garden, we have a lovely and generous rhubarb plant. The problem with rhubarb is that it is so tart most recipes require a heap of sugar. Since we prefer minimizing the glycemic load of our family's food, I wanted to develop a recipe that used this beautiful, tart fruit with much healthier ingredients than usual. The sweet-tart flavour combination of rhubarb, peach and apple is so unconventional, I almost decided not to include it in this collection. However, the deliciousness factor won this debate. If you are game for a unique flavour adventure, this delectable dish is for you. *Makes 3 cups*

DIRECTIONS

Stew all the ingredients in a covered saucepan over high heat (stirring frequently) until the fruit is soft and tender (about 5 minutes). Mash to the desired consistency. Serve the compote warm or chilled.

INGREDIENTS

2 cups chopped rhubarb

1 peach or nectarine, chopped

2 apples, chopped

1 cup water

1 tbsp *Chicory Root Inulin with Stevia* (page 324) or favourite sweetener, or to taste

1 tsp lemon juice (optional)

dash Himalayan salt

¼ tsp cinnamon, or to taste

Bev's Bit
Your eyes will love the antioxidant lutein in rhubarb!

INSTANT RAW APPLESAUCE

1 apple, cut into pieces
for processing

½ tsp cinnamon, or to taste

2–4 tbsp water

¼ tsp *Chicory Root Inulin with
Stevia* (page 324) or favourite
sweetener (optional)

If you haven't gathered it already, it makes me super-happy when I can make something in an absolute flash. This is as easy, delicious and healthy as it gets. If you want to fancy it up by adding a sprinkling of granola and maybe even a swirl of coconut or nut cream, go for it. This recipe was created one fall, when our wonderful friend Karen Bogdanovich generously shared organic apples and pears from her plentiful harvest. We felt like we had won the lotto—thanks so much, Karen! *Serves 1–2*

DIRECTIONS

Process all ingredients together in a blender or food processor to the desired consistency. Serve immediately.

GETTING FRESH
SALADS & DRESSINGS

RAW KALE & AVOCADO SALAD

INGREDIENTS

4 cups chopped baby
or de-stemmed kale

⅓–½ cup chopped chives

1 cup diced tomato

½–1 red bell pepper,
thinly sliced

1 avocado, chopped in
small pieces

juice from 1 lemon,
or 2–4 tbsp apple cider
vinegar, to taste

1 tbsp extra virgin olive oil

1 tbsp nutritional yeast

Himalayan salt and black
pepper, to taste

OPTIONAL GARNISHES

chopped chives and edible
flowers, *Herbed Croutons*
(page 316) or other favourite
gluten-free croutons

Here's a version of a kale salad we have been making for years. An important trick when working with fresh kale is to "cook" it by massaging it with your hands in the oil (in this case, olive oil combined with fresh avocado) and acid (lemon juice or vinegar), squeezing the kale as you do so. This process not only helps to make the kale softer, but also improves its taste—a fun method that most people have never heard of. It can take you back to your days of finger-painting in school. Kids will love this process too, and it's a great way to turn them on to eating this incredibly nutritious food. I used to think that kale was boring and didn't taste very good. It was this recipe and method that changed my mind forever, and it's been a great transformer for many others as well. Avocado-massaged kale = YUM!
Serves 2–3

DIRECTIONS

Toss together the kale, chives, tomato and red bell pepper, then add and massage with the avocado, lemon juice or vinegar, olive oil, nutritional yeast, salt and black pepper. Serve immediately, with the garnish of your choice.

Theresa's Tip

I know these directions sound weird. But as you massage in all these ingredients you are, in effect, creating the dressing for the salad. The tomatoes break down and blend with the avocado and other items, resulting in an amazingly delicious creation.

DANDELION QUINOA SALAD

Because it is so bitter, dandelion is a difficult green to use in culinary dishes. However, it offers incredible health benefits because it is rich in vitamins, minerals, antioxidants and prebiotics. Dandelion is also a detoxifier and blood purifier that supports the liver, gallbladder and several other functions. I was excited to develop a delicious recipe using this amazing plant along with other beautiful and healthy ingredients that bring the flavour of this salad to life. *Serves 4–6*

DIRECTIONS

Toss together all ingredients, except the sauce. Cover generously with *Creamy Sunflower Seed Sauce* and serve.

1 cup thinly sliced dandelion leaves

1 cup shredded carrots

½ cup finely chopped cilantro

2 cups cooked and cooled quinoa

¾ cup diced red bell pepper

½ cup pine nuts and/or sesame, hemp or favourite seeds (optional)

½ cup raisins and/or goji berries (optional)

1–2 tbsp thinly sliced fresh mint leaves (optional)

Himalayan salt, to taste (optional)

Creamy Sunflower Seed Sauce (page 318), to taste

PACHAMAMA SALAD

This simple and deliciously satisfying favourite is so multidimensional. It includes all of the tastes—sweet, savoury, astringent, bitter, pungent, salty—so the only name that could properly capture its essence is "Pachamama," Mother Earth in traditional Andean culture. *Serves 1*

INGREDIENTS

1½ cups mixed salad greens

1–2 tbsp *Creamy Sunflower Seed Sauce* (page 318)

5–8 fresh raspberries

1 tbsp sunflower seeds

2 tbsp cooked chickpeas

½–1 tsp finely chopped fresh garden herbs (optional)

DIRECTIONS

Drizzle the dressing over the salad greens, then top with the raspberries, sunflower seeds, chickpeas and fresh herbs.

Bee Bite

The bees' Waggle Dance, is sort of a compass dance, in which they waggle their little bums in a special manner, angling and stretching their bodies in the geographically precise direction of the food. This complex communication provides information about how far away the food is by the speed of the dance and the number of straight stretches they do in the dance. The other bees gather the information by mimicking the movements (like in line-dance class), integrating the information into their nervous system. This dance also explains what type of food the bees will find at the distant location and the characteristics of that food. Even if there are big obstacles along the way, such as mountains or buildings, the Waggle Dance will still accurately lead them to where the food is located. The intelligence of bees and their ability to navigate is absolutely mind-blowing!

BEET & CILANTRO SALAD

This recipe was inspired by the salad one of our friends made for a Thanksgiving meal we shared. The combination of beets, cumin and cilantro is an unforgettable flavour. When I experimented with adding carrots, green onions and red bell peppers, it was an absolute hit! If you like to eat raw-infused dishes that span the rainbow, this dish is a great one to add to your repertoire. You can make it ahead of time and refrigerate—it gets better as it marinates in the juices. Sometimes I like to also sprinkle on a few chia seeds, just to add another dimension of nutrition to this already power-packed salad. One of my test kitchens suggested that this recipe would be a good one for someone who is just trying out beets, since it is easy and likely to be a positive experience. I also like to use this salad as an alternative to salad dressing over leafy greens—colourful and delicious. *Serves 4–6*

DIRECTIONS

Steam or boil the beets for about 40 minutes or until you can stick a fork in them easily. Remove them from the water or steamer and, when they're cool enough to handle, peel (if desired) and cut into small pieces. Set aside in a medium-large bowl. Add the red bell pepper, green onions and carrots to the cooled beets. Dress generously with *Cumin Vinaigrette* and allow to marinate, refrigerated, for several hours or overnight. Before serving, stir in the cilantro and garnish with a few additional sprigs of cilantro.

INGREDIENTS

3-4 beets

¼–½ red bell pepper, cubed

¼–½ cup thinly sliced green onions

¼–½ cup shredded carrots

Cumin Vinaigrette (page 102)

½ cup chopped cilantro, plus a few sprigs for garnish

Bev's Bit
Don't throw away your beet greens! In addition to other nutrients, the greens have tons more vitamin A and C than the beets themselves!

ASIAN COLESLAW WITH KALE

INGREDIENTS

7–8 cups shredded cabbage (any combination of green, purple or savoy)

2 cups shredded kale, packed

1 cup grated carrots

Spicy Asian Dressing (page 102)

mixed seeds (pumpkin, sunflower, sesame, hemp, chia and/or flax), for garnish (optional)

Funnily enough, the development of this recipe was prompted by a friend who gave us some cut-up cabbage when she was cleaning her kitchen before moving. I don't know what makes the classic spicy Asian taste profile that I threw together so appealing, but this salad doesn't last very long in our house whenever we make it! *Serves 4–8*

DIRECTIONS

Toss the cabbage, kale and carrots in a large bowl. Dress with *Spicy Asian Dressing*. Serve fresh, garnished with a sprinkling of seeds.

RAINBOW QUINOA, BASIL & PEPPER SALAD

I felt like nothing less than a superhero when I created this incredibly nutritious, light, bright and protein-packed dish of deliciousness. For the longest time, it was a staple in our house—the favourite meal for lunch and dinner! Feel free to experiment with using vegetables that are in season (steamed cut green beans are amazing in it!), but the fresh basil is a must. Here's what one test kitchen had to say about this recipe: "It was very easy to make. It was pretty and healthy. Prepared it three times and recommend it to friends." *Serves 6-10*

DIRECTIONS

In a large pot sauté the onion on medium heat for about 5 minutes, then add the garlic and sauté another 1-2 minutes, until all are translucent. Add the water and quinoa, stir to combine, turn the heat to high and bring to a boil. Reduce the heat and simmer, covered, for 20 minutes. Turn off the heat and mix the kale and/or spinach into the quinoa until wilted. Remove from the stove and allow to cool. Once cooled, toss in all the remaining ingredients and dress with *Lemonette Dressing*. Garnish with some additional basil or any of the other ingredients in the salad.

INGREDIENTS

favourite cooking oil for sautéing

1 onion, finely chopped

2-3 garlic cloves, finely minced or microplaned

3½ cups water

1½ cups quinoa, rinsed

1½ cups chopped baby or de-stemmed kale and/or spinach leaves, packed

½-1 cup diced fresh tomatoes

1½ cups diced mixed bell peppers (any combination of red, orange and yellow)

½ cup chopped celery

½-1 cup chopped cauliflower

½ cup chopped fresh basil

½ cup pine nuts or chopped almonds (optional)

additional lemon juice (optional)

Himalayan salt, to taste

Lemonette Dressing (page 103)

LENTIL SALAD

What a satisfying and simple salad! When friends brought a lentil salad with vinaigrette to a holiday potluck, I knew I had to create one for this collection! I love it on its own, but also enjoy it as a nutritious and flavourful filling for wraps. It also makes a tasty topping for green salad instead of using a dressing. *Serves 6*

DIRECTIONS

Toss together the carrot, bell pepper, green onions, parsley and lentils, then dress with the vinaigrette. Finish by adding salt and pepper to taste. Serve chilled.

> **Bev's Bit**
> Lentils are a powerhouse of nutrition, with one cup of the cooked legumes boasting 17 grams of protein and 15 grams of fibre!

INGREDIENTS

1 cup grated, julienned or spiralized carrots, packed

⅓ cup diced red bell pepper

⅔–¾ cup thinly sliced green onions

1 cup finely chopped parsley

2 cups cooked green lentils, drained

Italian Vinaigrette Dressing (page 103)

Himalayan salt and black pepper, to taste

¼ tsp cayenne pepper, or to taste (optional)

TABBOULEH WITH MINT & CILANTRO

2 cups chopped parsley, firmly packed

1 cup chopped cilantro, firmly packed

½ cup chopped mint, firmly packed

3 cups diced cucumbers

2 cups diced tomatoes

1 cup chopped green onions, loosely packed

1 cup chopped red bell pepper

4 garlic cloves, finely diced or microplaned, or to taste

3 tbsp lemon juice

1 tbsp extra virgin olive oil

1 tbsp cold-pressed flax or hemp oil or more extra virgin olive oil

¼–½ tsp Himalayan salt, to taste

⅛ tsp black pepper

3 cups cooked and cooled *Quinoa Rice* (page 161, or millet variation) or *Cauliflower Rice* (page 163) or cooked and cooled millet

3 cups cooked chickpeas, rinsed (optional)

Fresh, fragrant and light, this salad is a delicious standby for anyone, especially those in busy households. I love to make this dish on the weekend and prepack it in glass jars for lunches during the week. You can use this salad as a filling for a quick wrap as a grab-and-go meal that is healthy and light, yet incredibly satisfying. This is delicious with or without the grains and chickpeas. So flavourful, it's hard to believe it is so low in fat and salt! *Serves 6–8*

DIRECTIONS

Place all ingredients except the grains in a very large bowl and toss together. Then add *Quinoa, Millet* or *Cauliflower Rice*, or cooked millet, along with the chickpeas (if using) and toss to completely combine. Serve immediately or refrigerate to enjoy later.

CUMIN VINAIGRETTE

While beautiful as a salad dressing, this vinaigrette also offers an intriguing flavour profile that can turn a simple pasta, rice or quinoa dish into something flavourful and exotic for a quick side dish, with or without added vegetables. Add a few nuts or seeds to turn the side dish into a main meal! *Makes about ¾ cup*

INGREDIENTS

2 tbsp apple cider vinegar

juice of ½ lemon, or to taste

¼ cup extra virgin olive oil

1 tsp ground cumin

1–2 garlic cloves

¼ cup chopped onion

½ tsp Himalayan salt

¼ tsp black pepper

pinch *Chicory Root Inulin with Stevia* (page 324) or favourite sweetener (optional)

pinch cayenne pepper (optional)

DIRECTIONS

Put all ingredients in a blender and purée until creamy.

> **Bev's Bit** 🌱
> Cumin is a good source of dietary iron.

SPICY ASIAN DRESSING

When I developed this recipe, I had a friend of mine in mind who cannot eat sesame yet loves Asian food. It can be adapted several ways to account for food sensitivities: sunflower seeds and extra virgin olive oil in place of sesame; if avoiding soy, use coconut aminos. This dressing thickens a bit with time, and is a wonderful condiment to enjoy with vegetable, pasta, stir-fries, rice and quinoa dishes. *Makes 1½ cups*

INGREDIENTS

2 garlic cloves, chopped

2 tbsp chopped onion

½ inch fresh ginger root, chopped

¼ cup sesame oil (optional)

¼ cup extra virgin olive oil (or ½ cup if not using sesame oil)

¼ cup plus 1 tbsp rice vinegar

¼ cup plus 1 tbsp water, or to desired consistency

4 tbsp sunflower or sesame seeds

2 tbsp tamari or coconut aminos

1 tbsp smooth, unsalted, unsweetened peanut butter or other nut/seed butter or soy (nut-free) nut butter alternative

¼ tsp Himalayan salt, or to taste

⅛ tsp black pepper

½–1 small Thai red hot chili pepper (optional)

DIRECTIONS

Put all ingredients in a blender and purée until creamy.

LEMONETTE DRESSING

Lemons are magical! They are so delicious—versatile for savoury or sweet dishes, and are incredibly good for you. I vividly remember growing up in a rural town in Southern California called Rancho Cucamonga (yes, there really is a place called that!) where old eucalyptus trees were grown as natural windbreaks to protect the citrus groves in our little community. The aroma of the blossoms, interwoven with the healing scent of the eucalyptus, was incredible. Daily life there was a spa-like, aromatherapy experience! *Makes ⅔ cup*

INGREDIENTS

3 tbsp lemon juice

3 tbsp extra virgin olive oil

3 tbsp water

1½ tbsp tamari or coconut aminos

1 tsp maple syrup or favourite sweetener (optional)

DIRECTIONS

Put all ingredients in a blender and purée until creamy.

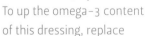

Theresa's Tip
To up the omega-3 content of this dressing, replace 1 tbsp of the olive oil with 1 tbsp cold-pressed flax or hemp oil.

ITALIAN VINAIGRETTE DRESSING

It's always nice to have a standard Italian vinaigrette. This one was inspired by my perennial herb garden, which always offers such a generous harvest. If you don't already grow oregano, thyme and winter savory, these are three winners that are virtually indestructible—great for accidental gardeners like me!

Makes about 1 cup

INGREDIENTS

½ cup plus 2 tbsp extra virgin olive oil

¼ cup red wine vinegar

2 tbsp apple cider vinegar

2 tbsp minced shallot or onion

2 garlic cloves

1 tsp fresh (or ½ tsp dried) oregano, thyme and/or savory, finely minced

¼ tsp Himalayan salt

⅛ tsp black pepper

1 tbsp lemon juice (optional)

DIRECTIONS

Put all ingredients in a blender and purée until creamy.

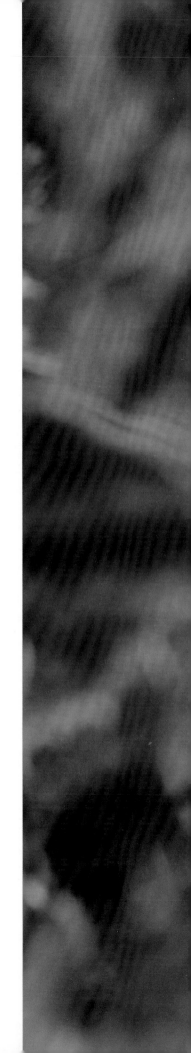

LIFE'S A BOWL OF SOUP

CHEESY BROCCOLI SOUP

INGREDIENTS

favourite cooking oil
for sautéing

1½ cups chopped
yellow onions

2 tsp miso (chickpea or soy)

Himalayan salt and black
pepper, to taste

4 cups chopped broccoli or
broccolini florets and stems

2 cups chopped celery

4 cups almond milk or
favourite non-dairy milk

1½ tbsp white vinegar

1 cup nutritional yeast

You will fool and delight everyone with this soup: it tastes so much like it has real cheese in it! When my husband tried it, knowing that I can't eat cheese, he looked at me quizzically and had to confirm that there wasn't any cheese of any sort (even non-dairy) in it. This soup is a real winner, hands-down, and can be on the table in less than 20 minutes, start to finish! *Makes about 7 cups*

DIRECTIONS

In a large soup pan over medium heat, sauté the onion in oil until it softens and starts to become translucent (about 5 minutes), stirring in the miso, salt and pepper while you sauté. Then add the celery and broccoli or broccolini, continuing to sauté 3–5 more minutes until the flavours begin to marry. Stir in the milk, vinegar and the nutritional yeast and cook for another 5 minutes, stirring. Season with more salt and pepper to taste. Serve hot.

Theresa's Tip

If you prefer a smooth cream soup, simply process some or all of the hot soup in a blender for 1 minute or until creamy before serving. You will have an amazing, low-fat and delectable cream soup in minutes!

CREAMY CARROT & GINGER SOUP

It was a longstanding dream of mine to make a soup like this, and it turned out even better than I had hoped! I was committed to making it super-simple and the idea of roasting the vegetables got me really excited. A bonus was finding a way to use cilantro stems, which otherwise often end up in the compost. This soup is sure to be a crowd-pleaser, filled with ingredients that most people are able to eat and have on hand. The only problem is that it doesn't last long: if you want to have leftovers or will be serving guests, you might consider doubling or tripling the recipe. If you do so, you'll need to blend it in batches. *Makes 5 cups*

DIRECTIONS

Place the carrots, onion, celery, garlic and green onions in a large baking dish. Drizzle with the olive oil and stir to coat evenly. Bake in a preheated 315°F oven for 45 minutes. Before the vegetables are done baking, purée the rest of the ingredients with the water in a high-speed blender, using the coconut cream can to measure the water. Then add the roasted vegetables and purée again until smooth and creamy. Serve warm directly from the blender or refrigerate for a chilled soup. This freezes well and can be gently reheated for future quick meals (don't overheat).

Haely's Hint ❀
Ginger is great for digestion.

INGREDIENTS

2 cups roughly chopped carrots

1 small or medium yellow onion, roughly chopped

2 celery stalks, roughly chopped

2–3 garlic cloves, halved

¼ cup chopped green onions

2 tbsp extra virgin olive oil

1 x 13.5 fl oz (400 ml) can premium full-fat coconut milk

13.5 fl oz (400 ml) water

¼ cup cooked chickpeas (optional)

2 tbsp roughly chopped cilantro stems

4 tsp lemon juice, or to taste

2 tsp grated ginger, firmly packed

1½ tsp white vinegar

1 tsp Himalayan salt, or to taste

¾–1 tsp dried dill, or to taste

½ tsp ground cumin

½ tsp black pepper

¼ tsp curry powder

⅛ tsp garlic powder

⅛ tsp cinnamon

CREAMY CUCUMBER & SORREL SOUP

INGREDIENTS

favourite cooking oil
for sautéing

2 cups chopped yellow
or white onions

1½ cups chopped green onions

1 cup chopped daikon

6 cups chopped cucumbers,
skin on

3 cups water

2 cups chopped fresh sorrel

¼ cup chopped dandelion
leaves (optional)

½ cup chopped
de-stemmed kale

¼ tsp nutmeg

½ tsp dry mustard

½ cup nutritional yeast

1 cup almond milk or favourite
non-dairy milk

1½ tsp Himalayan salt

½ tsp black pepper, or to taste

1–2 tbsp fresh dill, for garnish

The Dunbar Community Centre in Vancouver has an annual celebration called "Salmonberry Days" at the end of May, celebrating the harvest of these plentiful, wild, sweet berries. During the month, volunteers from the community share their knowledge about our local natural habitat—a great tradition. For the last few years, as part of this celebration, Hanno Pinder has organized what she calls a "Forager's Meal," teaching community members about local food and how it can be made into beautiful meals. One year, she made a nettle risotto and a chilled cucumber soup. This latter dish inspired me to develop a vegan and gluten-free variation with a few extra twists. I never would have dreamt of cooking cucumbers and puréeing them into a low-fat, creamy soup the way Hanno taught us. Thank you, Hanno—this recipe is dedicated to you! *Makes about 12 cups*

DIRECTIONS

Sauté the onions, green onions and daikon in the oil over medium heat in a large soup pot until the onions are translucent. Add the cucumbers and water, bring to a boil and simmer until softened (about 10–15 minutes). Remove from the heat and purée with an immersion blender until creamy (or purée in portions in a regular blender). Add the remaining ingredients (except the dill), and purée again until the desired creaminess is achieved. Serve garnished with a sprinkling of fresh dill. This is equally good served cold.

> **Bev's Bit**
> Daikon in Japanese means "great root," and with good reason! It is used in some cultures for aiding digestion, as well as for curing a hangover.

LOVAGE, LEEK & KALE SOUP

One day while out watering my garden, our dear friend Karin Mickelson came walking by with her adorable dog, Dillon. We were talking about some of the unusual plants in my garden when she spotted the lovage on the edge of the boulevard box. Lovage is an easy-to-grow perennial that is a great addition to any garden. Karin said that her absolute favourite soup was a lovage soup her mother-in-law Margaret makes. I have taken this very simple recipe and made several changes, including making it vegan- and grain-free. I've also added leeks and kale to give it a little different twist.

Makes about 6 cups

DIRECTIONS

In a soup pot, sauté the leeks and onion over medium heat in the oil until soft (about 5 minutes). Stir in the kale and lovage and continue to cook for another minute. Then stir in the water and milk, cover and simmer for 20 minutes. Add the vinegar, salt and pepper and serve. Never boil the soup when heating or reheating.

> **Theresa' Tip** 🌢
> With lovage, a little goes a very long way: a tiny bit, finely minced, added to salads or dips takes the flavour in entirely new directions. When you experiment with lovage, be sure to start with less than you think you will need, then gradually add more, so as not to overpower the dish.

INGREDIENTS

favourite cooking oil for sautéing

1½ cups finely sliced leeks (both green and white parts), packed

1 large yellow onion, finely diced

4 cups thinly chopped kale leaves (spines and all!)

4 tbsp finely chopped lovage leaves

1 cup water

4 cups almond milk or favourite non-dairy milk

1 tsp white vinegar

1–1½ tsp Himalayan salt, to taste

1 tsp coarsely ground black pepper, or to taste

ROSEMARY-INFUSED CREAM OF MUSHROOM SOUP

INGREDIENTS

favourite cooking oil
for sautéing

1 large yellow or white onion,
roughly chopped

4 cups chopped mixed
mushrooms

2 cups almond milk or
favourite non-dairy milk

¾ tsp rosemary

1½ tsp miso (chickpea or soy)

2 tbsp nutritional yeast

¼ cup chopped parsley stems
and/or leaves

½ tsp apple cider vinegar

½–¾ tsp Himalayan salt,
to taste

½ tsp black pepper

chopped fresh parsley and
fresh ground black pepper,
for garnish

For this recipe, I used shitake and crimini mushrooms. However, depending on what is available in your local area, have some fun playing with other mushroom varieties. Once you've chopped the vegetables, this recipe makes an incredibly fast meal—ready in less than 10 minutes! I almost always double this popular soup; it is so delicious and healthy. Here was what one test kitchen said about this recipe: "Despite the fact that 1) we don't use onion because Eric's allergic, and 2) I only had vanilla non-dairy milk, and 3) we're not usually wild about mushroom soup, this was really good. I know it would be even better *sans* vanilla." *Makes about 4 cups*

DIRECTIONS

Over medium heat, sauté the onion in oil until it softens and starts to become translucent (about 5 minutes). Then add the mushrooms and sauté for 3–4 minutes until the mushrooms just begin to cook down. While cooking the onion and mushrooms, put all of the other ingredients except the garnish in a blender (ideally a high-speed type, but any blender will do). Add the cooked onion and mushrooms to the other ingredients in the blender. Purée until creamy and serve warm directly from the blender or refrigerate until later, when the soup can be gently reheated. Garnish with parsley and ground black pepper.

Haely's Hint ❁

Mushrooms are full of antioxidants and will help boost your immune system. They are also the only vegan source of vitamin D, known as the sunshine vitamin!

FENNEL & TOMATO SOUP

This delicious recipe is one that I created a few years ago on my first attempt, after learning about how wonderful fennel can be for gut health. While we were crazy about it, unfortunately this is one recipe I'll never be able to enjoy again. I discovered with my first delicious bowl that I am quite allergic to fennel! A great example of bio-individuality in action—we are all so different. So, even though it is not a soup we make at home, I decided to share it here so that you can have the pleasure of enjoying this extremely low-fat, delectable soup. *Makes about 7 cups*

DIRECTIONS

In a large heavy saucepan, sauté the chopped fennel, celery, onions, shallot, garlic, salt and pepper in oil, stirring occasionally, until the onions begin to soften (about 5 minutes). Add the carrots and sauté about 5 minutes more, adding water as needed. Add the stock, tomatoes, vinegar and crushed hot pepper and jalapeño flakes (if using), then bring to a boil. Reduce the heat, cover and simmer for about 20 minutes or until the onions and fennel are tender. Serve hot, garnished with lots of fresh cilantro.

INGREDIENTS

favourite cooking oil for sautéing

1 bulb fennel, coarsely chopped

2–3 celery stalks, chopped

2 onions, or 1 onion and 1 shallot, chopped

4 garlic cloves, minced

½ tsp Himalayan salt, or to taste

½ tsp black pepper, or to taste

1 large carrot, chopped

4 cups vegetable stock

2 x 13.5 fl oz (400 ml) cans whole or diced tomatoes

½ tsp rice wine vinegar, or to taste

¼–½ tsp crushed hot red pepper flakes, to taste (optional)

¼–½ tsp jalapeño flakes, to taste (optional)

½ cup cilantro, chopped, for garnish

ROASTED RED PEPPER & TOMATO CREAM SOUP

INGREDIENTS

2 large red bell peppers,
roughly chopped

1 medium tomato,
roughly chopped

2 celery stalks,
roughly chopped

½ large onion,
roughly chopped

2–3 garlic cloves,
roughly chopped

1 medium carrot,
roughly chopped

1 large green onion, chopped

2–3 tbsp extra virgin olive oil

2 cups almond milk or
cream or favourite creamy
non-dairy milk

1 x 6 fl oz (175ml) can
tomato paste

2–4 tbsp nutritional yeast,
to taste

2 tsp lemon juice

2 tsp rice vinegar or
white vinegar

½ tsp dried oregano
(or 1 tsp fresh oregano)

¾ tsp Himalayan salt,
or to taste

¼ tsp dried
(or ½ tsp fresh) basil

¼ tsp black pepper

⅛ tsp ground nutmeg

This soup is incredibly versatile. In addition to being enjoyed as a soup, it can be used as a pasta sauce, a pizza sauce, a condiment in wraps or to enliven a rice or quinoa dish. You can also add a dash of cayenne pepper if you want a spicy twist. Enjoy experimenting with the possibilities! *Makes 5–6 cups*

DIRECTIONS

Place the chopped vegetables into a lightly greased large baking pan and drizzle with olive oil, stirring to coat well. Bake in a preheated 315°F oven for 45–60 minutes, until the vegetables are nicely roasted and beginning to caramelize. While the vegetables are in the oven, blend the remaining ingredients together in a high-speed blender until smooth. Once the vegetables are caramelized, add them to the blender with the other ingredients and blend until creamy. Serve warm directly from the blender or refrigerate until later. This soup freezes well.

SPICY THAI LEMONGRASS SOUP

This is my absolute favourite immune-boosting, pick-me-up soup for chilly days or when I feel a cold coming on. For those times when I don't have fresh shitake mushrooms on hand, I like to keep dehydrated shitake mushrooms and lemongrass in the pantry and fresh Thai chili peppers in the freezer, just in case I feel called to make this soup. It never lasts long, so if you're sharing it with others, you might want to double this recipe! *Makes about 7 cups*

DIRECTIONS

Sauté the onion, garlic, Thai chili peppers and ginger in a large soup pot over medium heat until the onions are translucent (about 5 minutes). Then add the water, lemongrass, tamari, broccoli, celery, shitake mushrooms, miso and rice vinegar. Cook over medium heat until the flavours begin to marry and the desired texture of the vegetables is almost achieved (about 5 minutes). Add the tofu, lemon juice and seasoning, and cook for another 5 minutes. Before serving the soup, place some of the prepared green onions, cilantro and carrots in the bowls and then ladle the soup on top. Garnish with the remaining cilantro or green onions and serve immediately.

Theresa's Tip

If you want to avoid picking out small pieces of lemongrass when eating the soup, tie the pieces in a piece of cheesecloth while cooking the soup and remove before serving.

Haely's Hint ❋

To get the most nutritional benefit from onions and garlic, let them sit for 5–10 minutes after chopping, before cooking them. Crushing or chopping garlic and onions causes a release of an enzyme called allinase that catalyzes the formation of allicin. Cooking reduces the potency of allinase and therefore reduces the health benefits of the onions and garlic. When you let them sit for 10 minutes after chopping, other enzymes are released that will help protect the allinase from heat.

INGREDIENTS

favourite cooking oil for sautéing

1 onion, chopped

1–2 garlic cloves, finely minced or microplaned

1–3 Thai red hot chili peppers, finely minced

½ inch fresh ginger root, finely minced or microplaned

4 cups water

2 tsp dried or fresh lemongrass, cut into pieces

1 tsp tamari or coconut aminos

1 broccoli stalk, sliced into thin sticks

2 celery stalks, thinly sliced

1 cup chopped shitake mushrooms

1 tbsp miso (soy or chickpea)

1 tsp rice vinegar

6 oz firm tofu, cubed or cut in thin batons

¼–½ cup lemon juice, to taste

Himalayan salt and black pepper, to taste

½ cup chopped green onions

1 cup chopped cilantro

1–2 cups shredded carrots

ITALIAN WEDDING SOUP

INGREDIENTS

favourite cooking oil
for sautéing

1 cup diced daikon

4 garlic cloves, finely minced

7–8 cups water

1 tbsp agar agar flakes

3 tbsp miso (chickpea or soy)

¾ cups thinly sliced celery

1 cup finely chopped
parsley, packed

2 cups baby spinach
leaves, packed

¾ cup finely sliced green onion

½ cup chopped basil,
firmly packed

20 small *Veggie Meatballs*
(page 169)

1 tsp Himalayan salt, or to taste

½ tsp dried oregano, or
to taste

About 15 years ago my husband Eric and I co-developed the most amazing Italian wedding soup, which was one of our favourite dishes to serve to guests. Even though it was a hit, it was about as gluten-loaded and non-vegan as they come! Needless to say, this recipe sadly became a mere memory for about five years. In addition to issues involved in creating a vegan broth, the lack of a satisfactory meatball was a hurdle we couldn't get past. After three years of trying to find or come up with the perfect veggie meatball, I gave up for about a year. When I finally was able to create one that met my standards, work on this recipe was at the top of my to-do list! We are so happy to be able to enjoy this favourite again and to be able to share its deliciousness with you. *Makes 8 cups*

DIRECTIONS

Over medium heat, sauté the daikon and garlic for about 6 minutes. Then add the water, sprinkle the agar agar on top and stir in the miso, celery and parsley. Increase the heat to high and bring to a boil, then reduce the heat to medium, cover and continue to cook for 10 minutes. Finally, reduce the heat to low and add the spinach leaves, green onion, basil, *Veggie Meatballs*, salt and oregano, continuing to simmer for 5 more minutes before serving. (If you are not serving this soup right away, the flavours will intensify and you may want to add some more water.)

INSTANT MINESTRONE SOUP MIX

When you live with dietary restrictions, travelling can be really stress-ful. This recipe is a great example of the old saying, "Necessity is the mother of invention." During the couple of years prior to *YUM*'s publication, I did a lot of travelling. On one of these trips, where there would be no store access, I had the idea of bringing a bunch of ingredients that I could experiment with to create soups using hot water in the hotel room. It was so exciting to develop this delicious, nutritious minestrone soup that only needs hot water to make—an amazing light food for travel or camping. The first person to share this soup with me was my dear friend, Dr. Synte Peacock, on our adventure in Philadelphia. This recipe is a great example of how to use dehydrated vegetables and herbs, as discussed in *Sustainable Kitchen Tips 101*. Feel free to make ingredient adjustments according to your dietary needs and preferences. *Makes about 5 cups dry mix*

DIRECTIONS

Mix together all the ingredients (except the noodles) in a bowl, making sure there are no lumps of tomato or mushroom powder. Store the mix in a large bag or jar until ready to use.

To serve 1, put ¼ cup of the mix into a mug or bowl and stir in 1 cup of boiling water. If you would like to add rice vermicelli noodles, stir the noodles (broken up) into the hot mixture. Cover for 4–5 minutes or until the vege-tables and noodles are soft. Remove the cover and enjoy!

> **Theresa's Tip**
> For a "meaty" minestrone, add 2 or 3 very dehydrated *Veggie Meatballs* (page 169) to the mix before adding the boiling water.

INGREDIENTS

1½ cups tomato powder

1 cup dehydrated spinach flakes

1 cup dehydrated leek flakes

⅔ cup shitake mushroom powder

⅔ cup nutritional yeast

½ cup dehydrated celery flakes

½ cup dehydrated parsley flakes

⅓–½ cup dehydrated bell pepper flakes

⅓ cup *Italian Seasoning* (page 319), or use 2 tbsp each oregano, basil and thyme

2 tbsp Vitamineral Earth (optional)

1 tbsp crushed hot red pepper flakes (optional)

1¼ tsp salt, or to taste

¼ cup extra-thin rice vermicelli noodles per serving (optional)

LIVING ON THE EDGE
SIDES & APPETIZERS

APRICOT BASIL APPETIZER STACKS

INGREDIENTS

8 very large basil leaves

2–4 ripe fresh apricots

½ cucumber

3–4 oz Daiya wedge cheese or favourite vegan cheese

16 blueberries or other small berries

With only five ingredients, this is a simple, delicious appetizer or quick snack—full of flavour contrasts that can be constructed in seconds for a brunch, dinner party or for unexpected guests. The multiple dimensions of flavour and colour make these stacks irresistible and the perfect party food! *Makes 8*

DIRECTIONS

Lay each basil leaf flat (shiny side down), allowing for the natural upturn of the edges. Remove the pits from the apricots, then slice into ¼-inch rounds (save any unused bits for fruit salads, smoothies, granola, etc). Cut the cucumber into 8 slices (about ¼-inch thick) and slice the cheese into slices ⅛–¼ inch thick. On top of each leaf, place (in order) 1 apricot round, 1 cucumber round, 1 cheese slice and 2 berries. Chill or serve immediately.

BASIL-WRAPPED STUFFED DATES

This simple and delicious dish can be served as an appetizer or as a dessert. When Alex and I took Lovena Galyide's Raw Food Chef course at her wonderful restaurant, the Indigo Food Café in Vancouver, she taught us this recipe. We loved the surprising experience of the multiple and intense flavour dimensions—and how easy it was to make. I have had fun extending the possibilities for different fillings and encourage you to do the same—let your creativity soar! Thank you, Lovena, for allowing me to include this here. *Makes 8*

INGREDIENTS

8 large fresh Medjool dates

savoury fillings of your choice (eg whole cacao beans, nuts, bell pepper slices, soft or hard vegan cheese)

8 medium-to-large basil leaves

8 toothpicks

DIRECTIONS

Slice each date partially through lengthwise, remove the pit and fill with the savoury item of your choice. Wrap a basil leaf around each date, securing it with a toothpick. Serve immediately or chilled.

CHEESY TOFU CUBES

INGREDIENTS

12 oz extra firm tofu, cut into ½-inch cubes

2–4 tbsp nutritional yeast

Himalayan salt (optional)

1–2 tsp favourite cooking oil, for coating the pan or baking dish

If you are able to enjoy some soy in your diet, these simple cubes of deliciousness will not disappoint: they are so good and so easy. On those extra-hectic evenings when you come home and are exhausted, but need to throw a meal together, you'll discover how well this protein-filled dish serves up in no time! *Serves 3–4*

DIRECTIONS

Place the tofu cubes in a medium-sized bowl and sprinkle with the nutritional yeast, plus a pinch of Himalayan salt, if desired. Completely coat all sides of the cubes.

STOVETOP METHOD Sauté the cubes over medium heat in a pan with the oil until the cubes are evenly browned and the desired texture is achieved (about 15 minutes).

OVEN METHOD Roast the cubes in the oven on an oiled baking sheet at 315°F, flipping occasionally until they are brown and the desired texture is achieved (about 20–30 minutes). Serve while hot.

RHO'S GIARDINIERA PICKLED VEGETABLES

INGREDIENTS

approx 1 lb of each of the following vegetables (no need for precision—use what you have on hand)

zucchini

celery

carrots

narrow string beans

1–2 tsp Himalayan salt (for weeping the vegetables)

5 cups apple cider or white vinegar

2½ cups water

1 whole garlic head, finely minced or microplaned

½ cup extra virgin olive oil or favourite oil, plus more to fill the jar

1 green onion or 1 inch of leek, minced or thinly sliced

2–3 x 1-quart mason jars, sterilized

When two Italian women who are both on elimination diets due to sensitivities get together, one thing is sure to happen—recipe-sharing of foods that the other can eat! This is one of Rho's favourites, which she generously shared with me and thought readers would enjoy. I agree—it is so yummy! The hardest part of this recipe is finding separate colanders for weeping the salted vegetables and places to put them. Don't worry if the vegetables need to share a colander, just keep them separate. They'll get over it! *Makes about 8–10 cups*

DIRECTIONS

Cut the zucchini, celery and carrots into ¼-inch julienned slices. Place the vegetables in separate colanders over pans. Sprinkle the salt over each of the vegetables and rub it over all the surfaces. Leave them to weep out the moisture for about 1 hour. Near the end of the hour, put the vinegar and water into a large pot over high heat. Once it is boiling, carefully drop the vegetables in, one type at a time and in the following order, so as to retain the colour of each vegetable. Time the cooking from when the water returns to a boil after adding the vegetable. Begin with the zucchini: cook for 1 minute (once it returns to a boil) then remove with a strainer and place in a large bowl. Next, add the celery, cooking for 2 minutes and then removing in the same way and adding to the zucchini. Then cook the carrots for 2 minutes, remove and transfer to the same large bowl. Finally, cook the string beans for 3 minutes, strain and transfer to the bowl. You don't want to overcook the vegetables; they are best when still crunchy. Stir in the garlic and leave to cool. When completely cool, add the oil and green onion or leek, and mix well.

Fill the mason jars with the vegetables and press them down firmly to pack in as much as possible. Add enough oil to each to completely cover all the vegetables. Close the jars and refrigerate overnight or for several days, allowing the flavours to penetrate the vegetables. These vegetables keep very well in the refrigerator for at least 2–3 weeks. Serve the pickled vegetables on their own as an appetizer or as a topper (instead of dressing) on salads. Mixed with quinoa or brown rice, they make for an instant tasty side dish.

> **Theresa's Tip** 🍃
> You can reserve the strained vinegar-water to use in soup or dressing recipes, if desired. I made a fabulous hot-and-sour soup with mine.
> If you're on a roll, you can also reuse the vinegar-water to make *Rho's Garlic Marinated Mushrooms* (page 136).

Sterilizing Jars

There are three common methods for sterilizing jars. The first is in a dishwasher that has a sterilization setting. You can also boil the jars and lids for five minutes, then remove them from the water and let them air dry. The third way is in the oven. Wash the jars and lids in warm, soapy water and rinse thoroughly. Place the jars and lids in a preheated 175°F oven and leave until completely dry. If you are using jars with loose rubber liners, boil these rather than putting them in the oven, because dry heat damages them.

CARROT & CABBAGE PROBIOTIC SAUERKRAUT

This classic recipe was passed along to me by my good friend Hody Lye. Many people don't realize that store-bought sauerkraut is processed using vinegar and doesn't have the same beneficial probiotic qualities that this recipe offers. Once you learn how simple it is to make, you'll never want to buy sauerkraut from the store again. While the carrots and miso aren't necessary for regular sauerkraut, they add a delicious taste dimension that my body delights in. Everything about this fermented cabbage recipe is healthy and goes way back to our early human ancestors, long before refrigeration existed. Let the tradition continue, and may our brains be the wiser for it. Thanks, Hody! *Makes about 4 cups*

INGREDIENTS

8-10 cups shredded green cabbage, setting aside 1 large leaf

2 tsp Himalayan salt

2 cups shredded carrots

1-2 tsp chickpea or soy miso (optional); otherwise add ½ tsp more Himalayan salt

1 quart mason jar with an air-tight seal and non-reactive lid (no plastic or metal), sterilized

Haely's Hint ✿
Sauerkraut that is naturally fermented (not using vinegar) is a great source of probiotics.

DIRECTIONS

Put the cabbage in a large bowl and sprinkle the salt over top. With gloved or very clean hands, aggressively massage the salt into the cabbage until it "cooks" down and becomes *very* wet. This will take several minutes, and it will surprise you how much the cabbage reduces in size and the amount of water that begins to pool in the bowl. *It is critical to continue to massage until there is a lot of liquid released from the cabbage*, because it will be that same liquid that will protect the vegetable and will also be the magical carrier of the friendly bacteria. Add the carrots and miso (if using) and mix in thoroughly again with your hands, massaging all the ingredients together, ensuring a thorough blending. Place the mixture in the glass jar and press down firmly, making sure that all of the cabbage mixture is completely submerged in the liquid. Top the filling in the jar with a whole cabbage leaf, folded over and pressed down firmly, to act as a semi-seal over the shredded contents. Seal the jar very tightly and leave on the countertop for 5-7 days (opening to release gasses every day) or until the vegetables obtain the desired taste. Discard the leaf on top and store in the refrigerator to enjoy whenever you like. Kept submerged in an airtight container in the refrigerator, sauerkraut can last for several months.

Theresa's Tip 💧
Recent research is demonstrating the important connection between our gut and our brain. Neurologist and nutrition expert Dr. David Perlmutter has been increasing our awareness of the relationship between intestinal flora and brain functioning, including neurodegenerative conditions. These studies are changing the way we think about food.

RHO'S GARLIC-MARINATED MUSHROOMS

INGREDIENTS

1½ cups apple cider vinegar or other favourite clear vinegar

3 cups water

5 cups small, or halved and quartered mushrooms (eg shitake, portabellini, crimini, oyster, etc)

4–6 garlic cloves, finely minced or microplaned

¾ cup extra virgin olive oil

2 tbsp finely chopped parsley or cilantro

Himalayan salt and black pepper, to taste

Another authentic Italian treasure from my dear friend Rho Tuttle, this classic recipe is one that my dad would have loved. They are just like the marinated mushrooms he used to buy at Claro's Italian Market in Upland, California, for special occasions. Here's what one test kitchen had to say about this insanely delicious recipe: "I didn't think I would like it, but I really did! I made this once and everyone liked it so much that I made it two other times—including for the teenager's slumber party (and her friends usually like meat, but ate vegan). I bought pizza crust from the store and rolled it out and used it with the pesto sauce once and with a vegan alfredo sauce two other times. I was pleasantly surprised by how tasty it was on pizza. Recommend highly to friends." *Makes about 2 cups*

DIRECTIONS

In a large covered saucepan, bring the vinegar and water to a full boil. Add the mushrooms and boil for 20 minutes, or until the mushrooms are tender and the flavour is well absorbed. Carefully scoop the cooked mushrooms out of the pot with a slotted spoon and place in a strainer with a bowl under it. Allow to cool for about 5 minutes, then put mushrooms into a bowl and stir the garlic and oils to completely saturate them. Stir in the cilantro or parsley and season with salt and black pepper to taste. Let the mushrooms marinate a couple of hours or more in the refrigerator to deepen the flavour. Garnish with more cilantro and/or parsley and serve. These marinated mushrooms are a wonderful addition to salads or wraps, as a pizza topping, chopped and added to pasta or as a topping to my *Garlic-Infused Polenta* (page 155). They keep very well in the refrigerator for at least 2–3 weeks.

Theresa's Tip

To up the omega-3 content of this recipe, replace up to ¼ cup of the olive oil with cold-pressed flax or hemp oil.

> TOP LEFT: *Rho's Garlic-Marinated Mushrooms* (this page)
TOP RIGHT: *Spicy Pickled Kale Seed Pods* (page 139)
BOTTOM: *Spicy Pickled Okra* (page 138)

SPICY PICKLED OKRA

INGREDIENTS

5 cups small- to medium-sized fresh okra

1¼ cups apple cider vinegar or other favourite clear vinegar

3 cups water

4–6 garlic cloves, finely minced or microplaned

¾ cup extra virgin olive oil

1 tsp crushed hot red pepper flakes, or to taste

Himalayan salt and black pepper, to taste

It has meant a great deal to me that Dr. Saul Pilar at Connect Health in Vancouver has been so supportive of this book and the recipes I've been developing. Given his love of food and also his knowledge about the potential healing properties it can offer, I asked him if he had any favourite recipes he would like me to try to create. Sauerkraut was one of them, but another ingredient he mentioned was okra. I stopped in my tracks... I'd never cooked with okra before and didn't have any idea how it behaved. Okra is very mucilaginous—a fancy way of saying "extremely gooey." From a culinary perspective, this can be really great or really not-so-great, because it needs special treatment to be turned into something that has a delightful texture. That same quality, though, also makes this unusual food a wonderful friend to the gut. Being someone who loves a challenge, Saul's suggestion sent me on a mission and the end result was incredible, without the "goo" effect. If you're able to get your hands on some okra (it can be difficult to find at times), this is a recipe you'll surely want to try! *Makes about 4 cups*

DIRECTIONS

Remove the stems from the okra carefully, so as to leave the caps on the tops of the vegetable. In a large saucepan, bring the vinegar and water to a full boil, then add the okra and let boil for 15–30 minutes, or until tender. Drain and cool, then toss in the garlic, oils and hot pepper flakes, and season with salt and black pepper to taste. Serve this as an appetizer or side dish, add it to salads, slice it for pizzas or use it as a unique and delicious garnish for main dishes. Cut it into smaller pieces and add it with other vegetables, such as bell peppers and tomatoes, to quinoa or brown rice for a special side dish.

SPICY PICKLED KALE SEED PODS

This may be the craziest recipe I've ever developed and is only for the gardeners who grow kale, which produces beautiful, edible, little yellow flowers that the butterflies, bees and other insects feast upon. Kale then develops a plethora of skinny little seed pods that the birds love to devour. It's a big kale party, but a lot of seed pods usually just find their way to the compost pile! However, after reading one of Joshua Evan's blog posts (hearthstrung.wordpress.com) about making nasturtium seed pickle capers, I realized that pickling those kale seed pods might also be a great idea. It's extremely important to use only very young seed pods (the older ones are too tough and dry) and to snip them from the plant at the end of the seed pod itself, making sure there is no hard stem attached. *Makes about 3 cups*

INGREDIENTS

1¼ cups apple cider vinegar or other favourite clear vinegar

3 cups water

2 cups very young kale seed pods

2–3 garlic cloves, finely minced or microplaned

6 tbsp extra virgin olive oil

½ tsp crushed hot red pepper flakes, or to taste

Himalayan salt and black pepper, to taste

DIRECTIONS

In a large saucepan, bring the vinegar and water to a full boil, then add the young kale seed pods and let boil for 30-40 minutes. Drain and cool, then toss in the garlic, oils and hot pepper flakes, and season with salt and black pepper to taste. A fun condiment and a great conversation piece!

CHEESY ITALIAN HERB TOMATOES

Growing up in an Italian home, I've made garden-fresh tomatoes and herbs a beloved mainstay. It makes me happy to be able to pick the ingredients from my garden and present such a flavourful and wonderful dish with only a moment's notice. *Serves 4*

DIRECTIONS

Slice the tomatoes in ¼-inch slices and place in a single layer on a plate or platter. Lightly sprinkle with Himalayan salt and the chopped fresh garden herbs. Then sprinkle the tomatoes with the *Raw Parmesan*, nutritional yeast or grated Brazil nuts, followed by the lemon juice and a drizzle of the oil. Scatter a few fresh basil leaves on top as a garnish and serve immediately.

Haely's Hint ❁
Herbs not only add amazing flavour to your food, they are great sources of micronutrients as well.

Theresa's Tip 🌢
If you don't have access to fresh herbs or they aren't in season, you can still enjoy this dish using dried Italian herbs.

INGREDIENTS

2 large (or 4 medium) tomatoes

¼ tsp Himalayan salt, or to taste

1–2 tbsp chopped mixed fresh herbs (eg oregano, thyme, savory, rosemary)

1–2 tbsp *Raw Parmesan* or *Nut-Free Raw Parmesan* (page 314), nutritional yeast or grated Brazil nuts

2 tbsp lemon juice, or to taste

2 tbsp extra virgin olive oil, or to taste

fresh basil leaves, for garnish

ITALIAN STUFFED ARTICHOKES

INGREDIENTS

2 globe artichokes

2 cups *Raw Parmesan*
(page 314), or ½ cup *Raw
Parmesan* plus 1½ cups
Herbed or Spicy Breadcrumbs
(page 316)

3 tbsp dried parsley

3 garlic cloves, finely minced
or microplaned

1½ tsp dried oregano

¾ tsp dried minced onion

3 tbsp extra virgin olive oil
(plus more for drizzling)

When I was a kid, this messy-to-eat, flavourful and fun traditional dish was an even bigger hit than the *Roasted Garlic* (page 163) in our home! Making these delicacies is super-simple, but they do take a bit of time; you need to put a little filling in each leaf of the artichoke before baking. My mom was an amazing cook and we spent countless hours in the kitchen together. I learned more from her than I realized at the time about cooking. I remember filling artichoke leaves when I was a little girl—it was one of my rites of passage. This photo is one that I'm particularly proud of, as it reflects the beauty as well as the deliciousness of this incredible treat. I am so happy that this recipe captures the exact taste I remember. Thanks, Mom! *Serves 2*

DIRECTIONS

Wash the artichokes well, then cut 1–1½ inches off the top of each artichoke plus trim the bottom stem as well. (The bitter stem can be cooked in the same pan beside the stuffed artichokes, or reserved to make a healing tea or for other culinary purposes.) Mix together all of the ingredients except the artichokes in a large bowl, then set aside. Tug and flare the leaves of the artichoke outward, to create more space for the filling. One at a time, put the flared artichokes in the bowl with the crumb mixture and, with a relatively flat teaspoon, fill each leaf with the mixture, working up from the bottom. The more you press into each leaf, the yummier the end result. When you reach the top of the artichoke, fill the centre area with more of the crumb mixture, then place the stuffed artichoke upright in a cooking pan filled with about ½ inch water. Lightly drizzle the artichokes with olive oil, cover tightly with aluminum foil, being sure not to let the foil touch the vegetables. Cook in a preheated 315°F oven for about 1¼–1½ hours, or until the leaves come off easily. The larger, heavier and denser the artichoke, the longer the cooking time will be. To eat, pull off individual leaves and use your teeth to scrape the tender part of the artichoke along with the tasty filling into your mouth. When you get to the prickly part in the middle of the artichoke, use a spoon to remove the fuzzy part, then enjoy the amazing heart of the vegetable with all of its goodness!

PIMENTO CHEESE STUFFED MUSHROOM CAPS

INGREDIENTS

4–6 cups crimini and/or shitake mushroom caps, stems removed

¼ cup extra virgin olive oil

1 tbsp brown rice syrup, coconut nectar or favourite sticky syrup

Spicy Breadcrumbs (page 315) or *Raw Parmesan* (page 314)

1–2 cups *Pimento Cheese Dip* (page 242)

sprigs fresh dill (optional)

Except for stir–fries, I'm generally not a huge fan of fried food because of the health implications. Because of this, I've made a concerted effort to create recipes that offer a similar mouth–feel and taste, but without the dark side of frying! This recipe is a great example of one such success. *Serves 4–6*

DIRECTIONS

In a medium bowl, whisk together the oil and sticky syrup. One by one, dip each mushroom cap in the bowl to coat with the mixture. Then transfer each cap to a second bowl containing *Spicy Breadcrumbs* or *Raw Parmesan*, gently coating them with the crumbs. Place each mushroom cap on a parchment-covered baking sheet. Fill each cap generously with *Pimento Cheese Dip* and top with some fresh dill. Cook in a preheated 315˚F oven for 30 minutes, or until desired tenderness has been achieved. The larger the mushroom caps, the more cooking time required. Serve immediately.

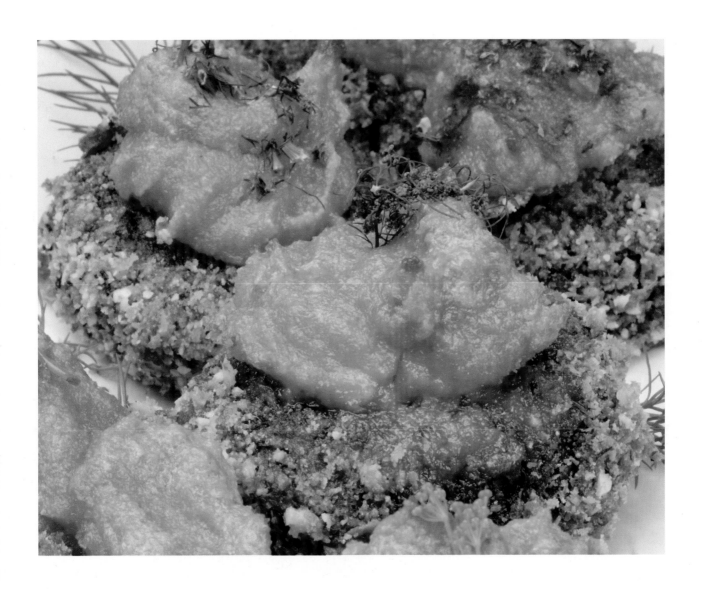

ITALIAN ZUCCHINI & ONIONS

Even though he died when I was just six years old, my memories of Papa Ralph (my dad's father), couldn't be more vivid. As an Italian immigrant barber and shoeshiner, he had very few material things, yet his loving and doting presence made us feel like royalty. I remember how Papa Ralph would always arrive at our home bearing gifts of pennies and Baby Ruth bars for us kids, delighting in our excitement to see and embrace him. Then, he would take over the garden. With his green thumb, this sweet grandfather planted fig and other fruit trees with each visit. Finally, we would watch him floating around the kitchen, transforming it into an incredibly magical wonderland of smells and tastes from the Old Country, which only filled the air when he was around. This is one of the dishes I remember him cooking—the sweet fragrance of the onions sautéing with the zucchini was intoxicating! I don't know what other ingredients he used or whether lemons were ever in it, but when I developed this recipe in memory of him, their brightness mirrored his soul and provided the final touch to the dish. When you have access to an abundant zucchini harvest, be sure to try this simple dish, knowing that the memory of my kind, white-haired grandfather is with you while you do. *Makes about 5–6 cups*

INGREDIENTS

¼ cup avocado oil

2 medium-to-large white or yellow onions, chopped

3 large zucchini

½ tsp Himalayan salt, or to taste

juice of ½ lemon, or to taste

½ tsp cracked black pepper, or to taste (optional)

DIRECTIONS

Over medium heat, sauté the onions until very translucent (about 5-6 minutes). Cut the zucchini in quarters lengthwise, then slice ¼ in thick and add to the pan, stirring well to mix completely with the onions. Cover and cook, stirring occasionally for another 6-10 minutes, removing from the heat once the flavours have all married beautifully and sweetness permeates the dish. Avoid overcooking—this dish is best when the zucchini still has body and doesn't turn to mush. Add the lemon juice, salt and black pepper to taste and serve warm. (I also love this dish chilled.)

CHEESY BAKED BROCCOLI & CAULIFLOWER

INGREDIENTS

7–8 cups bite-sized broccoli florets or broccolini and/or cauliflower pieces

2–3 tbsp extra virgin olive oil

½ cup nutritional yeast, or to taste

When this ultra-simple dish is baking in the oven, even the sleeping souls of the house will rise and want to know what's cooking and when it will be ready! Because of its water content, broccoli shrinks *a lot* during cooking, so I recommend making at least double the amount of this popular dish than you think you will need—it's that good! Here are some comments from the test kitchens about this dish: "It was really good. I never massaged oil into broccoli before—made a huge difference;" and "There wasn't enough to feed my whole family. I would have to double the recipe at least." This is a dish you'll find yourself wanting to make over and over, it is so incredible and easy to whip into the oven in a flash. *Makes about 4 cups*

DIRECTIONS

Place the broccoli and/or cauliflower in a bowl and drizzle with the olive oil. Use your hands to massage the vegetables, ensuring that they are well covered, but not too oily. Place the vegetables in a single layer on a baking sheet and sprinkle them generously with the nutritional yeast, stirring thoroughly to cover all surfaces. Bake in a preheated 315°F oven for 30 minutes (stirring occasionally), or until the vegetables are the desired tenderness. Serve hot.

Theresa's Tip

Like kale, broccoli and cauliflower are in the cruciferous family, which can provide countless health benefits for many people. These anti-inflammatory foods are rich in wonderful nutrients, full of antioxidants and fibre, and are great for the cardiovascular and digestive systems, as well as protective against cancer. They are true powerhouses and so delicious as well!

STUFFED GRAPE LEAVES (DOLMAS)

Anyone who knows me well knows my passion for sustainable living and my desire to reduce waste. For me, this recipe using the leaves from the grapevine is a great example of how our ancestors similarly liked to find ways to use otherwise wasted materials. What a great discovery it was! A few years ago, I had a grapevine in the ground that took over an entire region of our small garden (the accidental gardener strikes again!), so we had to dig it up and put it into a large pot. Poor plant! It needs more space and will likely never again produce fruit. However, this dear soul is a great example to all of us—a real survivor that still makes tender leaves. In fact, the dolmas in this photo are from that very vine and my, they are seriously delicious! *Makes about 30*

DIRECTIONS

Thoroughly wash the grape leaves and allow to dry on a towel. One at a time, remove the stem at the base and, with the shiny side facing down, spoon 1–1½ tbsp of *Portobello Quinoa* near the base of the leaf. Fold each side of the leaf in diagonally, then snugly roll up the leaf toward the tip, folding the sides in more completely as you roll. Place the dolmas in a glass baking dish, with the tip of the leaf on the bottom. Squeeze the lemon juice over the dolmas, then lightly drizzle with the oil. Cover and bake in a preheated 315°F degree oven for 45–50 minutes, or until a fork can pierce the rolls with ease. Serve warm, at room temperature or chilled from the refrigerator.

INGREDIENTS

2½—3 cups *Portobello Quinoa* (page 156)

approx 30 young and tender grape leaves, depending on the size of the leaves

juice of 1 lemon

extra virgin olive oil, for drizzling

Theresa's Tip

You may notice that I break the conventional rules for dolma making here, because I don't soak the leaves in salt as is the traditional practice. Personally, I find that soaking the leaves in this way makes dolmas taste way too salty. This lower–salt version of the dish is wonderful and not missing anything!

GARLIC-INFUSED POLENTA

From the age of 16, I worked for five years at the most charming little Italian restaurant called La Piccoletta in Claremont, California, right next to the Claremont Colleges. At the time, Enzo and Linda Biscardi owned it and Linda's sister, Rosie, worked there and was one of my dearest friends. They were beautiful years with wonderful memories. Developing this recipe took me right back to my days there and those people I loved like family. They touched my life in ways they'll never realize and will always live in my heart. It was because of them that I later decided to change my career direction from engineering to psychology, which was one of the most soul-inspired decisions of my life. My memories of them are reflected in this dish, even though this recipe is made differently than the polenta we made there. Thank you for the light and love you brought into my life. *Makes 18 triangles*

INGREDIENTS

favourite cooking oil for sautéing

3–4 garlic cloves, finely minced or microplaned

3 cups water

½ tsp Himalayan salt

1 cup cornmeal

¼ cup *Raw Parmesan* (page 314), grated Brazil nuts or grated vegan cheese (optional)

parsley and/or cilantro, to garnish

DIRECTIONS

In a medium-large saucepan over medium heat, sauté the garlic until it begins to soften and become translucent, but do not overcook. Add the water and salt and bring to a boil over high heat. Reduce the temperature to low and whisk in the cornmeal, adding it very gradually (to avoid clumping). Keep whisking continuously until the polenta becomes very thick and begins to move from the bottom and sides of the pan (about 1 minute more). Immediately pour it into an oiled 9-inch square baking dish or into a silicone pan form. Sprinkle the top with the *Raw Parmesan*, grated Brazil nuts or grated cheese (if using) and allow the polenta to set.

To serve, cut into triangles and enjoy as they are or with a topping of your choice. Try *Rho's Garlic-Marinated Mushrooms* (page 136), *Spicy Pickled Okra* (page 138) or *Spicy Szechuan Eggplant* (page 204). Garnish with parsley or cilantro.

◄ *Garlic-Infused Polenta topped with Rho's Garlic Marinated Mushrooms, page 136*

PORTOBELLO QUINOA

INGREDIENTS

3 cups chopped Portobello mushrooms

favourite cooking oil for sautéing

⅔ cup diced onion

⅔ cup diced daikon or parsnips

⅔ cup diced celery

2 garlic cloves, minced or microplaned

½ tsp fresh turmeric root, finely minced or microplaned (or ⅛ tsp dried turmeric)

¾ tsp Himalayan salt

pinch black pepper

1 cup rinsed quinoa

2 cups water

Really now, how can you go wrong with this combination of ingredients? So good and so good for you. It is versatile and has a distinctive, but not overpowering, flavour, so it can be a side dish as well as a stuffing. You may notice that there is turmeric in this recipe—one of the most anti-inflammatory foods on the planet. But did you know that for the curcumin in the turmeric to do its anti-inflammatory magic, it also needs to be paired with black pepper and heat? If that question ever comes up in Trivial Pursuit, you'll nail it! By the way, daikon is no slouch either. If you want to be impressed sometime (or impress someone special), check out the health benefits of that humble radish. I can almost guarantee that when you do, you'll want to start to eat more of it and maybe grow some of your own!

Makes about 5 cups

DIRECTIONS

Pulse the chopped Portobello mushrooms in a food processor until they are in small bits, but not overprocessed. (If you don't have a food processor, no worries: just finely dice them with a knife.) Set aside. In a large skillet, sauté the onion, daikon or parsnips, celery, garlic, turmeric and salt and pepper over medium heat, until the onions become translucent and begin to caramelize. Add the mushrooms to the skillet and continue to sauté until they start to soften. Add the quinoa and water and bring to a boil. Cover, reduce the heat and simmer for 25 more minutes or until the liquid is mostly absorbed. Enjoy as a side dish, in wraps, in salads, as a stuffing or in other recipes.

MASHED NO POTATOES

As you've been moving through this book, you may have noticed that none of the recipes contain regular potatoes. This is no coincidence! Like many others who struggle with autoimmune challenges, I have a problem with potatoes. My digestive system shows signs of trouble, and my joints become arthritic, with the discomfort of this lasting over a week after eating them. As yummy as they are, potatoes are not for me. So I developed this delicious recipe that, while not an exact replication of conventional mashed potatoes, does have the same creamy texture, appearance and a flavour profile that, while distinctly different, is reminiscent of this popular potato dish.
Makes about 2½ cups

DIRECTIONS

In a preheated 375°F degree oven, bake a whole head of cauliflower uncovered on a baking dish until it is soft when pierced with a fork. Because heads of cauliflower vary so much in size, the time for this will be between 1–1½ hours. While it is baking, blend all the other ingredients, holding back on half of the lima beans and the lima bean cooking liquid until later. Once the cauliflower is softened, roughly chop it into pieces and add it to the blender. Blend on high until creamy, using the tamper to ensure even puréeing, adding as much of the reserved lima bean liquid and lima beans as you need to achieve your desired consistency. Blend until extremely creamy. Enjoy immediately while hot or use in recipes calling for mashed potatoes.

INGREDIENTS

1 cauliflower

1–1½ cups cooked lima beans, in ¼–¾ cups cooking liquid

1 tbsp coconut oil

1 tbsp extra virgin olive oil

2½ tsp lemon juice

1 tsp Himalayan salt, or to taste

1 tsp maple syrup or other favourite sweetener, optional

½ tsp tamari or coconut aminos

⅛ tsp onion powder

⅛ tsp rice vinegar

⅛ tsp cumin powder

Bev's Bit
Cauliflower is an excellent source of vitamin C.

SWEET POTATO FRIES

INGREDIENTS

1–2 sweet potatoes or yams

1–2 tbsp extra virgin olive oil or favourite cooking oil

Himalayan salt, to taste (optional)

Sweet potatoes are not members of the nightshade family and are only distant relatives of white potatoes, so usually can be enjoyed by those who are unable to eat regular potatoes. They are not only delicious, but also have some wonderfully nourishing qualities, such as being high in fibre and rich in minerals and other nutrients. Sweet potatoes have a lower glycemic index than white potatoes. *Serves 2–4*

DIRECTIONS

Wash, peel and cut the sweet potatoes or yams into long stick shapes (about ¼ inch wide). Place in a baking dish and use your hands to rub just enough oil over the sticks to lightly cover all the surfaces. Spread out in a single layer in a baking dish, leaving a little space between the fries (not squished together) and sprinkle lightly with salt. Bake in a preheated 315°F oven for 1¼–1½ hours, or until desired crispiness and tenderness is achieved (turning once or twice during cooking). There are lots of variations possible for these fries: sprinkle with cayenne pepper, either before or after cooking for spicy fries; for herbed fries, before cooking sprinkle in a small amount of your favourite herbs (eg rosemary, oregano, savory or thyme) and rub in with the oil. Serve hot.

Theresa's Tip

If you are in a hurry, you can cook the fries at a higher temperature (425°F) and they will be ready in about 30–40 minutes. If you do so, please avoid using olive oil or any other oil with a similarly low smoke point. Choose instead an oil with a higher smoke point, such as avocado, almond, apricot kernel, carmelina or sesame.

THE ULTRA-BASICS

I remember growing up and loving *The Joy of Cooking*, which I knew contained just about any recipe I wanted, even the ultra-simple basic ones. Inspired by *The Joy of Cooking*, the first working title for this book was *The Joy of Delish*! While clearly this volume has a much smaller scope than *The Joy of Cooking*, my desire for it to serve a similar function remains. I would like young people and inexperienced cooks to feel more empowered to prepare their own food, as well as offer new dishes for those more experienced in the kitchen. Because I'd like all readers to feel confident in the kitchen, I've included instructions for these six key basics.

If you already know how to make these basics, that's wonderful— just skip over these pages. However, if you are newer to cooking whole, unprocessed foods or are a young person wanting to learn useful basic cooking skills, these recipes using universal, nutritious and relatively inexpensive ingredients are here for you to enjoy. Since they are used in many of the recipes in this collection, I don't want there to be any unnecessary hurdles for anyone. Let's keep this journey easy and fun!

BASIC COOKED QUINOA

The versatility of quinoa is amazing. Add salad dressings, sauces or even soups to the basic recipe for simple and colourful side dishes. Experiment with adding nuts, seeds, dried fruit or goji berries, mixed or marinated vegetables—be fanciful and let your creativity be your guide! *Makes 2–2 ½ cups*

INGREDIENTS

1 cup quinoa, rinsed

2½ cups water

Himalayan salt and black pepper, to taste (optional)

DIRECTIONS

In a medium saucepan, stir together all ingredients and cook on high to bring to a boil. Cover and reduce the heat to simmer the quinoa for 20–25 minutes, until the liquid is absorbed. Enjoy as a side dish or in recipes that call for cooked quinoa.

> **Theresa's Tip** 🌢
> Quinoa tastes better when it has been thoroughly rinsed to remove the saponins as much as possible. See *Funky Ingredients* (page 20).

QUINOA RICE

This dish is very versatile and can be used hot as a side dish for stir-fries, in soups, in wraps, in burritos, etc. Not a rock-star recipe, but an amazing supporting one that can be the wind beneath the wings of other culinary show-offs. Combining brown basmati rice with quinoa offsets their respective slight bitterness, resulting in a delightfully mild flavour. Some companies are now packaging the two together (they must have discovered this too), which wasn't the case several years ago when I developed this simple recipe. This dish can also be cooled and used for quinoa salads, such as tabbouleh, or as a topper for green salads and in countless other dishes. Adding a few nuts or seeds, with some ribboned greens or diced vegetables, perhaps with a small sprinkling of raisins or dried cranberries, turns this easy dish into a quick snack or light meal. Season with a bit of tamari or a favourite condiment or sauce. *Makes about 5 cups*

DIRECTIONS

Place all ingredients in a medium-to-large saucepan and stir together. Bring to a boil over high heat, stirring occasionally to keep the grains free from the bottom of the pan. Once the water begins to boil, immediately reduce the heat and cover the pan. Simmer for 20–25 minutes, or until the liquid is nicely absorbed, then turn off the heat. Enjoy with your favourite seasonings or use in recipes as indicated.

INGREDIENTS

1 cup quinoa, rinsed

1 cup basmati brown rice, rinsed

5 cups water

Theresa's Tip
As an alternative to quinoa, use millet and prepare this dish in exactly the same way to create Millet Rice.

LENTILS

Packed with protein and nutrients, lentils are one of the quickest and easiest legumes to cook and to digest. They can be used cooled in salads or in cooked dishes, such as soups, chili, pasta sauces and stews. *Makes about 2 cups*

DIRECTIONS

In a medium saucepan, bring all ingredients to a boil, then simmer for 20 minutes, or until the lentils are cooked but still hold their shape well. Lift out the bay leaf and remove the pan from the heat. Drain off the excess water, which you can reserve to use as a soup broth, or as a replacement for water when cooking rice, millet or quinoa or in other recipes.

INGREDIENTS

1 cup dried green or brown lentils, rinsed, removing any stones or irregular lentils

2 cups water

1 bay leaf

2 garlic cloves, minced

1 cup dried lima beans, rinsed, removing any stones and irregular beans

6 cups water

Theresa's Tip 🌢

To save time, make some extra lima beans that you can freeze in pre-measured amounts to use when wanting to whip up a recipe with lima beans in a flash.

QUICK-COOK LIMA BEANS

Fresh-cooked lima beans have the double benefit of being less processed than those in a can and are much more affordable. However, unlike other dried beans, lima beans are prone to falling apart and turning to mush. Given this characteristic, I developed a simple quick-cook method for these delicate and creamy beans. Especially useful for those with busy lives, this method combines the benefits of soaking and rinsing beans with speedy preparation. In addition, it yields a fantastic cooking liquid that can be used for soups and in other dishes. I hope this recipe helps you to feel more empowered to prepare lima beans in this wholesome way. *Makes about 3 cups, including the juice*

DIRECTIONS

Put the lima beans and 3 cups of the water into a large saucepan. Bring to a full boil over high heat. Reduce the heat to medium and cook for 6 more minutes (stirring occasionally), and then pour through a strainer to drain. Rinse the beans again thoroughly with cool water and return to the pan, along with the other 3 cups of water. Bring to a full boil over high heat again, then immediately reduce the heat to low and simmer in the covered pan for 1 hour, or until tender.

ROASTED GARLIC

In our Italian–American household, my mom used to leave our home-grown garlic cloves whole in the pasta sauce and in many other dishes she made. My brothers and I would all fight over who could enjoy those precious garlic cloves. It still makes me laugh when I think about it! My first year growing garlic, I was so excited when I could braid the tops and hang them in our kitchen. Of course, my husband had to take photos of this proud mama with her braided babies that day!

DIRECTIONS

Slice off the wide root end of each head of garlic, exposing the garlic meat within. Cut off enough of the pointy side so that the garlic head can sit upright in the baking dish with the wide end facing upward. Remove the excess white peel from each garlic head. (You can save all of these removed parts in the freezer for a future broth—see *Sustainable Kitchen Tips 101*, page 330.) Pour the oil into a small bowl and dip in the wide cut side of the garlic head to coat. Set each head, oiled side upward, in a glass baking dish or garlic roaster. Sprinkle with the herbs and a tiny bit of salt. Cover the baking dish with a lid or foil tent and cook in preheated 315°F oven for 1 hour, or until the garlic becomes soft and creamy. (If using foil to cover the dish, be sure it's not in direct contact with the garlic.) Check on it halfway through cooking, and drizzle a little more olive oil over the top if the heads are looking dry.

To use, squeeze the garlic out from the cloves and enjoy warm or refrigerate for use later in wraps, mashed as a spread on bread, as a pizza topping or in other recipes.

INGREDIENTS

1 or more whole garlic heads

½–1 tsp extra virgin olive oil per garlic head

pinch mixed fresh or dried Italian herbs (eg thyme, oregano, savory, rosemary or sage) per head

Himalayan salt, to taste

CAULIFLOWER RICE

A staple in raw food circles, an easier rice substitute isn't possible! This is especially good in my *Tabbouleh with Mint & Cilantro* (page 98) and in other chilled salads and wraps. As simple and versatile as it is, this awesome grain-free substitute is not well known. *Makes 3-6 cups, depending on the size of the cauliflower*

DIRECTIONS

Cut the cauliflower into florets, saving the core and stem for other recipes. Pulse the florets in a food processor until they achieve a rice-like texture, scraping the sides frequently to ensure even processing. Use as a grain-free alternative in many of your other favourite rice recipes.

INGREDIENTS

1 cauliflower

Theresa's Tip 🌢

To make Cauliflower Cous Cous, use this same method, only pulse the cauliflower just a little bit more to achieve the right texture.

CHOW TIME!
MAIN DISHES

BEST NO-MEAT MEAT (YUM)

INGREDIENTS

2 cups roughly chopped
Portobello mushrooms

2 cups roughly chopped
crimini mushrooms

2 cups roughly chopped shitake
and/or oyster mushrooms,
or more crimini mushrooms

1 tbsp tamari or coconut
aminos

1 tsp rice vinegar

1 tsp lemon juice

NUT MIXTURE

2 cups raw walnuts

¼ cup roughly chopped
parsley, firmly packed
(stems and all)

½ cup chopped green onions,
packed

½ tsp Himalayan salt

¼ tsp dried oregano

¼ tsp black pepper

⅛ tsp powdered sage

This is an amazing recipe that you'll probably want to double once you've tried it. The flavour and texture will knock your socks off and it can be used in a host of recipes to make burgers, sausages, ground round substitute and more. When I created this recipe, it opened the door to a culinary paradise! It's the ultimate go-to base for so many recipes. *Makes about 3 cups*

DIRECTIONS

In a food processor, pulse the Portobello mushrooms until they reach a small gravelly texture (don't overprocess), scraping the sides of the food processor a few times along the way to ensure even processing. Place in a medium-sized bowl. Without cleaning the food processor, repeat the same procedure with the other mushrooms, tamari or coconut aminos, vinegar and lemon juice, all at the same time, and add these to the bowl with the Portobello mushrooms. Next, again without cleaning the food processor, do the same with all of the nut mixture ingredients. Processing these will take longer (at least 60–120 pulses) and will require scraping the sides of the vessel much more frequently. Even though this takes a lot of pulses, avoid the temptation to leave the food processor running without pulsing, because that would result in some of the mixture turning to mush with other bits unprocessed. Continue to pulse until the nut mixture reaches a somewhat wet and lumpy, meal-like consistency (smaller pieces than for the mushrooms). Add to the rest of the ingredients in the bowl. With clean or gloved hands, massage the lumpy mixture until well combined.

> **Theresa's Tip** 🌢
> Use more shitake if you want a stronger flavour, more oyster or crimini mushrooms if you want a milder flavour. Feel free to switch these mushrooms, depending on your taste preferences and also which mushrooms are available. If you are sensitive to walnuts, you could try pecans or Brazil nuts as an alternative.

MEATLESS GROUND

Makes about 1½ cups

Spread the *Best No-Meat Meat* mixture on a silicone baking mat or on a parchment-covered baking sheet, or on a teflex dehydrator sheet.

BAKED VERSION Bake in a preheated 315°F oven for about 30-40 minutes, turning the ground meat a couple of times through the cooking time.

RAW VERSION Dehydrate at 105°F on a teflex dehydrator sheet for about 10-14 hours, breaking up with a fork and turning the ground meat a couple of times during the dehydration process.

Serve hot directly from the oven or dehydrator. Can be enjoyed in any favourite recipe calling for ground meat.

MEATLESS TACO GROUND

Makes about 1½ cups

DIRECTIONS

Prepare as for the *Meatless Ground* recipe, with the additional spices massaged in before baking or dehydrating. A Mexican hit!

ADDITIONAL INGREDIENTS

2 tsp dried cilantro

2 tsp chili powder

¼ tsp onion powder

⅛ tsp cayenne pepper

1/16 tsp garlic powder

BEST VEGGIE BURGERS

Makes about 6 standard-sized patties

Use about ½ cup of the *Best No-Meat Meat* mixture per patty to form about 6 burger patties. Place on a silicone baking mat or parchment paper-covered baking sheet, or on a teflex dehydrator sheet.

BAKED VERSION Bake in a preheated 315°F oven for about 40-50 minutes, carefully flipping over about 30 minutes into the cooking.

RAW VERSION Dehydrate at 105°F on a teflex dehydrator sheet for about 12 hours, flipping onto a mesh dehydrator sheet and removing the teflex sheet about ⅔ of the way through the dehydration process.

Serve hot directly from the oven or dehydrator. If you like, very lightly brush the surface of the patties with some extra virgin olive oil. These burgers can be enjoyed as is on a bed of lettuce, on a gluten-free bun with burger condiments or in any other favourite burger recipe.

VEGGIE MEATBALLS

Makes 24–30 meatballs

Prepare the *Best No-Meat Meat*, then form into meatballs, ¾-1 inch in diameter. Place the meatballs on a silicone baking mat or on a parchment-covered baking sheet, or on a teflex dehydrator sheet.

BAKED VERSION Bake in a preheated 315°F oven for about 40-50 minutes (or until desired doneness is achieved), turning the meatballs about ⅔ of the way through the cooking time.

RAW VERSION Dehydrate at 105°F on a teflex dehydrator sheet for 16-24 hours (they take more time than the burgers to dehydrate because the burgers are thinner and flat, with a larger surface area), turning the meatballs a couple of times throughout the dehydration process.

Serve hot directly from the oven or dehydrator. Enjoy in your favourite recipes calling for meatballs.

> **Theresa's Tip** 🌢
> For meatballs that will store and travel very well, dehydrate them for at least twice the time, until no moisture remains. These make a great addition to the *Instant Minestrone Soup Mix* (page 123).

SHEPHERD'S PIE

1 recipe *Mashed No Potatoes*
(page 157) or 2½ cups
mashed potatoes

1 yellow onion,
roughly chopped

1–2 garlic cloves,
roughly chopped

1 Portobello mushroom,
roughly chopped

1½ cups roughly chopped
crimini mushrooms

1 cup roughly chopped
shitake mushrooms

favourite cooking oil
for sautéing

1½ cups *Meatless Ground*
(page 167)

1 cup finely diced carrots

½ cup shelled peas

½ cup corn kernels (optional)

2 tbsp tomato paste

2 tsp rice vinegar

2 tsp lemon juice

2 tsp tamari or coconut aminos

½ tsp ground sage

½ tsp Himalayan salt

¼ tsp black pepper

¼ tsp thyme

¼ tsp turmeric powder

After so many years, it's wonderful to enjoy this richly flavoured take
on the old classic once again. *Serves 4–6*

DIRECTIONS

Put the onion, garlic and all the mushrooms in a food processor and pulse
about 20 times, scraping the sides of the vessel if needed to ensure even
processing. In a very large frying pan over medium heat, sauté the mixture for
about 6–7 minutes. Remove from the heat, stir in the remaining ingredients
except for the *Mashed No Potatoes* or mashed potatoes, pressing them evenly
on the bottom of a 10-inch square baking dish. Spread the *Mashed No Potatoes*
or mashed potatoes evenly over the meaty mixture and bake in a preheated
315°F oven for 1 hour. Serve hot.

CAJUN SAUSAGE JAMBALAYA

favourite cooking oil
for sautéing

2 small onions, chopped

2 green onions, thinly sliced

1 red bell pepper, chopped

2 garlic cloves, chopped

2 stalks celery, sliced on
the diagonal

3 medium tomatoes, chopped

¾ cup uncooked brown
basmati rice or favourite rice

1½ cups water

1 tbsp *Cajun Spice Mix*
(page 174), or to taste

1 recipe *Herb-Infused
Breakfast Sausages* (page 75),
cut into pieces

Spicy and simple, this fast and delicious one-pot meal is a fantastic option for the meat-eaters in the crowd. Best of all, if you have the sausages on hand, it is easy to whip together at the end of a long workday. *Serves 4*

DIRECTIONS

In a large skillet sauté the onions, green onions and bell pepper on medium heat for about 3 minutes, then add the garlic and celery and sauté for another 3 minutes, until all start to become translucent. Stir in the tomatoes, rice, water and the *Cajun Spice Mix* and increase the temperature to high until it begins to boil. Cover, reduce the temperature and simmer for about 30 minutes or until the rice is cooked and most of the water is absorbed. Stir in the sausage pieces and continue to simmer another 5–10 minutes. Serve hot.

CAJUN SPICE MIX

INGREDIENTS

4 tsp paprika

2 tsp Himalayan salt

2 tsp crushed hot red pepper flakes, or to taste

2 tsp dried parsley flakes

2 tsp garlic powder

1 tsp onion powder

1 tsp dried oregano

1 tsp dried thyme

1 tsp black pepper

1 tsp cayenne pepper, or to taste

I've only visited New Orleans once in my life, but I was struck by the distinctive flavours of Cajun cooking. This spice mix has the classic spicy flavour profile that I loved while in New Orleans. It's amazing how just a sprinkle takes me right back to the sights and sounds of Bourbon Street! *Makes about ¼ cup*

DIRECTIONS

Put all ingredients in a bottle and shake to mix. Use to spice up rice, salads, vegetable dishes or in Cajun-style recipes. Store in a little jar in a cool, dry place.

SPAGHETTI & VEGGIE MEATBALLS

A classic dish every spaghetti and meatball fan will love. *Serves 6–8*

DIRECTIONS

COOKED VARIATION In a medium-sized pan, heat the *Marinara Sauce* over low or medium-low heat. Once warm, add the meatballs and continue to heat for another 5–10 minutes, until the meatballs are heated through. Put the hot spaghetti in a very large pasta serving dish or bowl and spoon over the sauce and meatballs, carefully tossing together (reserve a little extra sauce to add to individual servings). Sprinkle the *Raw Parmesan* or grated Brazil nuts on top. Serve hot.

RAW VARIATION In a medium-sized bowl or large glass jar, heat the *Marinara Sauce* (raw version) in the dehydrator until warm. On a separate tray in the dehydrator, warm the raw meatballs. During the last 20–30 minutes before serving, add the meatballs to the sauce in the dehydrator and continue to warm. Prepare zucchini "noodles" or other favourite raw pasta and put into a very large pasta serving dish or bowl. Remove the sauce and meatballs from the dehydrator and spoon over the pasta, carefully tossing together (reserve a little extra sauce to add to individual servings). Sprinkle the *Raw Parmesan* or grated Brazil nuts on top. Serve hot.

INGREDIENTS

1 recipe *Marinara Sauce* (page 322)

1 recipe *Veggie Meatballs* (page 169)

8–10 cups prepared gluten-free pasta

2–4 tbsp *Raw Parmesan* or *Nut-Free Raw Parmesan* (page 314) or 2–4 Brazil nuts, finely grated or microplaned

Theresa's Tip 🌢

Use the *Marinara Sauce* and *Veggie Meatballs* to make meatball sandwiches on gluten-free buns, with or without bell pepper slices, vegan cheese and/or *Raw Parmesan* or grated Brazil nuts added. Served either hot (to melt the cheese) or cold, this is a wonderful comfort food.

RAW ZUCCHINI "PASTA" WITH CREAMY SUNFLOWER SEED SAUCE

If you are not already familiar with zucchini pasta, this recipe may make you do a double-take! This very simple dish is one of my favourite (virtually instant) suppers, using condiments that I like to keep on hand. I can make this dish in less than 5 minutes—start to finish—without even needing to boil water! This pasta works well with other hot or cold sauces and in salads topped with other vegetables. It is a super-quick meal at the end of a long day. *Serves 2–4*

DIRECTIONS

Place the prepared zucchini in a large bowl and toss gently with the remaining ingredients. Serve immediately (important), garnished with a little more *Raw Parmesan*, grated Brazil nuts or nutritional yeast and fresh herbs.

Why Raw Noodles?

In the raw food world, raw zucchini "noodles" are a common main dish. This idea can seem quite unusual to those who eat primarily mainstream diets, who might see this recipe as a salad rather than a main course. In general, folks who eat a lot of raw food do so because they value eating not only nutrient-dense food, but also food with a very high water content as well. When I was initially introduced to the world of raw food living, I was really surprised by how filling and satisfying the food could be. So as I share this recipe with you, I am aware that you may be raising your eyebrows in disbelief—that's great! I want you to be curious and begin to realize that there is a much broader range of food to choose from than you may have thought. Learn more about spiralizers for preparing vegetables in *Terrific Tools* (page 34).

INGREDIENTS

1 medium-to-large zucchini, peeled, then spiralized, julienned or grated

1–2 cups sliced, grated, diced or chiffonaded vegetables (bell peppers, carrots, tomatoes, kale, arugula, etc)

handful fresh herbs (basil, oregano, thyme, savory, sage), plus a few more for garnishing

½ cup *Creamy Sunflower Seed Sauce* (page 318), to taste

¼ cup *Raw Parmesan* or *Nut-Free Raw Parmesan* (page 314), 2–4 Brazil nuts, finely grated or microplaned, or 2 tsp nutritional yeast

½ cup cooked chickpeas (optional)

dash cayenne pepper (optional)

MAC 'N' CHEESE

INGREDIENTS

½ tsp garlic powder

2 tbsp starch (tapioca or potato) or arrowroot powder

½ cup nutritional yeast

2 cups almond milk or favourite non-dairy milk

1 tbsp lemon juice

1 tbsp tamari or coconut aminos

1 tbsp melted coconut oil

1 tbsp extra virgin olive oil

2 cups grated Daiya cheddar cheese or favourite vegan cheese

5 cups cooked gluten-free macaroni

Our vegan daughter Alex had a brainstorm for this masterpiece, and she really nailed it! Some test kitchen comments: "It was really good and cooked much faster than it appeared from reading the recipe..." "The baby (11 months old) also liked it and we cooked the macaroni long enough for it to be soft for her." "My husband was quite skeptical because it wasn't baked mac and cheese, and he actually eats cheese... he really really liked it. He wanted to serve the cheese sauce separately from the macaroni, so individuals could regulate how much sauce they wanted. I didn't like that idea, but it could be done, I guess. I suspect it was his way of rationing out the tasty cheese sauce." *Serves 4–6*

DIRECTIONS

In a small bowl, mix together the garlic powder, starch, and nutritional yeast. Set aside near the stove. In a medium-sized bowl, mix together the milk, lemon juice and tamari or coconut aminos. Set aside near the stove. Place the oils in a medium-large saucepan over medium heat. Once heated, add the milk mixture, followed by the dry yeast mixture, and whisk continuously until quite thick (about 10 minutes). Remove the pan from the heat, add the vegan cheese and mix well for about 1 minute until the cheese has melted and is thoroughly integrated into the sauce. Finally, stir in the cooked macaroni. Serve immediately while hot.

Theresa's Tip

Once you have measured out and prepared all of the ingredients, put them close to the stove because as soon as you start cooking you will need to stir continuously. Also, feel free to replace the macaroni with any other gluten-free pasta of your choice.

EGGPLANT PARMESAN

This dish is simple to make and impressive even for your most fussy dinner guests. It could become a family favourite in no time.

Serves 2–3

DIRECTIONS

In one flat-bottomed bowl, stir together the oil and maple syrup. Put the breadcrumbs in a second flat-bottomed bowl. Brush or dip each round in the oil mixture, then in the breadcrumbs, covering all surfaces. Place the coated rounds on a baking sheet and place in a preheated 450°F oven for 30 minutes, carefully flipping each over halfway through cooking. After the 30 minutes, remove the baking sheet from the oven. In the bottom of a large glass baking dish, spread about ½ cup of the *Marinara Sauce* and then place the eggplant rounds on top of the sauce. Cover the rounds with about 1½ cups of *Marinara Sauce*. Sprinkle with the chopped fresh basil, followed by the remaining sauce. Top evenly with the shredded vegan cheese, followed by a sprinkling of the grated Brazil nuts (if using). Bake for 15 minutes at 450°F and serve hot.

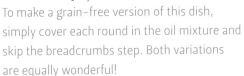

Theresa's Tip

To make a grain-free version of this dish, simply cover each round in the oil mixture and skip the breadcrumbs step. Both variations are equally wonderful!

INGREDIENTS

2 tbsp maple syrup or favourite sticky syrup

¼–½ cup avocado oil or favourite cooking oil

1–1½ cups gluten-free breadcrumbs (optional)

1 very large eggplant, sliced into ½ inch thick rounds

1 recipe *Marinara Sauce* (page 322, cooked version)

½ cup finely chopped fresh basil, packed

½ cup shredded Daiya mozzarella cheese or other favourite vegan cheese

1–2 Brazil nuts, finely grated or microplaned (optional)

1⅓ cups *Raw Curry Paste*

1 sweet potato or yam, sliced in ⅛–¼ inch slices

2 celery stalks, chopped

1½ cups puréed, crushed or diced tomatoes

1 cauliflower, cut into pieces

1½ cups cooked chickpeas

2 cups finely chopped leafy greens (kale and/or collard greens)

1 cup coconut milk or favourite non-dairy milk (optional)

GARNISH

chopped cilantro leaves

dash rice vinegar and black pepper, to taste (optional)

INGREDIENTS

1 tbsp chopped fresh ginger

1 large or 2 small-medium yellow or white onions, roughly chopped

1 tsp Himalayan salt

1 tsp chopped or grated fresh turmeric root, or 1 tsp dried turmeric

1 tbsp ground coriander

1 tbsp ground cumin

2 tsp cayenne pepper

3–5 garlic cloves, to taste

CURRIED CAULIFLOWER & CHICKPEA STEW

Anyone who has ever been to Vancouver knows that it has some of the best Indian restaurants in the world. This wonderful and hearty dish was a result of my craving to enjoy Indian food again, in all its wonder. It can be served as a stew or made into a soup by adding more milk, water or broth. Once you have the basic Indian flavour-profile of spices using the curry paste, it is incredible how creative you can be with incorporating lots of healthy ingredients! *Serves 6–10*

DIRECTIONS

In a very large saucepan, sauté the *Raw Curry Paste* over medium heat for 2–3 minutes, then add the sweet potato or yam and continue to cook, covered, until the potatoes begin to soften, stirring frequently. Add the celery and cook an additional 3–4 minutes, stirring occasionally. If necessary to prevent sticking, add a small amount of water to the pan while cooking. Stir in the tomatoes, cauliflower and chickpeas and continue cooking over low-medium heat, covered. Once the cauliflower begins to soften (about 8 minutes), add the greens. For the creamy variation, add the coconut or other non-dairy milk and cook an additional 5–10 minutes. Serve hot on its own, or over cooked quinoa, brown rice or *Cauliflower Rice*, and garnish with cilantro and a dash of rice vinegar and black pepper.

RAW CURRY PASTE

A wonderful condiment to have on hand to make any curry dish or to use in other recipes as a spicy flavour enhancer.
Makes about 1⅓ cups

DIRECTIONS

Process all ingredients in a food processor or blender until they form a paste. This paste can be stored in the refrigerator for up to two weeks.

> **Theresa's Tip** 🌢
> To make curry powder, spread the curry paste on a teflex tray, dehydrate until completely dry and then pulse to a powder in a blender. Store in an airtight container to enjoy sprinkled on rice, quinoa, steamed vegetables and salads as a delightfully spicy condiment.

ERIC'S FAMOUS CHILI

INGREDIENTS

16 oz plain tempeh

1 jalapeño pepper or 2 serrano peppers, chopped (optional)

2 sweet yellow onions, chopped

1¼ cups daikon, chopped

4 garlic cloves, chopped

1 tbsp ground cumin

2–3 tbsp Mexican chili powder

½ tsp ground dried (or 1–1½ tsp fresh grated) turmeric

favourite cooking oil for sautéing

6 cups cooked beans (kidney, black and/or pinto), liquid included

4 cups tomatoes, diced

¾ celery stalk with leaves, chopped

½ cup green or red dried lentils

1 tsp dried crushed hot red pepper flakes, or to taste (optional)

1 green bell pepper, chopped

1 red bell pepper, chopped

1 green onion, chopped

Himalayan salt and coarse-ground black pepper, to taste

My dear husband, Eric, is an amazing, intuitive one-pot cook. He effortlessly whips together these dishes in no time. Before our family shifted to a gluten-free lifestyle, one of his favourite large-gathering dishes was a fabulous chili using a vegetarian ground round. While it took a bit of tweaking to get the flavour and texture just right, we have been thrilled with his gluten-free vegan chili recipe. The daikon is fantastic in this dish! *Serves 7–9*

DIRECTIONS

Sauté the tempeh, jalapeño or serrano peppers, onions, daikon, garlic, cumin, chili powder and turmeric in a large, heavy soup pot with just enough oil to keep the ingredients from sticking. Cook for about 5 minutes, or until the onions are translucent. Add the rest of the ingredients, bring to a light boil, then reduce the heat and simmer for 1 hour, stirring frequently. Serve hot with the garnishes of your choice.

Haely's Hint ❁
Cumin and turmeric are both anti-cancer agents.

Garnishes
chopped green onions or cilantro,
nutritional yeast or grated Daiya chedder
cheese or favourite vegan cheese

CABBAGE ROLLS

INGREDIENTS

8–10 very large Savoy cabbage leaves or favourite green cabbage leaves

1 recipe *Portobello Quinoa* (page 156)

1 recipe *Tomato Sauce* (page 319)

¼ cup *Raw Parmesan* (page 314) or 4 Brazil nuts, finely grated or microplaned (optional)

A great comfort food, cabbage rolls go way back in history. Because of its touted anti–tumour, anti–inflammatory and antioxidant qualities, cabbage is the subject of much recent investigation. This is a filling and delicious dish with general appeal. *Serves 4–5*

DIRECTIONS

Lightly steam or boil the cabbage leaves (do not overcook) so they are pliable, then carefully remove them from the water or steamer and place on towels to dry. When the leaves are cool enough to handle, place ⅓ cup of the *Portobello Quinoa* about 1 inch from the base of a leaf, then firmly and carefully roll the base over the quinoa. Fold in the 2 sides to complete the cabbage roll. Place the cabbage rolls snugly side by side in a baking dish. Cover with the *Tomato Sauce*. If desired, also sprinkle some *Raw Parmesan* or grated Brazil nuts over the sauce. Cover the dish and place in a preheated 315˚ F oven for 75–80 minutes, or until a fork easily pierces the cabbage. Serve hot.

CLASSIC MARGHERITA TORTILLA PIZZA

Gluten-free flour tortillas make a quick and easy base for pizza. Using this method, it's important to remember not to pile on as many toppings as you might get away with on a regular crust. It's a delicious meal you can make at the end of a long day or enjoy for a family pizza-and-movie night. It also makes a great appetizer or snack for brunches or game-day parties. Keeping tortillas and shredded vegan cheese in the freezer means instant, easy meals, anytime. *Serves 1*

DIRECTIONS

Place the tortilla on a pizza stone or parchment-covered cookie sheet and brush the entire top surface with the olive oil. Sprinkle or spread the surface with the garlic or creamy *Roasted Garlic*. Cover the tortilla evenly with the vegan cheese, followed by the tomato slices in a single layer. Sprinkle the fresh herbs, *Raw Parmesan* and red pepper flakes (if using) evenly across the surface. Place in a preheated 315°F oven and bake for about 20 minutes, or until the cheese has melted. Serve hot.

INGREDIENTS

1 gluten-free flour tortilla

extra virgin olive oil

1–2 garlic cloves, crushed, finely minced or microplaned, or *Roasted Garlic* (page 163)

⅔ cup shredded Daiya cheese or favourite vegan cheese

1 large tomato, very thinly sliced

fresh Italian herbs (eg basil, oregano, thyme, savory and/or rosemary)

2 tbsp *Raw Parmesan* (page 314), optional

crushed hot red pepper flakes (optional)

POLENTA PIZZA

INGREDIENTS

favourite cooking oil
for sautéing

3–4 garlic cloves, finely minced

2 cups water

1 tsp Himalayan salt

½ tbsp rosemary

1 cup organic cornmeal

avocado oil

Marinara Sauce (page 322)
or favourite pizza sauce

TOPPING OPTIONS

Daiya wedge cheese or
favourite vegan cheese

mushrooms (*Rho's Marinated
Mushrooms,* page 136, or fresh
sliced mushrooms)

sliced peppers (hot and/
or sweet)

sautéed marinated
tempeh slices

sliced tomatoes, fresh
or sun–dried

Spicy Pickled Okra (page 138)

...or any other toppings that
your heart desires!

Have a blast being creative with this recipe! Making mini–pizza crusts that guests can top themselves is a great party idea. You can also make the pizza in a 10-inch square pan and cut it into 2–inch squares as a fantastic hot appetizer for a get–together. This pizza is delicious and really simple to make. However, unlike the traditional variety, polenta pizza is not a grab–and–go meal: it is softer, so you'll want to eat it with a fork! YUM! *Serves 2–4*

DIRECTIONS

In a medium-large saucepan, sauté the garlic over medium heat until it starts to become translucent (do not overcook). Add the water, salt and rosemary and bring to a boil over high heat. Reduce the temperature to low and whisk in the cornmeal, adding it very gradually. Keep whisking continuously until the polenta becomes very thick; cook for about 1 more minute, until it begins to move away from the bottom and sides of the pan.

Pour it onto a parchment-covered baking sheet or in a silicone pan form and *very quickly* spread it to make a 12-inch diameter round, about ¼-inch thick. (For mini-pizzas, make several smaller rounds.) It is really important to move quickly in the spreading process because the polenta begins to set super-fast. Allow the polenta to set fully, which only takes 5–10 minutes. Brush the whole top surface with some oil and bake the crust in preheated 425˚F oven for 15 minutes. Remove and allow to cool before adding the sauce and toppings of your choice. After topping, return to a preheated 425˚F oven for about 20 minutes, or until the toppings are heated and the cheese has melted. Serve immediately.

CRUSTLESS CHEESY BROCCOLI QUICHE

Perfect for brunch or lunch or anytime! I created this mouth-watering quiche when our broccolini plants were abundant and at their prime. Our wonderful neighbour Jenny Chapman had given us seedlings she'd grown in her greenhouse from her previous year's crop. All that loving care infused every special bite. *Serves 4–6*

DIRECTIONS

Blend together the tofu, salt, pepper, nutritional yeast and herbs until creamy, then set aside. In a skillet, lightly sauté the onions, garlic and jalapeño pepper (if using) until the onions are translucent. Turn off the burner and stir in the broccoli, green onions, 1 cup of the cheese and the prepared tofu mixture. Spoon into greased ramekins. Sprinkle the remaining cheese on top of the ramekins and bake in a preheated 350°F oven for 30-45 minutes. Remove from the oven and serve hot.

INGREDIENTS

12 oz firm silken tofu

½ tsp Himalayan salt

⅛ tsp black pepper

2 tbsp nutritional yeast

½ tsp fresh (or ¼ tsp dried) thyme

½ tsp fresh (or ¼ tsp dried) oregano

½ tsp fresh (or ¼ tsp dried) rosemary

favourite cooking oil for sautéing

1 small onion, chopped

2–3 garlic cloves, finely minced or microplaned

1 tsp finely minced jalapeño pepper (optional)

2 cups chopped broccoli and/or broccolini

⅓–½ cup finely chopped green onions

1½ cups Daiya cheddar or favourite vegan cheese, grated

ALEX'S TAHINI KALE WITH TOFU

INGREDIENTS

favourite cooking oil
for sautéing

1 small garlic clove, minced
or microplaned

1 inch fresh ginger root,
peeled and minced, grated
or microplaned

½ cup finely chopped
yellow onion

12 oz extra-firm tofu
or tempeh, diced into
¼–½ inch cubes

6–8 cups de-stemmed kale,
torn into small pieces

¼–½ cup water,

½ cup *Alex's Tahini Sauce*
(page 198)

Himalayan salt, to taste
(optional)

This invention by Alex is nothing less than pure genius! While the taste is slightly different than saag paneer, the look and texture remind me of that beloved Indian spinach and pressed cheese dish. It is so rewarding to witness my daughter in her creative element and to celebrate with her these awesome moments of success. This one became an instant family favourite! *Serves 3–4*

DIRECTIONS

Warm up a large skillet over medium heat, then add the oil and wait a minute for the heat to build up. Add the garlic, ginger, onion and tofu or tempeh to the pan and cook, stirring occasionally, until the onions begin to caramelize and it start to smell really wonderful. Add the kale and water and cover, cooking until the kale turns bright green. Turn off the heat, add the tahini sauce and stir until evenly coated. Season with salt if desired.

Haely's Hint ✿

Kale is definitely one of the healthiest foods around. If you eat it raw you will get more vitamins and enzymes; if you steam it lightly you will get more minerals. Kale is a known cancer-fighter, helps lower cholesterol and supports the body's detoxification system and much more. It's versatile and readily available—you can't go wrong with kale!

Theresa's Tip 🍃

Warming the pan, then warming the oil for 1 minute before adding the vegetables prevents them from sticking.

PAD THAI

There is something about the combination of a complex flavour profile, varied textural qualities, beautiful colours and the light quality of this raw–infused dish that is truly wonderful. *Serves 4*

DIRECTIONS

In a large skillet over high heat, lightly sauté the green onions and bok choy or cabbage for 5 minutes. Stir in the snow peas and bean sprouts and cook about 2 minutes longer. Remove from the heat and stir in the prepared noodles, carrots, red bell pepper, *Raw Pad Thai Sauce* and hot red pepper flakes.

To serve, place on a large serving platter (or individual plates) and top with the garnishes. Serve hot.

INGREDIENTS

peanut oil, sesame oil or favourite cooking oil for sautéing

3 green onions, thinly sliced

4 cups shredded bok choy or Chinese cabbage

½ cup snow peas, cut in half diagonally

3 cups long Asian bean sprouts

4 cups cooked wide rice noodles or other gluten–free noodles

½ cup shredded or julienned carrots

½ cup julienned red bell pepper

1 recipe *Raw Pad Thai Sauce* (page 318), or to taste

½–1 tsp crushed hot red pepper flakes, or to taste

GARNISHES

cilantro, chopped peanuts or almonds, lemon or lime wedges

ALEX'S TAHINI SAUCE

¼ cup lemon juice

1 tbsp tamari
or coconut aminos

¼ cup tahini, or to
desired texture

Tahini is sesame seed butter, much like peanut butter, with a distinctive taste that can take recipes in surprising new directions. Alex fell in love with Gourmet Raw Food Chef Cherie Soria's "Bon Bon Sauce," which we learned while studying at the Living Light Culinary Institute. Inspired to play with this flavourful ingredient, Alex created this simple sauce for her kale and tofu recipe. *Makes ½ cup*

DIRECTIONS

Combine the ingredients in a small bowl and mix together with a fork. Can be stored in the refrigerator for up to two weeks.

Theresa's Tip 🍃

My substitution trick for anyone allergic to sesame seeds is to replace them (or tahini) with sunflower seeds (or sunflower seed butter). Both share a similar flavour profile that makes more beautiful things possible for those sensitive to sesame!

RAW PAD THAI SAUCE

This sauce is a delicious and flexible condiment to add spice to salads, rice, quinoa and pasta dishes. It's also good as a marinade for tofu, tempeh or vegetable stir-fries. A little can also be sprinkled in wraps, spring rolls and burritos to add a surprising new dimension of flavour to dishes. *Makes 1 cup*

DIRECTIONS

Process all ingredients thoroughly in a blender. Can be stored in the refrigerator for up to 2 weeks.

Bee Bite
It's estimated that the honey bee contributes more than $14 billion to the economy in the United States alone.

INGREDIENTS

⅓ cup rice vinegar

2 garlic cloves, chopped

1 shallot or small onion, chopped

¼ cup lime juice

2 tbsp tamari or coconut aminos

1 small Thai red hot chili pepper or similar, chopped

⅛–¼ inch fresh ginger root, peeled and chopped

⅛ tsp *Chicory Root Inulin with Stevia* (page 324) or favourite sweetener (optional)

1-inch-square piece nori paper or other seaweed

pinch white pepper

dash paprika

SESAME CABBAGE STIR-FRY

1 tsp sesame or peanut oil,
plus 1 tsp favourite cooking oil
for sautéing

2–3 cups shredded purple
cabbage

2–3 cups shredded green
cabbage

1 small onion, chopped into
medium-large pieces

1 garlic clove, minced or
microplaned

1 carrot, thinly sliced

1 fresh jalapeño pepper,
finely diced (optional)

1 cup snow peas

½ cup shitake mushrooms,
cut in pieces

3 large kale leaves,
de-stemmed and torn
into pieces

1 tbsp tamari or coconut
aminos, or ½ tsp miso
(chickpea or soy)

Himalayan salt (optional)

sesame or hemp seeds

I have so much admiration for my husband, Eric. He is a respected leader in the field of energy and the environment, doing what he can to make a difference in the world while he's here on the planet. A champion for diversity and human rights, he never hesitates to step up to the plate when the voice of truth and integrity needs to be heard—especially when those being harmed are individuals unable to advocate for themselves and need someone to fight for them. On top of that, he's an incredible dad and partner! This rainbow-coloured dish is his creation, filled with lots of our favourite ingredients and love. *Serves 2–4*

DIRECTIONS

Sauté the cabbage, onion, garlic, carrots and jalapeño in the oils for about 5 minutes, until the onion start to soften and the flavours begin to marry. Then add the snow peas, mushrooms, kale and the tamari (or alternative). Continue to cook another for 3–5 minutes. Add salt to taste. Serve on its own or over rice, quinoa or noodles, sprinkled with the seeds as a garnish.

Bev's Bit
While all cabbages are great for your health, the deep red-purple cabbage comes with even more health-protective phytonutrients than its siblings.

TERIYAKI UDON STIR-FRY

Here's another raw-infused recipe that Eric and I love and like to share with friends who enjoy spicy Asian food. You can have a lot of fun creating variations of this dish by using different ingredients: shredded cabbage, bean sprouts, peanuts or cashews, and tofu or tempeh. You can also use grated or spiralized zucchini or kelp noodles for the "spaghetti" to increase the raw ingredient content. Here was what one of the test kitchens had to say about this dish: "Made it without onion per husband's allergy. Still delish. Also added cashews. I also cooked up some steak separately for the meat-eaters and they just added it to theirs and loved it. Very fun and flexible recipe."
Serves 4

DIRECTIONS

Sauté the onion, ginger, garlic or leeks, and the jalapeño in the oils for about 5 minutes over medium heat, until the onions start to soften. Then add the rice vinegar, tamari (or alternative), broccoli, celery and snow peas, and cook for about 5 more minutes with the lid on until the broccoli and peas brighten in colour and begin to slightly soften. Remove the lid and stir in the dark green leafy vegetables, the red bell pepper and the carrot. Finally, stir in the prepared noodles or spaghetti and season with salt and pepper. Garnish with the seeds and serve immediately while still hot.

INGREDIENTS

1 tsp sesame or peanut oil, plus 1 tsp favourite cooking oil for sautéing

½ onion, sliced into julienne arches

1 inch fresh ginger root, peeled and grated or microplaned

2–3 garlic cloves, or ½ cup chopped leeks

1 small fresh jalapeño pepper, finely diced

1 tbsp rice vinegar, or to taste

2–4 tbsp tamari or coconut aminos, or ½ tsp miso (chickpea or soy), to taste

1½– 2 cups broccoli florets

2 celery stalks (and leaves, if desired), chopped

½–1 cup snow peas, cut into bite-sized pieces

2 cups chopped dark green leafy vegetables (eg kale, spinach, bok choy, etc)

1 red bell pepper, julienned

1 cup julienned or shredded carrot

2 cups prepared noodles or gluten-free spaghetti

Himalayan salt and black pepper, to taste

sesame or hemp seeds, for garnish

SPICY SZECHUAN EGGPLANT

INGREDIENTS

2 small or medium eggplants,
or 3–4 medium Japanese
eggplants

2 tbsp sesame or peanut oil,
or favourite cooking oil

1 tbsp grated fresh ginger root

3–4 garlic cloves, finely minced
or microplaned

3 green onions, sliced

1 tsp rice vinegar

¼ tsp crushed hot red pepper
flakes, or to taste

½ cup water

1 recipe *Raw Hoisin Sauce*
(page 318)

¾ cup shredded carrot,
or to taste

GARNISHES

fresh cilantro and sesame
or hemp seeds (optional)

Since learning that I couldn't have any gluten, dining out at our favourite restaurants became a thing of the past. One of the dishes that I dearly missed was Szechuan spicy eggplant. Now I can enjoy it again! Here's what one of the test kitchens said about this recipe: "This is an excellent recipe. Easy to make, easy to double, easy to eat on a whole range of things. It made a great lunch. It's super versatile, because you can even eat the eggplant cold, so it would also be good for a picnic. We'll make this over and over again. It has all the qualities of a soon-to-be-beloved recipe." I so agree! *Serves 2–4*

DIRECTIONS

Cut the eggplant into wedges about ½ inch at their widest point. If using larger eggplants, there will be some strips without any peel (and that's fine). Lightly sauté the eggplant strips, ginger and garlic in the oil for 1 minute over medium heat. Then add the green onions, vinegar and crushed pepper flakes and continue to sauté for another 1–2 minutes. When the vegetables start to dry, add half the water and continue to cook for another minute. Add the *Raw Hoisin Sauce* and the rest of the water and reduce the heat, simmering 2–4 more minutes, until the eggplant is soft but not overcooked. Remove the pan from the heat, stir in the shredded carrot and serve immediately, garnished with the cilantro and seeds. Serve hot on its own or with rice, quinoa, noodles or pasta. You can also chill and use on salads, in wraps and as a topping.

STUFFED PORTOBELLO MUSHROOMS

Reminiscent of French cuisine, this herb- and wine-infused, meaty dish is so rich and decadent, it's hard to believe it's so healthy! This is a meal we enjoy on special occasions, perfect for a romantic candle-light dinner. *Serves 4*

DIRECTIONS

In a skillet over medium heat, sauté the onion, garlic and green onions until the mixture begins to soften. Add the shitake and crimini mushrooms, the chopped reserved Portobello mushroom stems and the herbs. Once all of the vegetables begin to soften, add the white wine and continue to sauté until the flavours have begun to marry and the ingredients are soft. Season with salt and pepper. Fill the Portobello mushroom caps with the cooked vegetable mixture. Generously cover with the Daiya or vegan cheese and bake uncovered in a preheated 350°F degree oven for 45–60 minutes, or until the cheese melts and the Portobellos are soft and juicy. Garnish with some chopped fresh herbs and serve while hot.

INGREDIENTS

favourite cooking oil for sautéing

1 onion, chopped

2–3 garlic cloves, minced

4 green onions, thinly sliced

1 cup sliced shitake mushrooms

1 cup sliced crimini mushrooms

4 large Portobello mushrooms, stems removed, chopped and reserved

1 tsp fresh (or ½ tsp dried) oregano or thyme

1 tsp fresh or dried rosemary, finely chopped

½–⅔ cup white wine

Himalayan salt and black pepper, to taste

1½–2 cups Daiya or favourite vegan cheese

chopped fresh herbs, for garnish

RAW CORN & AVOCADO LETTUCE BOATS

INGREDIENTS

kernels from 1 raw corn cob

1 avocado, diced

1 carrot, shredded

juice of 1 lemon

Himalayan salt and black pepper, to taste

2 large whole lettuce leaves

2 tbsp chopped fresh basil or cilantro, plus sprigs for garnish

The first time Alex made this dish and brought it to the table, I had to do a double-take! The first hit was the bright and fresh aroma; the second was the beautiful display of the glorious fresh vegetables and avocado. Before taking raw culinary courses, I never knew that uncooked corn could be so delicious and sweet, straight off the cob! Corn needs a lot of space to grow, so we feel blessed to be able to buy it fresh at our local summer farmer's market. *Makes 2 boats*

DIRECTIONS

Combine all of the ingredients (except for the lettuce leaves and the herb sprigs for garnish) in a bowl. To serve, divide the mixture between the two lettuce leaves and garnish with basil or cilantro.

Haely's Hint ✿
Corn is a crop that is frequently GM, so buy organic whenever possible.

CHEESY BEAN & KALE QUESADILLAS

We love beans with the fresh kale and other garden vegetables in this easy, cheesy, raw-infused family favourite. Test kitchen feedback: "Loved it. Can't wait to make it again..." "We love quesadillas; they are perfect for our busy lifestyle. Quick and little prep required..." "This worked great as supper for a week. We just varied it to keep it interesting... We had never had vegan cheese and had to buy it, but it was really delicious! ... It was a hit." *Serves 1*

DIRECTIONS

Place the tortilla flat in a large dry skillet over medium heat, then sprinkle the cheese over the whole surface, followed by a strip of beans evenly distributed along the middle. Generously spread the kale over the tortilla. Cover the skillet to allow the cheese to melt and to warm the beans. Once the cheese has melted, lay any of the optional additions on top along the middle of the tortilla. (If you choose to add avocado, do so only at the last moment.) With a pancake turner, fold the tortilla in half, carefully transfer it from the skillet to a plate and serve immediately.

INGREDIENTS

1 gluten-free flour tortilla

$\frac{1}{4}$–$\frac{1}{2}$ cups Daiya cheese (wedge or shredded) or favourite vegan cheese

3 tbsp mixed beans (black, refried and/or pinto)

1 cup de-stemmed kale, torn into pieces

OPTIONAL ADDITIONS

cilantro, basil, arugula, peppers (hot and/or sweet), tomatoes, avocado and/or green onions

TACOS

1 corn tortilla

shredded Daiya cheddar cheese or favourite vegan cheese

2 tbsp *Meatless Taco Ground* or *Meatless Ground* (page 167), refried beans or cooked black/ pinto beans

very thin onion slices

1 tbsp finely diced jalapeño pepper (optional)

fresh cilantro sprigs

very thin red bell pepper slices

1–2 tbsp *Salsa* (page 237) or diced fresh tomato

1–2 tbs *Guacamole with Cilantro & Basil* (page 238), optional

You can fill these tacos with just about anything. For example, you can add fresh sliced tomatoes, avocado slices, shredded lettuce, more bell peppers, hot sauce or non–dairy plain yogurt or any other fillings you like. You can also use different beans—we especially like refried beans or pinto beans. Be inventive with this easy and hearty meal that is a great transition food for those having a difficult time reducing or eliminating meat from their diets. Expect requests for seconds! *Serves 1*

DIRECTIONS

Place the tortilla flat in a skillet over medium heat and cover generously with the cheese and *Meatless Taco Ground* or beans. Cover the skillet to melt the cheese. Meanwhile, in another pan, dry sauté the onions and jalapeño pepper. Once the cheese has melted, place the sautéed onion-pepper mixture on top, add a generous amount of fresh cilantro and thinly sliced red bell peppers. Garnish with fresh cilantro and serve immediately while still hot, along with some salsa, diced fresh tomato, guacamole or other favourite fillings.

BLACK BEAN & KALE CHEESY ENCHILADAS

A great rich and cheesy Mexican dish that can be multiplied and easily prepared for a large number of guests or enjoyed at a potluck supper. *Serves 6–8*

INGREDIENTS

⅓ cup chopped onion

2 tsp finely chopped jalapeño pepper

1 cup cooked black beans

¼ cup red bell pepper, diced small

2 tbsp finely sliced green onions

¼ cup finely chopped kale

1 tbsp chopped cilantro

2 cups shredded Daiya cheese or favourite vegan cheese

⅓ cup sliced black olives

6–8 gluten-free flour tortillas or organic corn tortillas

1 recipe *Enchilada Sauce*

DIRECTIONS

In a medium bowl, stir together the onion, jalapeño pepper, beans, bell peppers, green onions, kale and cilantro, together with 1 cup of the shredded cheese and 2 tbsp of the sliced black olives. Spoon a line of filling in each of the tortillas, roll them up and place in a baking dish. Slather the rolls with the *Enchilada Sauce*, and sprinkle over the rest of the cheese and olives. Bake in a preheated 375°F oven for 20 minutes. Serve hot.

> **Bev's Bit** 🌿
> Your gut loves the fibre in black beans, as it helps to support an ideal balance of the micro-organisms needed for a healthy digestive system.

ENCHILADA SAUCE

An authentic and healthy sauce created for the popular Mexican dish. *Makes 4 cups*

INGREDIENTS

2 tsp minced garlic

1 tbsp minced onion

3 tbsp chili powder

3 tbsp favourite gluten-free flour

1 tsp cacao powder or cocoa powder

1 tsp dried oregano

3 cups water

1 x 6 oz (175 ml) can tomato paste

½ tsp Himalayan salt, or to taste

¼ tsp black pepper

1 tsp apple cider vinegar

¼ tsp blackstrap molasses

DIRECTIONS

Process the onion and garlic thoroughly in ¾ cups of the water in a small blender, then place in a medium saucepan with all of the other ingredients. Stir well and cook on medium heat until the sauce thickens. Use immediately, refrigerate for up to 2 weeks or freeze.

STUFFED BELL PEPPERS

4 red, yellow, and/or orange medium-to-large bell peppers

4 cups *Portobello Quinoa* (page 156)

1½ cups *Tomato Sauce* (page 319)

1 cup *Meatless Ground* (page 167), optional

1 x 8 oz can fire-roasted green chiles, drained and diced small, or 2 tbsp finely diced jalapeno or serrano peppers (optional)

¾ cup *Raw Parmesan* (page 314)

My childhood friend since kindergarten, Lisa Gray (now Lindsey Rehfeld), and I reconnected recently after 30 years. When she heard about this book, Lisa requested that I include a stuffed bell pepper recipe, which she fondly remembered my mom making. This one's for you, Lisa. Enjoy! *Serves 4*

DIRECTIONS

Cut a circle in the top of each bell pepper to remove the stem and create a hole large enough to spoon in the filling, leaving in the pith and seeds. In a medium bowl, combine the *Portobello Quinoa*, 1¼ cups of the *Tomato Sauce*, the *Meatless Ground* and green chiles (if using), and all but about 2 tbsp of the *Raw Parmesan*. Gently press about 1¼ cups of the Portobello Quinoa mixture into each pepper, filling to the top, then place the peppers side by side in an ungreased baking pan. Top each filled pepper with 1 tbsp of *Tomato Sauce* and sprinkle with the remaining *Raw Parmesan*. Cover the pan with a lid or aluminum foil. (If using foil, be sure to make it into a tent to avoid contact with the food.) Bake in a preheated 315˚F oven for 80-90 minutes, or until a fork easily pierces the peppers. Serve hot.

WRAPS

NORI RICE PAPER WRAPS

This convenient invention was born out of the frustration of making nori or rice paper wraps that were difficult to travel with, because they so often fell apart. The lightness of traditional rice paper combines with nori (seaweed paper) for a fantastic structural soundness. These wraps are a light, delicious and convenient travel food. Sturdy and practical, they are one of my absolute favourite lunchbox or hiking meals. The options for filling them are endless. Enjoy! *Makes 1 wrap*

DIRECTIONS

Wet the rice paper with water and place on a plate. Place a nori sheet on top of the wet rice paper and gently press it onto the rice paper to fuse them together. Place leafy greens flat along the middle of the nori sheet, followed by the *Hummus* or other dip, and then add your other fillings (don't overfill and be sure not to place filling along the outer edges of the nori). Finally, wrap one corner tightly over top of the centre mixture, and fold the edges in on top of the first fold before finishing by snugly rolling up the wrap. If the nori doesn't seal, lightly dab with water and then press closed. Serve immediately or take as a wonderful on-the-go, fresh and satisfying meal.

Theresa's Tip 🌿

These wraps offer wonderful flexibility and are terrific for when you are on the road. You can even whip them together in your hotel room. Just get a pack of nori sheets and rice paper, some fresh veggies, salad or leftovers, and you're good to go!

WRAP INGREDIENTS

1 round rice paper sheet

1 nori sheet (raw or roasted)

FILLING INGREDIENTS

leafy greens

2–3 tbsp *Hummus* (page 241), *Guacamole with Cilantro & Basil* (page 238) or favourite dip

Plus any combination of the following

watercress

pea shoots

cilantro or parsley

shredded carrots

shredded or julienned zucchini, cucumbers, daikon or other radishes

diced tomatoes or peppers

avocado slices

raw or cooked corn kernels

roasted red peppers or eggplant slices

Rho's Marinated Mushrooms (page 136) or *Rho's Giardiniera Pickled Vegetables* (page 132)

bean or grain salad

Spicy Szechuan Eggplant (page 204)

... anything else that you are moved to put in!

COLLARD WRAPS

INGREDIENTS

1 collard leaf (the bigger the better), halved and spine removed

fillings (see *Nori Rice Paper Wraps*, page 217)

The idea of creating wraps using fresh collard leaves is a classic in the raw food world. It is hard to know where to begin to describe the health benefits of steamed and raw collard greens. This nutrient-dense, antioxidant superfood also provides detoxifying, anti-inflammatory, cancer-preventative and cholesterol-lowering benefits for the body. Easy to grow in most climates (except the perennial tree collards, which grow up to 5–6 feet tall and are unable to tolerate as much chill as the more familiar annual varieties), these brassicas are definitely a food you might want to consider growing in your garden! *Makes 2 wraps*

DIRECTIONS

On a flat surface or plate, lay one of the halves flat on a plate or cutting board surface, vein-side up. Then fill with your choice of ingredients and roll the leaf up snugly and firmly. Enjoy immediately.

> **Theresa's Tip** 🌿
>
> In the middle and late summer, when the choices for fillings in the garden are at their best, nothing beats a fresh lettuce wrap, which is similar to the collard wrap, but much lighter. You can use large lettuce leaves, such as Butter Leaf, Green Leaf or Red Leaf instead of collards for these light meals or snacks. Secure with toothpicks or tie with a long chive or a "string" cut from a leek.

KALE & BEAN COLLARD WRAPS

INGREDIENTS

2 cups baby or de-stemmed kale

Creamy Sunflower Seed Sauce (page 318), to taste

1 collard leaf, halved and spine removed

4 tbsp refried beans, cooked beans, *Hummus* (page 241) or favourite bean salad

While the possibilities for collard wraps are endless, here is one ultra-simple and nutritious version that uses beans and our favourite sauce—both staples we usually have on hand in the refrigerator. *Makes 2 wraps*

DIRECTIONS

Tear up the kale and put it in a bowl, then liberally dress with the *Creamy Sunflower Seed Sauce*, massaging well with your hands to cover all the kale and soften its texture.

Lay one of the collard leaf halves flat on a plate or cutting board, vein-side up. Spread 2 tbsp of beans, *Hummus* or bean salad across the short width of the leaf, midway on the leaf or closer to you. Cover the beans with some of the prepared kale, then fold the leaf side closest to you over the top of the filling and snugly roll the leaf the rest of the way closed. Repeat with the other collard leaf half. If you are taking these wraps out, rather than eating at home, also fold the outer sides of the leaf closed before completing the wrapping process.

VIETNAMESE SPRING ROLLS

These are light, fun, and delicious—plan to make more than you expect to need! When I lived in Las Vegas, my friend Kim Twitchell, who grew up in Vietnam, showed me how to make the authentic version of these. I loved them and was determined to create a plant-based, gluten-free version. The test kitchens approved my efforts: "Everyone loved these and wanted more than one... Well, I had three adult males and me. One is a very picky eater and he loved his. The other wanted several, even though he'd already eaten dinner. I kept making them—I'd say I made 10–12 of them. They would have eaten more, but were absorbed in a Seahawks game... I actually ended up making it without tempeh...and without onion in the sauce. Both turned out more than fine. Like I said, everyone loved them and wanted more than one." A bonus is that you can prep the ingredients and just use what you want, then refrigerate the leftovers for another meal later. Your kids will love making these wraps with their friends. They make a terrific take-out lunch or dinner too! *Makes 12 rolls*

DIRECTIONS

If using the tempeh, sauté over medium heat and set aside. Dip a rice paper wrap in water and place on a plate. (If using seaweed sheets, leave them dry!) Put a row of the vermicelli or other thin noodles in a line in the middle of the rice paper and set a tempeh strip (if using) on top. Spoon 1–2 tbsp *Raw Hoisin Sauce* along the strip, then put the 2 basil leaves, 2 mint leaves, some cilantro and a tiny bit of dill along the top. Finish the filling by adding about 2–3 tbsp of the shredded carrots and some of the cucumber and jicama (if using) sticks. Carefully wrap one side of the rice paper over the top of the vegetable mound. Fold each of the ends in to close them and then finish rolling the wrap. Repeat this process for each wrap. Serve immediately or take as a fresh and satisfying on-the-go meal.

INGREDIENTS

8 oz tempeh, cut into ¼-inch matchstick strips (optional)

favourite cooking oil for sautéing

12 rice paper wraps or seaweed sheets

2–3 cups cooked Asian rice vermicelli, bean thread noodles, bean spaghetti or favourite thin raw or cooked thin pasta noodles

1 cucumber, seeds removed, cut into matchstick-shaped strips

1 cup julienned jicama (optional)

2 cups shredded carrots

24 basil leaves

24 mint leaves

1 medium bunch of cilantro

1 tbsp finely chopped fresh dill (optional)

1 cup *Raw Hoisin Sauce* (page 318)

FOR THE MUNCHIES
CHIPS, DIPS &
SAVOURY SNACKS

QUICK KALE CHIPS

Nothing exotic here—just old-fashioned quick kale chips, for those times when instant gratification is the name of the game!
Makes about 2 cups

INGREDIENTS

2 cups baby or de-stemmed kale, firmly packed

1 tbsp extra virgin olive oil

dash Himalayan salt (optional)

¼ cup nutritional yeast

cayenne pepper (optional)

DIRECTIONS

Place the kale in a large bowl then massage the oil into the leaves with your hands, coating thoroughly. Lightly sprinkle with salt if desired, then toss with the nutritional yeast, mixing well to coat the kale. Place the kale in a single layer on a baking sheet (with minimal overlapping). Sprinkle with cayenne pepper (if using) and bake in a preheated 315°F oven for 15–20 minutes or until the chips have the desired consistency. Serve immediately or enjoy as a snack later.

Theresa's Tip

If you decide to use any salt, be sure to use only about ¼ of the amount you think you'll need, because when the kale cooks it loses its water content, which intensifies the impact of the salt.

DELUXE KALE CHIPS

Once you make these, they will become a staple in your home, especially during kale harvest time! They are irresistible and disappear so fast, you might find yourself making them every day for a while, as we did! Remember to keep the stems to use for making green juice or in stir-fries, soups or smoothies. *Makes about 4 cups*

DIRECTIONS

Place the kale in a large bowl. With your hands, massage all of the remaining ingredients thoroughly into the kale (reserve 2 tbps hemp seeds). Spread the dressed kale out onto a dehydrator tray or on a parchment-lined baking sheet or silicone mat. The mixture will be mushier than you would expect, but this is important to make the final chips extra-yummy: luscious, colourful and flavourful. Sprinkle with the reserved hemp seeds. Dehydrate at 105°F for 24-48 hours, or until the chips are the desired texture. If you don't have a dehydrator, use the Oven Dehydration Method (page 233). The low-temperature dehydration helps the chips retain their awesome nutritional value, respects the omega-3 oils in the hemp seeds and keeps their lovely colour.

INGREDIENTS

4 cups baby or de-stemmed kale, firmly packed

¾–1 cup *Creamy Sunflower Seed Sauce* (page 318)

¼ cup nutritional yeast

4 tbsp hemp seeds

⅛ tsp cayenne pepper (optional)

¼ cup cooked lima beans or favourite creamy white beans, mashed (optional)

CRUNCHY CHICKPEAS

INGREDIENTS

1½ cups cooked chickpeas

1 tbsp extra virgin olive oil

2 tbsp nutritional yeast

½ tsp Himalayan salt

Alex was so cute when she made these fun snacks. Because we typically use olive oil for this recipe, we cook them at 315˚F to keep the oil from exceeding its smoke point. However, if you'd rather cook them at a higher temperature, just be sure to use oil with a smoke point higher than the temperature you bake them at, and cook them for less time. These are a great snack for any time you have the munchies. *Makes 1½ cups*

DIRECTIONS

Theresa's Tip
For a spicy version, sprinkle a little cayenne pepper on top.

Put the chickpeas into a rimmed baking sheet or glass baking dish and coat thoroughly with the oil. Sprinkle on the nutritional yeast and Himalayan salt, and stir to coat well. Spread the chickpeas in a single layer and bake in a preheated 315˚F oven for 45–60 minutes, stirring every 10 minutes, until they are crispy. Enjoy as a crunchy snack or as a topping for salad. These lose their crunchiness over time, so they are best enjoyed immediately or later the same day.

BAKED EGGPLANT ROUNDS

While I haven't had much success growing these beauties in the Pacific Northwest, fibre-rich eggplant is full of valuable nutrients (vitamins, mineral, and antioxidants). In addition to its anti-cancer benefits, eggplant reportedly supports the skin and hair, as well as the heart, brain and digestive systems. You and your kids won't believe how tasty these chips are until you try them. Angeline is crazy about them. *Serves 2–4*

INGREDIENTS

1 globe eggplant or 3 Japanese eggplants, sliced into rounds, $1/8$–$1/4$ inch thick

½ cup extra virgin olive oil

Himalayan salt

DIRECTIONS

Very lightly brush both sides of the eggplant slices with the oil and place them in a single layer on cookie sheets. Bake in a preheated 315°F oven until they reach desired texture (about 45-60 minutes, baking longer for crispier chips). Because of their high water content, make a lot more than you think you'll need—they really shrink! Serve while still hot.

VEGETABLE FLAX CRACKERS

INGREDIENTS

2 cups roughly chopped carrots

2 large red or orange bell peppers, roughly chopped

3 cups ground flax

1 cup flax seeds

1–2 tsp *Italian Seasoning* (page 319), to taste

¾ tsp Himalayan salt, or to taste

⅜ tsp onion powder

¼–½ tsp cayenne pepper, to taste

⅓ tsp fenugreek (optional)

3½ cups water

¼ cup lemon juice

2 tomatoes, roughly chopped

¾–1 cup roughly chopped basil (stems included), packed

2 ½ tsp balsamic vinegar, or to taste

During one of my stays at the Living Light Inn in Fort Bragg, California, I got the idea to experiment with vegetable flax crackers. With all of the information about the importance of omega–3s, any opportunity to increase these in our home is welcome! My friend Nikki Shattuck (one of the innkeepers) became my partner in crime—tasting and helping me brainstorm around the flavour–balancing and enhancement. Amazingly, the first go hit the mark. Unfortunately, I hadn't recorded any of the amounts, so a few days later, we repeated the process and were happy with the outcome: light, crispy, textured and delicious crackers, which have endless possibilities for variation by experimenting with different herbs and spices. Have fun playing with this versatile cracker. *Makes about 100–300 crackers*

DIRECTIONS

Pulse the carrots in a food processor into small to very small pieces and put into a very large bowl. Without cleaning the food processor, process one of the peppers by pulsing in the same way and add to the bowl with the carrots. In another bowl, stir together the ground flax, flax seeds and seasonings, then add to the carrot-pepper mixture, combining well. Process the water, lemon juice, tomatoes, remaining pepper, basil and vinegar in a blender until smooth. Stir into the flax-carrot-pepper mixture until completely combined. With an offset or other spatula, spread the mixture as thinly as possible onto 5–6 teflex dehydrator trays. With a dull knife or offset spatula, score into small squares or triangles and dehydrate at 105°F for 12 hours. Carefully flip the crackers over onto a mesh dehydrator sheet, removing the teflex sheet. Dehydrate for 12 more hours, until crispy. Break into pieces and serve as a snack or side dish with soups, or as an appetizer with your favourite dips.

Oven Dehydration Method

If you don't yet have a dehydrator, you can still make these crackers and other dehydrator recipes using the oven dehydration method. Simply set your oven to its lowest temperature (on most ovens, this is usually around 150°F) and prop open the oven door slightly, perhaps using a wooden spoon to help it stay in position. While this isn't the most energy-conserving method, it is a great alternative until you are able to get a dehydrator. Once you learn about all the wonderful things you can make with these amazing machines, you will definitely put it on your wish list!

Bev's Bit 🌱
Super-versatile chia seeds are so chock-full of antioxidants that they can be stored for quite a while—2 to 4 years in a cool cupboard—without becoming rancid.

CHIA CHIPS

Excited by my *Vegetable Flax Crackers* (page 232), I decided to up the omega–3 ante with these ultra–light chia chips. Full of healthy goodness, the crispy texture of these chips remind me of Indian papadaums, often enjoyed with chutneys or other dips. These are a great snack on their own, and are also wonderful with dips or with some salad spooned on top. They are so delectable, it's hard to believe how good they are for the body! *Makes 3 sheets of chips*

DIRECTIONS

Place all of the dry ingredients into a very large bowl, stir to combine and set aside. Place all wet ingredients in a high-speed blender and process until smooth. Pour into the bowl with the dry ingredients and stir quickly until completely combined. With an offset or other spatula, spread as thinly as possible (tiny holes are not a problem) onto 5–6 teflex dehydrator sheets. Score into desired shapes and then dehydrate at 105°F for 12 hours. Carefully flip the crackers over onto the mesh dehydrator sheet, removing the teflex sheet. Dehydrate for a further 12 hours, until crispy. Because these chips curl quite a bit during the dehydration process, it is best to leave extra space above each tray, if possible. After they are fully dehydrated, break the chips into pieces.

DRY INGREDIENTS

1 cup chia seeds

2 tbsp nutritional yeast

1 tbsp golden flax seeds (optional)

¼ tsp *Italian Seasoning* (page 319)

¼ tsp Himalayan salt, or to taste

¼ tsp onion powder

WET INGREDIENTS

1½ cups water

1½ cups chopped kale (with stems), firmly packed

½ cup chopped basil (with stems), firmly packed

3 Roma tomatoes, roughly chopped

1 tbsp lemon juice

1½ tsp balsamic vinegar

NACHOS

This is another dish that will make you forget that you aren't eating dairy! It is a simple extension of Alex's brilliant *Mac 'n' Cheese* recipe (page 178). Make sure to have all of the ingredients close to the stove before starting to cook because you will need to stir continuously once you begin. *Serves 4*

INGREDIENTS

¼ tsp garlic powder

1 tbsp starch (potato or tapioca) or arrowroot powder

¼ cup nutritional yeast

1 cup almond milk or favourite non-dairy milk

1½ tsp lemon juice

1½ tsp tamari or coconut aminos

1½ tsp coconut oil

1½ tsp extra virgin olive oil

1 cup shredded Daiya cheddar cheese or favourite vegan cheese

1–2 tbsp minced fresh jalapeño pepper, to taste (optional)

5–7 cups tortilla chips or other favourite chips

ADDITIONAL TOPPINGS

Guacamole with Cilantro & Basil (page 238)

sliced black olives

refried beans

green onions or chives, thinly sliced

Salsa (page 237)

thinly sliced jalapeño peppers

shredded lettuce

diced tomatoes

DIRECTIONS

In a small bowl, mix together the garlic powder, starch and nutritional yeast. Set aside near the stove. In a medium-sized bowl, mix together the milk, lemon juice and tamari or coconut aminos. Set aside near the stove. Place the oils in a medium-to-large saucepan over medium heat. Once heated, add the milk mixture, followed by the dry yeast mixture, and whisk continuously until quite thick (about 10 minutes). Remove the pan from the heat and add the cheese and jalapeño pepper. Mix well for about 1 minute until the cheese has melted and is thoroughly integrated into the sauce. Pour the jalapeño-cheese sauce over the chips and add the additional toppings of your choice. Serve immediately while hot.

SALSA

Like guacamole, salsa is a great standard to have and super-simple to make. There really is no reason to ever buy salsa again. Use as a light dip with chips or as a condiment for tacos, burritos, nachos or other dishes where you'd like to add a Mexican touch. You can even add this salsa and a little Mexican seasoning to cooked beans for a quick and easy chili dish or to refried beans for a Mexican bean dip. *Makes about 1½ cups*

DIRECTIONS

For a chunky version, simply stir all ingredients together. If you prefer a smoother salsa, pulse in a blender to your desired consistency.

Bev's Bit
Along with spicing up your life, vitamin C–rich jalapeños help to keep your immune system healthy!

INGREDIENTS

1 cup chopped tomatoes

¼ cup chopped onions

¼ cup chopped cilantro, loosely packed

1–2 tbsp minced fresh jalapeño pepper, to taste (optional)

1 tbsp lemon juice

Himalayan salt, to taste

GUACAMOLE WITH CILANTRO & BASIL

INGREDIENTS

1 avocado

2–4 tbsp lemon or lime juice, to taste

¼ cup finely chopped cilantro

¼ cup finely chopped green onions

¼ cup finely chopped tomato, seeds removed

¼ cup finely chopped red bell pepper

1 tbsp finely minced basil leaves

1–3 tsp minced jalapeño, to taste (optional)

Himalayan salt, to taste

This twist on an old favourite is an instant crowd–pleaser. Use as a dip or condiment with wraps, sandwiches, burritos, nachos, tacos, salads, toast, crackers, chips or anything else your heart desires. Perfect for a quick snack for unexpected guests. *Makes about 2 cups*

DIRECTIONS

In a bowl, mash the avocado just a little bit (you want it to still be chunky). Then stir in the rest of the ingredients, adding the salt sparingly only at the very end.

Haely's Hint ✿
Avocado is a great source of healthy fat.

> *Vegetable Flax Crackers* (page 232) dipped in *Guacamole with Cilantro & Basil*

HUMMUS

Even though sunflower and sesame seeds and tahini paste are chock-full of minerals and other nutrients, I opt to use sunflower seeds, because many people are sensitive to sesame and because it is so commonly used in other foods. For those who are unable to enjoy hummus because they are sensitive to chickpeas, I have suggested the alternative of lima beans—a delicious variation of this classic dip. *Makes about 1½ cups*

DIRECTIONS

Blend all ingredients together until very creamy, using the tamper as needed. Enjoy as a dip or spread with crudités, crackers or bread, or use as a filling for wraps.

Theresa's Tip

After you've made the hummus, don't clean out the blender. Use it to to make *Creamy Sunflower Seed Sauce* (page 318)—the flavours and textures are very compatible, plus doing so reduces waste and makes clean-up of the blender a cinch.

INGREDIENTS

1–2 garlic cloves

1½ cups cooked chickpeas or *Quick-Cook Lima Beans* (page 162)

¼ cup lemon juice

½–1 tsp Himalayan salt, to taste

2 tbsp tahini or 2 tbsp raw sunflower or sesame seeds

2 tbsp cold-pressed flax or hemp oil or extra virgin olive oil

water, to desired consistency

cayenne pepper (optional)

ground cumin (optional)

CHEESY PIMENTO DIP

INGREDIENTS

2 cups raw cashews, soaked
and rinsed well

1 cup chopped red bell pepper,
packed

3 tbsp nutritional yeast

2 tbsp chopped onion

2–4 tbsp lemon juice, to taste

1 tbsp apple cider vinegar

1 tsp miso (chickpea or soy)

1 tsp vegan probiotic
(eg acidophilus), or the
contents of 5–6 capsules

1–1½ tsp Himalayan salt,
to taste

½ tsp crushed hot
red pepper flakes

black pepper

¼ tsp *Chicory Root Inulin with
Stevia* (page 324) or favourite
sweetener (optional)

As anyone who has chosen or needed to eliminate dairy from their diet knows, the hardest part is often giving up cheeses and cheese spreads. There are a lot of raw pimento recipes using cashews, bell peppers, lemon juice and probiotic powder. Being the cheese lover that I am, I wanted to take the dairy-free pimento cheese experience to the next level, reflecting the depth, intensity, slight sweetness and other flavour dimensions I remember from regular pimento cheese dips. When I created this, I was so happy—it's an awesome dip.
Makes about 3 cups

DIRECTIONS

Blend all ingredients in a food processor until creamy. Serve as a dip with crudités, chips or crackers, or as a filling in wraps. Also delicious stirred into quinoa or rice as a cheesy side dish.

Bee Bite

Have you ever noticed how hairy bees are?
The hairs that cover the bee's body pick up pollen
from the flowers they visit, which the bees then put
into a little pollen sack on their back leg.

RAW SWEET & SAVOURY TRAIL MIX

Simple, delicious and easy. For this recipe you can omit and substitute any of the ingredients to suit your personal needs and preferences. *Makes about 3 cups*

DIRECTIONS

Mix all ingredients and enjoy on the run. Can be stored for 1 month or so in an airtight container.

> **Theresa's Tip**
> It is generally better to soak, rinse and dehydrate raw nuts before using them. While most people suggest soaking raw nuts for at least 7 hours, some recommend soaking nuts for at least 18 hours, with frequent rinses, before dehydrating them, to reduce the phytic acid levels even more. When prepared in this way, you not only maximize the bio-availability of the awesome nutrients in the nuts, you also reduce the enzyme-inhibiting quality that is present in unsoaked nuts (see *Funky Ingredients*, page 22).

INGREDIENTS

1 cup almonds

½ cup pecans

¼ cup jungle or other organic peanuts

¼ cup chopped dried apricots

¼ cup dried golden berries (Inca berries) or other dried berries

¼ cup raisins

¼ cup goji berries or other dried fruit

2 tbsp raw sunflower seeds

2 tbsp raw pumpkin seeds

¼ cup cacao nibs (optional)

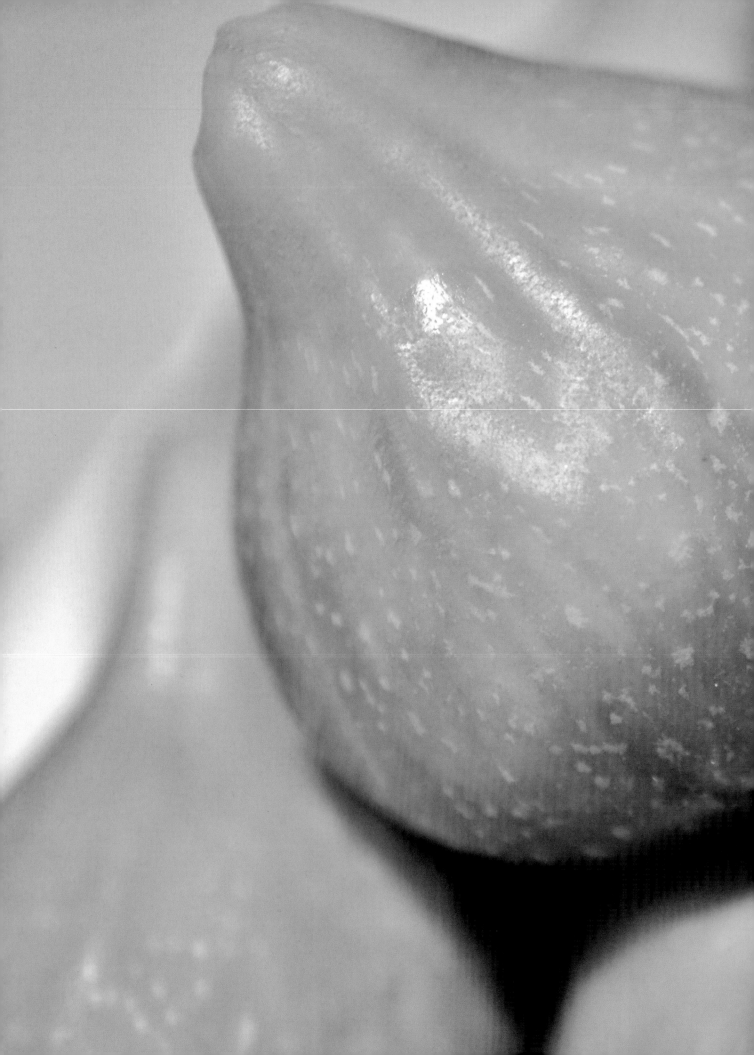

PURE DECADENCE
DESSERTS

FRESH FIGS

Okay, I admit it—this is me being a little cheeky. But seriously, many of the yummiest foods on the planet are the simplest. And what can beat the deliciously succulent and juicy joy of a fresh fig? Or if figs aren't your thing, take your pick of any other fresh fruit that transports you to new heights. These incredible prepackaged delights provided by nature are perfect and too often overlooked. Against the better judgement of more than a few, I felt they deserved an entry of their own! *Serves 1–2*

INGREDIENTS

1–2 fresh figs, stems removed, or other favourite fresh fruit

DIRECTIONS

Wash and enjoy immediately. If you desire a more delicate variation, remove the peel from the figs before eating.

BAKED CINNAMON PLANTAINS

On our adventure to the Living Light Culinary Institute in 2013, Alex and I met up with an old friend, Kim Yasuda, to share lunch together. Knowing our dietary needs, Kim suggested we go to Andy Nguyen's Vegetarian in Sacramento, a popular traditional Vietnamese restaurant with lots of gluten-free and vegan dishes. Boy, we were not at all disappointed! The food there was fabulous. After our main dish, we ordered their plantain dessert. It was steamed in its peel and then slathered with a delicious coconut cream sauce. This recipe was very much inspired by my memory of the creamy deliciousness we enjoyed that day. Since plantains can sometimes be difficult to come by, you can use bananas, which are equally delicious. *Serves 2*

INGREDIENTS

1 large ripe plantain or 2 large bananas, peeled

1 tbsp coconut sugar

½ tsp cinnamon

1 tbsp melted coconut oil

DIRECTIONS

Slice the plantain or bananas into ¼-inch-thick slices and place in a lightly oiled glass baking dish. In a small bowl, stir together the coconut sugar and cinnamon. With a pastry brush, generously paint all surfaces of the plantain or banana with the oil, and then sprinkle the cinnamon sugar evenly to coat the slices. Cook the fruit in a preheated 350°F oven for 50 minutes (30 minutes if using bananas) or until the fruit is extremely soft and creamy. If desired, serve topped with *Coconut Whipped Cream* (page 329) or ice cream (pages 275–279).

BAKED APPLES WITH PECAN CRUMBLE TOPPING

The test kitchens feedback says it all: "Let the kids make it. It's super easy for 6–10 year olds, and they could easily be left in charge of this recipe with a melon baller and directions to let me know when it's ready to go in the oven." "This is a great way to get around all the butter in baked apples. I never bother with baked apples—fresh ones are so delicious with cinnamon – but this I would make again." "The pecans really are tasty, and it is a healthful dessert that looks fancy but takes zero effort. Great for fooling friends who are food nitwits and need to be awed from time to time." *Serves 4*

INGREDIENTS

2 apples (eg Honeycrisp, Ambrosia, Fuji, Cortland or other crisp variety), halved and cored

¼ tsp cinnamon

1 recipe *Pecan Crumble Topping*

DIRECTIONS

Place the apple halves cut-side up in a large baking dish in a single layer. Lightly sprinkle with the cinnamon. Fill the cored areas with *Pecan Crumble Topping*, then spread any remaining crumble evenly over the apples. Bake in a preheated 350°F oven for 50–60 minutes. If desired, serve with ice cream (pages 275–279) or *Coconut Whipped Cream* (page 329).

PECAN CRUMBLE TOPPING

A super–easy and delicious topping for many desserts. *Makes ½ cup*

INGREDIENTS

½ cup crumbled pecans

¾ tsp cinnamon

2 tbsp maple or yacon syrup, or favourite sweetening syrup

DIRECTIONS

In a small bowl, stir all the ingredients together. Double or triple the quantity, as needed.

Theresa's Tip ◖
This topping is also good with walnuts instead of pecans.

BLUEBERRY CRUMBLE

You can make endless variations of this crumble by using different fruits or berries, alone or in combination. Try whatever sweet fruit is available and in season. Here's what the test kitchens had to say about this recipe: "It was yummy... I was generous with amounts, but stuck more or less to the recipe. When the crumble was in the oven, unexpected company showed up! Ended up serving small bowl each to 14 people—of course everyone wanted more because it was so yummy!" "Easy peasy... Loved by all... Great recipe."
Makes 9–12 squares

DIRECTIONS

Place the blueberries in an 8-inch or 9-inch greased or silicone baking dish. In a small bowl, mix together 2 tbsp of the sweetener with the starch then sprinkle the mixture evenly on top of the fruit. In a separate bowl, mix the oats, remaining sweetener, nuts (if using), salt, cinnamon and coconut oil together for the crumble. Sprinkle this evenly on top of the blueberry mixture. Bake in a preheated 350°F oven for 1 hour, then allow to cool. Serve warm as is, or top with ice cream (pages 275–279) or *Coconut Whipped Cream* (page 329). This dessert is also delicious chilled.

INGREDIENTS

6 cups blueberries, fresh or frozen

1/3–1/2 cup coconut sugar, xylitol or favourite granular sweetener

1–2 tbsp starch (tapioca, corn or potato)

1½ cups gluten-free rolled oats

1/2 cup Bob's Red Mill or favourite gluten-free all-purpose flour

1/2 cup crumbled walnuts or almonds, or 1/2 cup more rolled oats

dash Himalayan salt (optional)

1 tsp cinnamon

1/2 cup coconut oil

Bee Bite
Did you know that at least 1/3 of our food supply is dependent on the work of bees? The fruit and seeds produced from flowering plants rely on our hard-working friends to pollinate them in order to come to fruition.

JUICE JELLY

1 cup water

2½ tbsp agar agar flakes

1½ cups non-acidic organic fruit juice (eg cherry, blueberry, lychee, etc)

favourite sweetener, to taste (optional)

Theresa's Tip 🌿

For a freakish and fun Halloween treat, make a translucent red jelly (eg cherry) and add peeled lychee fruit with their pits still in to the jelly before it has set— they look a lot like eyeballs! (Just be sure to let your guests know to remove the pits when they eat the dessert!)

Since most gelatin (jelly) is derived from animal products, it's great to have a plant-based alternative (agar agar) that can also do the trick! Working with the sea vegetable agar agar is a lot of fun, but also requires some knowledge (see *Funky Ingredients*, page 30). You can make gelatin (jelly) from lots of different fresh juice varieties. However, it's important to know that high-acid juices may need quite a bit more agar agar to set properly, and the enzymes found in some uncooked fresh fruits such as papaya, mango and pineapple work against agar agar's gelling action. *Makes 2½ cups*

DIRECTIONS

In a medium saucepan over high heat, bring the water with the agar agar flakes to a boil, then reduce the heat to medium or medium-low and soft-boil for 4–5 minutes, stirring constantly, or until agar agar is fully dissolved. Remove from the heat and add the fruit juice and sweetener (if using). Pour into silicon gelatin moulds or beautiful glassware and chill in the refrigerator until set. If using moulds, remove from the refrigerator just before serving and invert onto dessert plates. Garnish with fresh fruits, seasonal berries or *Coconut Whipped Cream* (page 329), if desired.

STRAWBERRY JELLY

Strawberries are one of the easiest fruits to maintain in the garden and are so delicious! This beautiful, edible ground cover plant can survive in very small spaces and in a variety of climates. The test kitchens said it all about this recipe: "Loved it. Can't wait to make it again." "Easy peasy... Perfect as-is." " My young daughter loved it and I love the healthy ingredients... it was great." *Makes about 5 cups*

DIRECTIONS

In a high-speed or regular blender, purée the strawberries with the lemon juice and zest, vanilla, sweetener, molasses and salt until smooth and set aside. In a medium saucepan over high heat, bring the water with the agar agar flakes to a boil, then soft-boil for 4–5 minutes, stirring constantly, until the agar agar is dissolved. Remove from the heat and add the strawberry purée to the saucepan and stir to combine. Pour into silicon gelatin moulds or beautiful glassware and chill in the refrigerator until set. If using moulds, remove from the refrigerator just before serving and invert onto dessert plates. Enjoy as is or garnish with *Coconut Whipped Cream* (page 329), seasonal berries and fresh mint leaves.

Theresa's Tip

For a creamy, mousse-like variation, whip 2 cups *Coconut Whipped Cream* (page 329) into 2 cups of chilled jelly and serve immediately.

INGREDIENTS

4–5 cups strawberries, fresh or frozen

½ peeled lemon, seeds removed

½–1 tsp lemon zest

½ tsp vanilla extract

2 tsp *Chicory Root Inulin with Stevia* (page 324) or favourite sweetener

¼ tsp blackstrap molasses

pinch Himalayan salt

1½ cups water

¼ cup agar agar flakes

NO-BAKE PUMPKIN PIE

INGREDIENTS

1 x 13.5 fl oz (400 ml) can
premium full-fat coconut milk

2½ tbsp agar agar flakes

1½ tsp blackstrap molasses

1 cup maple syrup

1½ tsp cinnamon

¾ tsp Himalayan salt

½ tsp ginger

½ tsp nutmeg

⅛ tsp cloves

2 x 13.5 fl oz (400 ml) cans
pumpkin

2 prepared baked *Shortbread
Pie Crusts* (page 264) or other
favourite prepared baked
pie crust

With its unique shortbread crust, this traditional holiday dessert is
sure to become a new family favourite!
Makes 1 deep-dish or 2 standard-sized pies

DIRECTIONS

Place all the ingredients except the pumpkin into a medium-to-large
heavy saucepan over high heat and bring to a boil, stirring frequently. Stir
continuously while it boils for the next 7 minutes to ensure it doesn't stick
to the bottom of the pan. Stir in the pumpkin, reducing the temperature to
medium, and cook for another 7 minutes, stirring continuously. Remove from
the heat and immediately pour the filling into the pie shell(s). Refrigerate for
4–6 hours, or until completely set.

Unlike traditional pumpkin pie, the filling will only set after it has fully
chilled and the agar agar has taken effect. The crust will be a bit like cutting
a cookie, so you will need to use a sharp knife. If desired, top with some ice
cream (pages 275–279) or with *Coconut Whipped Cream* (page 329).

Theresa's Tip 🌿

If you prefer a grain-free pie, use *Pecan Date Butterball
Raw Pie Crust* (page 303) or *Basic Raw Crust* (page 325)
instead of the *Shortbread Pie Crust*. If you have any extra
filling, it can be used to make individual chilled pudding
cups. For an extra creamy dessert, you can fill the pie shells
with the super-light *Extra-Creamy Pumpkin Pudding*
(page 261).

NO-PUMPKIN PUMPKIN PIE

INGREDIENTS

1 recipe *Basic Raw Crust* (page 325)

1 cup raw cashews

1 cup baked and cooled yam (optional)

1½ large carrots, shredded

1 tsp cinnamon

1 tsp Himalayan salt

1 tsp tamari or coconut aminos or ¼ tsp miso (chickpea or soy)

¼ tsp ground ginger

¼ tsp ground cloves

¼ tsp ground nutmeg

juice and zest from ½ lemon

½ cup Medjool (or other) dates, pitted

1 small banana

½ avocado

½ cup raw nut milk or cream, or favourite non-dairy milk

1 tsp *Chicory Root Inulin with Stevia* (page 324) or favourite sweetener, or to taste

1 tbsp blackstrap molasses

1 vanilla bean, or 1 tsp vanilla extract or powder

2 tbsp yacon or maple syrup (optional)

2 recipes *Pecan Crumble Topping* (page 250)

This recipe took quite a few attempts to nail. As you may have gathered, pumpkin pie is pretty sacred around our house—it has to taste just right. The final critical ingredient to achieve that authentic pumpkin pie flavour was, surprisingly, tamari! Colour was also an issue for a while. The magic of the orange yam did the trick. I love that it is a pumpkin pie without any pumpkin—it makes for fun party conversation.

The test kitchens had a lot to say about this recipe: "It was yummy... This is a good addition! Keep it!" "Tested on kids prior to freezing. Loved it. Looks and tastes like pumpkin pie!" "Love all the healthy ingredients in it. Liquid recommendations for filling were perfect for Vitamix. Great taste. I like the recipe as is... would not change." "I used only 1 tsp of stevia as I don't like things too sweet and it was fine. I might even try without stevia at all or cut back on the maple syrup and use 2 tsp stevia for less sugar." "It was very good—Hubby liked it too and love the wholefood ingredients, gluten-free, etc!" *Serves 10–12*

DIRECTIONS

Press the *Basic Raw Crust* into 10-12 individual silicone forms and set aside. If you don't have these, you can use well-greased or non-stick muffin tins or tart pans with removable bottoms for more shallow pies. Then blend all of the ingredients for the filling in a food processor until smooth and creamy (about 5 minutes), scraping down the sides a few times while processing. Spoon into the silicone forms on top of the prepared crusts. Sprinkle the *Pecan Crumble Topping* on top of each pie to finish and freeze. To serve, remove from the freezer and moulds and let thaw on serving plates for about 15-30 minutes before enjoying. If desired, top with ice cream (pages 275-279) or *Coconut Whipped Cream* (page 329).

EXTRA-CREAMY PUMPKIN PUDDING

This delicious pudding is a creamy heaven that embraces everyone!

Serves 4–6

DIRECTIONS

Place all the ingredients except the pumpkin into a medium-to-large heavy saucepan over high heat and bring to a boil, stirring frequently. Stir continuously while it boils for the next 7 minutes to ensure it doesn't stick to the bottom of the pan. Stir in the pumpkin, reducing the temperature to medium, and cook for another 7 minutes, stirring continuously. Remove from the heat and immediately pour the filling into individual pudding dishes and refrigerate 2–4 hours or until fully set.

INGREDIENTS

1 x 13.5 fl oz (400 ml) can premium full-fat coconut milk

4 tsp agar agar flakes

¾ tsp blackstrap molasses

⅓ cup maple syrup

½ tsp cinnamon

¼ tsp Himalayan salt

⅛ tsp ginger

⅛ tsp nutmeg

1 x 13.5 fl oz (400 ml) can pumpkin

ZUCCHINI CARROT CRUMB CAKE

This recipe was an adventure. In fact, it wasn't even meant to be a crumb cake at all! Originally, it was going to be a Zucchini Carrot Pudding Bread. Everyone thought it was fantastic and wanted it in the book just as it was. However, while the bread tasted amazing and was super-moist, something just wasn't quite right. I fiddled and fiddled with the recipe so much, I got tired of making it and decided I would leave it for my next book. However, a last-minute brainstorm, a few changes and a surprise ending resulted in this most delectable crumb cake! I hope you love it as much as we do!

Makes 1 crumb cake or 12 muffins

DIRECTIONS

In a large bowl, cream together the wet ingredients with a fork and set aside. In a separate bowl, whisk together all the dry ingredients. Add the dry mixture to the wet mixture and stir together with a spatula until well combined. Stir in the zucchini, carrots, raisins or currants, shredded coconut and nuts. Press the mixture into a silicon or lightly greased 8-inch square baking pan, standard-sized bundt form or muffin tin. Sprinkle the crumble topping evenly over the top and cook in a preheated 350°F oven for 60-70 minutes (30 minutes for muffins) or until a toothpick comes out clean. Allow to cool. If desired, serve garnished with an extra sprinkling of shredded coconut.

Walnut Crumble Topping

A versatile, easy, and delicious topping for many baked desserts. *Makes 1 cup*

INGREDIENTS

½ cup crumbled walnuts

½ cup coconut sugar or xylitol

¾ tsp cinnamon

2 tbs maple or yacon syrup, or favourite sweetening syrup

DIRECTIONS

In a small bowl, stir all ingredients together. Double or triple the quantity, if needed. This topping is also good made with pecans.

WET INGREDIENTS

1 cup mashed banana

½ cup melted coconut oil

2 tbsp maple syrup

¾ tsp apple cider vinegar or lemon juice (optional)

DRY INGREDIENTS

2 cups Bob's Red Mill or favourite gluten-free all-purpose flour

⅓ cup coconut sugar or xylitol

1 tbsp *Chicory Root Inulin with Stevia* (page 324) or favourite sweetener

1½ tsp cinnamon

¾ tsp baking powder

½ tsp baking soda

½ tsp Himalayan salt

ADD-INS

1¼ cup grated zucchini, packed

½ cup grated carrots, packed

⅔ cup raisins or currants, packed

⅔ cup unsweetened shredded coconut

1 cup chopped raw nuts (walnuts, pecans and/or Brazil nuts)

1 recipe *Walnut Crumble Topping*

SHORTBREAD PIE CRUST

This delectable shortbread cookie pie crust is unlike any other crust you have ever eaten. You and your guests will be transported to pie paradise! *Makes 1 standard-size pie crust*

DRY INGREDIENTS

2½ cups Bob's Red Mill or favourite gluten-free all-purpose flour

¾ tsp baking powder

⅛ tsp baking soda

½ tsp Himalayan salt

¼ tsp cardamom

1 cup coconut sugar or xylitol

WET INGREDIENTS

¾ cup unmelted coconut oil

½ cup coconut butter

¼ cup maple syrup

DIRECTIONS

In a medium bowl, whisk together the dry ingredients, except the coconut sugar, and set aside. With a stand mixer (my favourite method) or in a large mixing bowl, cream together the coconut sugar or xylitol, coconut oil and coconut butter. Then with the beaters still going, slowly add the maple syrup and continue to mix until very well blended. Add the mixed dry ingredients and use just a few strokes to combine them all. It will not look very mixed and you won't believe it is time to stop, but you must. This is very important to keep the crust light and not tough. When you work the dough to shape the crust, the ingredients will be mixed just the right amount.

To prepare the crusts, oil 2 10-inch standard-sized pie pans (oil all the way up, including the top edges of the pie pan). Put half of the dough into the bottom of each pan and, with your hands, start by first building up the edges of the pie crust relatively thinly, pressing it up to form zig-zag fluted edges. Then form the bottom of the pie crust, making it as thin as you can, while ensuring complete pan coverage. The thinner you can make the crust, the easier it will be to cut the pie after it's cooked. However, if you prefer a thicker and crunchier cookie crust, that is fine too. This process will become easier with practice. The great thing is that you don't need to roll anything out and transfer—all you need to do is just press and go. Either bake in a preheated 350°F oven for 15–20 minutes or store in the freezer until ready to use (defrost before filling and baking).

NOTE If making a pie where the filling needs to be baked in the crust, only pre-cook the crust for 10–12 minutes.

RAW PINEAPPLE BANANA DREAM PIES

I was in a whimsical mood when I developed this recipe. After several failed attempts to make a raw banana cream pie, I had the idea of layering bananas with a creamy pineapple filling and walnuts on a delicious raw crust. The result was magical. Here is what the test kitchens had to say: "It was delish and Hubby loved it…" "I would not change—it was delicious…" "Very good, will definitely make again… It was a hit." *Makes about 12 mini pies*

DIRECTIONS

In a blender, process the nuts, pineapple chunks, vanilla bean or extract, salt, lemon, lemon zest, carob powder, sweeteners (if using) and avocado until the mixture reaches a creamy consistency. To assemble the pies, press *Basic Raw Crust* into the bottoms of individual silicone muffin forms. Cover each base with some banana slices. Spread a layer of the pineapple cream over the bananas and top with some of the walnut halves or pieces. Spread the rest of the filling over the nuts. Sprinkle the tops with the chopped walnuts to decorate. Place in the freezer until firm. To serve, remove from moulds and let thaw on serving plates for about 15–30 minutes before enjoying. Garnish with fresh fruit, if desired.

> **Bev's Bit**
> Pineapple is an excellent source of manganese, which your body needs for energy production!

INGREDIENTS

1 cup raw macadamia nuts, cashews or pine nuts

2 cups fresh or frozen pineapple chunks

1 small or ½ large vanilla bean or 1 tsp vanilla extract or powder

¼–⅓ tsp Himalayan salt

¼ small lemon, peeled and quartered, seeds removed

¼–½ tsp lemon zest

½ tsp carob powder

½ tsp *Chicory Root Inulin with Stevia* (page 324) or favourite sweetener (optional)

2 tbsp maple syrup or favourite syrup (optional)

½ avocado

1 recipe *Basic Raw Crust* (page 325)

2 ripe bananas, sliced into ¼ in round slices

1 cup walnut halves or pieces

⅓ cup chopped walnuts

FUDGE LAVA CAKE

1 cup Bob's Red Mill
or favourite gluten-free
all-purpose flour

7 tbsp cacao or cocoa powder

1 tsp baking powder

¼ tsp baking soda

½ cup coconut or almond milk,
or favourite non-dairy milk

1¼ cup coconut sugar, xylitol
or other favourite sweetener

3 tbsp melted coconut oil

½ cup chopped walnuts
(optional)

¼ tsp Himalayan salt

1¾ cups boiling water

With its gooey goodness, this recipe may be one of my favourite chocolate cake recipes ever! Be prepared, though, because once you make it, you might find you get barraged with hugs and smiles of delight! It's incredibly easy to make this dessert in a slow cooker (my favourite method), but you can also prepare it as individual servings in ramekins. *Serves 6–8*

DIRECTIONS

SLOW COOKER METHOD Grease the slow cooker liberally with some coconut oil and add the flour, 3 tbsp of the cacao or cocoa powder, the baking powder, ½ cup of the sweetener and the coconut oil and mix together. Next, stir in the non-dairy milk and walnuts (if using). In a separate bowl, mix together the remaining sugar and cacao or cocoa powder, then sprinkle evenly on top of the batter. Finally, gently pour in the boiling water, without stirring. Turn the slow cooker to high and cook for 2–3 hours, until the top is firm to the touch, but the hot lava sauce below is bubbling along the edges.

OVEN METHOD Grease individual ramekins, then prepare as above, only dividing evenly between each of the ramekins for each step. Bake in a preheated 350˚F oven for 35–40 minutes, until the desired consistency is achieved.

Serve the cake while still warm straight from the slow cooker or oven. Great on its own or with *Coconut Whipped Cream* (page 329) or ice cream (pages 275–279). This cake is best enjoyed immediately, but will keep for 1 day refrigerated.

LEMON CUPCAKES

INGREDIENTS

1½ cups Bob's Red Mill
or favourite gluten-free
all-purpose flour

1 cup coconut sugar or xylitol

¾ tsp baking soda

¾ tsp psyllium husk powder

½ tsp baking powder

½ tsp Himalayan salt

¼ cup melted coconut oil

½ cup favourite non-dairy milk

⅓ cup lemon juice

½ tbsp lemon zest, packed

1 tsp vanilla extract

¾ tsp lemon extract

Lemon, oh glorious lemon... How we love thee, let us count the ways!

This is another cupcake recipe that Alex and I collaborated on, and we still can't get over how much we love it. The colour is a brighter yellow and the texture slightly lighter when made with xylitol rather than with coconut sugar, but it's good to have the option to use either, and both versions taste great. Choose what is best for you based on your sensitivities, needs and preferences. *Makes 10–12 cupcakes*

DIRECTIONS

In a bowl, whisk together the flour, sweetener, baking soda, psyllium husk powder, baking powder and salt. Then, using a fork or a pastry blender, mix in the melted coconut oil and set aside. In a separate bowl, mix together the milk, lemon juice, lemon zest and the extracts. Then add the wet ingredients to the dry, whisking until thoroughly combined with only very small clumps. Immediately fill prepared baking cups ¾ full with batter, and bake in a preheated 350°F oven for about 35–40 minutes, until a toothpick inserted in the centre comes out clean. Leave to cool completely. If desired, top with the frosting of your choice. You can also sprinkle the frosted cupcakes with lemon zest, shredded coconut, berries or other favourite toppings.

Bee Bite
Did you know that the tiny brain of one honey bee contains almost one million neurons?

CHOCOLATE CUPCAKES

This is a recipe my daughter Alex and I worked on together, and it's our first choice for birthday parties for kids. No one can believe that these moist and delicious cupcakes are entirely vegan and free of both gluten and regular refined sugar. *Makes 12–14 cupcakes*

DIRECTIONS

In a bowl, whisk together the flour, sweeteners, cacao or cocoa powder, baking soda, baking powder and salt. Then, using a fork or a pastry blender, mix in the melted coconut oil and set aside. In a separate bowl, mix together the milk, water and vanilla extract. Then add the wet ingredients to the dry, whisking until thoroughly combined with only very small clumps. Immediately fill prepared baking cups ¾ full with batter, and bake in a preheated 350°F oven for about 35–40 minutes, until a toothpick inserted in the centre comes out clean. Leave to cool completely. If desired, top with the frosting of your choice. You can also sprinkle the frosted cupcakes with shredded coconut, fruit or cacao nibs.

Haely's Hint ✿

Thankfully for all of us chocolate lovers, raw cacao is actually a superfood! It's high in iron, magnesium and antioxidants and will help boost your serotonin! No wonder we love it!

INGREDIENTS

1½ cups Bob's Red Mill or favourite gluten-free all-purpose flour

1 cup coconut sugar or xylitol

¾ cup cacao or cocoa powder

2 tsp *Chicory Root Inulin with Stevia* (page 324) or favourite sweetener

¾ tsp baking powder

¾ tsp baking soda

½ tsp Himalayan salt

⅔ cup melted coconut oil

1 cup favourite non-dairy milk

½ cup warm water

2 tsp vanilla extract

BUTTERCREAM FROSTINGS

These are the lowest glycemic index (GI) frosting recipes ever! The coconut cream used in the frostings means that any cakes or items must be refrigerated and enjoyed within 3–4 days. If you need to store them longer, freeze the frosting or frosted desserts in a sealed container.

COCONUT VANILLA BUTTERCREAM FROSTING

Deliciously smooth and creamy basic frosting for cakes or cookies. *Makes about 2½ cups*

INGREDIENTS

1⅓ cup coconut butter

1⅓ cups coconut cream (see page 31 for method)

3–5 tbsp maple syrup, to preferred sweetness

1 tbsp *Chicory Root Inulin with Stevia* (page 324) or favourite sweetener

2 tsp vanilla extract

¼ tsp cardamom

¼ tsp Himalayan salt

DIRECTIONS

In a food processor, pulse all the ingredients until creamy, scraping the edges very frequently (do not overprocess). You can use the frosting immediately on cooled cakes, cupcakes or cookies, or refrigerate for up to 3–4 days. Allow the chilled frosting to warm to room temperature before using to frost cakes or cookies.

"To dream the impossible dream..."—THERESA

LEMON BUTTERCREAM FROSTING

This lemon frosting literally takes the cake. What is also incredible is how little sweetener there is in it, and you would never guess its low GI value. Unless you have sensitivity to the ingredients or an aversion to desserts of any sort, this is a recipe you will want to try. *Makes about 3 cups*

INGREDIENTS

1½ cups coconut butter

1⅓ cups coconut cream (see page 31 for method)

⅔ cup shredded coconut

¾ cup lemon juice

2 tbsp lemon zest, packed

2 tbsp maple syrup

1 tbsp *Chicory Root Inulin with Stevia* (page 324) or favourite sweetener

1 tsp lemon extract

1 tsp vanilla extract

¼ tsp Himalayan salt

¼ tsp turmeric, for colour (optional)

DIRECTIONS

In a food processor, pulse all the ingredients until creamy, scraping the edges very frequently (do not overprocess). You can use the frosting immediately on cooled cakes, cupcakes or cookies, or refrigerate for up to 3–4 days. Allow the chilled frosting to warm to room temperature before using to frost cakes or cookies.

PEANUT BUTTER BUTTERCREAM FROSTING

This rich and creamy delectable frosting will be a favourite in any home where peanuts can be enjoyed. Created for the *Peanut Butter Cookie Sandwiches* (page 300), it can be used for other desserts as well. Let your imagination be your guide. *Makes about 2½ cups*

INGREDIENTS

1⅓ cups coconut butter

1⅓ cups coconut cream (see page 31 for method)

⅔ cup smooth, unsalted, unsweetened peanut butter or other nut/seed butter or soy (nut-free) nut butter alternative

⅔ cup maple syrup, or to taste

1 tbsp *Chicory Root Inulin with Stevia* (page 324) or favourite sweetener

¼ tsp cardamom

¼ tsp Himalayan Salt

DIRECTIONS

In a food processor, pulse all the ingredients until creamy, scraping the edges very frequently (do not overprocess). You can use the frosting immediately on cooled cakes, cupcakes or cookies, or refrigerate for up to 3–4 days. Allow the chilled frosting to warm to room temperature before using to frost cakes or cookies.

> **Theresa's Tip** 🌢
> For those of you who cannot enjoy peanut butter: I haven't experimented yet with other creamy nut, seed or soy butters, but have a feeling they could work as well. If you give them a whirl, be sure to let me know how the frosting turns out!

LIGHT CHOCOLATE BUTTERCREAM FROSTING

When I created this creamy gem, our friend Leonard Bashun tried it and at first thought it was delicious chocolate ice cream! You won't believe how simple this decadent frosting is to make. *Makes about 2⅓ cups*

INGREDIENTS

1 cup melted coconut butter

1 cup coconut cream (see page 31 for method)

⅓–½ cup cacao or cocoa powder, to taste

⅓ cup maple syrup

2½ tsp *Chicory Root Inulin with Stevia* (page 324) or favourite sweetener

¼ tsp Himalayan salt

DIRECTIONS

In a food processor, pulse all the ingredients until creamy, scraping the edges very frequently (do not overprocess). You can use the frosting immediately on cooled cakes, cupcakes or cookies, or refrigerate for up to 3–4 days. Allow the chilled frosting to warm to room temperature before using to frost cakes or cookies.

ICE CREAM!

VANILLA COCONUT ICE CREAM

Simple, creamy and insanely delicious!
Makes about 2½ cups

INGREDIENTS

1 x 13.5 fl oz (400 ml) can premium full-fat coconut milk

½ tsp *Chicory Root Inulin with Stevia* (page 324) or favourite sweetener, or to taste

3–4 large dates, pitted, to taste

½ tsp vanilla extract, vanilla powder or ½ vanilla bean

⅛ tsp Himalayan salt, or to taste

pinch cardamom

DIRECTIONS

In a blender, process all the ingredients until very creamy. If using the chilled canister type of ice cream maker, refrigerate the blended ingredients for 1–2 hours before processing for the best results. If you don't have an ice cream machine, use the Freezer-Stir Method (see panel below).

Ice Cream Freezer–Stir Method
No Ice Cream Machine? No Problem!
While more time intensive than an ice cream machine, the freezer–stir method can be used to make ice cream. Simply pour the blended mixture into a large bowl or flat pan and set in the freezer, stirring or whisking it every 15–20 minutes to break up the crystals until it reaches your desired consistency.

RAW VANILLA ICE CREAM

No one will believe how delicious and creamy this ice cream is, right out of the ice cream maker! *Makes about 3 cups*

INGREDIENTS

2 cups *Brazil Nut Almond Pecan Nut Cream* or other *Raw Nut Cream* (page 50)

¼ cup maple or yacon syrup

1 tbsp *Chicory Root Inulin with Stevia* (page 324) or favourite sweetener

½ cup raw macadamia and/or cashew nuts, soaked and rinsed

3 large dates, pitted

1–2 whole vanilla beans, or 1–2 tsp vanilla extract or powder, or to taste

⅛ tsp cardamom

¼ tsp Himalayan salt

DIRECTIONS

In a blender, process all the ingredients until very creamy. If using the chilled canister type of ice cream maker, refrigerate the blended ingredients for 1–2 hours before processing for the best results. If you don't have an ice cream machine, use the Freezer-Stir Method (left).

Theresa's Tip
You can flavour-shift in many directions by using different nut creams in this recipe. My favourite is a combination of equal amounts of Brazil nuts, almonds and pecans (see *Raw Nut Milk*, page 50).

RAW ICE CREAM OR COCONUT ICE CREAM VARIATIONS

BUTTER PECAN

If you love butter-pecan like we do, just add broken pecan halves for a whole new treat.
Makes about 3 cups

DIRECTIONS

Make *Raw Vanilla Ice Cream* per the recipe instructions, adding ½ cup broken pecan halves 5 minutes before completion of the ice cream in the machine. If using the Freezer-Stir Method (page 275), stir the pecans into the mixture before putting the ice cream into the freezer.

STRAWBERRY VANILLA

Just adding one more ingredient changes everything!
Makes about 3½ cups

DIRECTIONS

Make *Raw Vanilla Ice Cream* or *Vanilla Coconut Ice Cream* per the recipe instructions, adding 1 cup fresh or frozen strawberries to be creamed in the blender with the other ingredients before being poured into the ice cream machine or use the Freezer-Stir Method (page 275).

SALTED CARAMEL SWIRL

I got the biggest hug from my daughters when I created this ice cream. It didn't hurt that salted-caramel coconut ice cream is one of Alex's all-time favourites.
Makes about 2½–3 cups

DIRECTIONS

Make *Vanilla Ice Cream* or *Vanilla Coconut Ice Cream* per the recipe instructions but at the very end, drizzle in ¼–⅓ cup of room-temperature *Caramel Sauce* (page 328) and let the machine stir it in for 5-10 seconds, just long enough to give the ice cream the caramel swirl. (Letting the machine run for longer than a few seconds results in *Caramel Ice Cream*, which is also delicious.) If using the Freezer-Stir Method (page 275), drizzle in the caramel sauce during the final stir.

PEANUT BUTTER CHOCOLATE COCONUT ICE CREAM

One of our family favourites! *Makes about 2½ cups*

INGREDIENTS

1 x 13.5 fl oz (400 ml) can premium full-fat coconut milk

⅓ cup smooth, unsalted, unsweetened peanut butter or other nut/seed butter or soy (nut-free) nut butter alternative

2–3 tbsp cacao or cocoa powder, to taste

½ tsp *Chicory Root Inulin with Stevia* (page 324) or favourite sweetener (optional)

4–7 large dates, pitted, to taste

⅛ tsp ground cardamom

⅛ tsp Himalayan salt, or to taste

DIRECTIONS

In a blender, process all the ingredients until very creamy. If using the chilled canister type of ice cream maker, refrigerate the blended ingredients for 1–2 hours before processing for the best results. If you don't have an ice cream machine, use the Freezer-Stir Method (page 275).

PINA COLADA ICE CREAM

There's nothing like the tropical magic of this ice cream on a hot summer's day! *Makes about 4 cups*

INGREDIENTS

1 x 13.5 fl oz (400 ml) can premium full-fat coconut milk

1½ cups pineapple chunks, fresh, frozen or canned

2 tsp pineapple juice

2 tsp maple syrup, or to taste

1 tsp lemon juice

½ tsp *Chicory Root Inulin with Stevia* (page 324) or favourite sweetener

pinch cardamom (optional)

⅛ tsp Himalayan salt, or to taste

DIRECTIONS

In a blender, process all the ingredients until very creamy. If using the chilled canister type of ice cream maker, refrigerate the blended ingredients for 1–2 hours before processing for the best results. If you don't have an ice cream machine, use the Freezer-Stir Method (page 275).

CHOCOHOLIC'S CHUNKY DELIGHT RAW ICE CREAM

This chunky, chocolatey, creamy deliciousness is every chocoholic's dream!

Makes about 3 cups

DIRECTIONS

In a blender, process all the ingredients until very creamy. If using the chilled canister type of ice cream maker, refrigerate the blended ingredients for 1–2 hours before processing for the best results. If you don't have an ice cream machine, use the Freezer-Stir Method (page 275). Add the cacao nibs 5 minutes before the end of the processing time. If using the Freezer-Stir Method, stir the cacao nibs into the mixture before putting the ice cream into the freezer.

Theresa's Tip

Add 1 tsp of finely ground coffee or espresso beans before blending to make a mocha version of this ice cream.

INGREDIENTS

2 cups *Raw Nut Cream* (page 50) or *Raw Hemp Cream* (page 52)

1 avocado

¼ lemon, peeled and seeds removed

½ cup maple syrup

½ cup raw cashews, soaked and rinsed

3 large dates, pitted

6 tbsp cacao or cocoa powder

1 tbsp *Chicory Root Inulin with Stevia* (page 324) or favourite sweetener

2 whole vanilla beans, or 2 tsp vanilla extract or powder

⅛ tsp ground cardamom

¼ tsp Himalayan salt

⅓ cup cacao nibs

4 cups banana pieces, frozen

almond milk, coconut milk or
favourite non-dairy milk or
cream (if necessary)

INSTANT BANANA RAW ICE CREAM

If you are blessed with a single- or double-auger juicer (one day we'll get one, even if just for this recipe), making this ice cream is super-easy. In the meantime, like our family, you can still enjoy this delicious, simple, nut-free and healthy treat by using the food processor method. If you don't have a food processor, you can use a blender, but will need to add more milk in order to blend smoothly and have the right consistency. *Makes about 3½–4 cups.*

DIRECTIONS

FOOD PROCESSOR/BLENDER METHOD Pulse the frozen banana pieces in the food processor until creamy. If necessary for your machine to process, add a little non-dairy milk or cream—just enough to allow the machine to process. The amount of milk or cream you need to add will depend on the power of your food processor.

JUICER METHOD Put the blank plate into a single- or double-auger juicer. Turn on the machine, press the frozen bananas through the chute, and voilà— perfect ice cream comes out of the other side! (Who would have known that a juice machine could make the most incredibly creamy ice cream? You've got to see this one to believe it!)

Theresa's Tip
We like to buy the ripe organic "baking bananas" when we can. Not only are they usually a better price, but riper bananas have a higher antioxidant content and are easier to digest than less ripe bananas.

INSTANT BANANA RAW ICE CREAM VARIATIONS

FRUITY

Makes about 4 cups

Add 1 cup of your favourite frozen fruit (eg strawberries, peaches, raspberries, mango, pineapple chunks, etc) for a delicious fruity variation.

CHOCOLATE

Makes about 3½ – 4 cups

Add ½ cup cacao or cocoa powder when processing the frozen banana pieces. (Food Processor/Blender Method only.)

NUTS & NIBS

Makes about 3½ – 4 cups

Add ¼ cup cacao nibs and/or chopped nuts to the *Chocolate-Banana Variation* near the end of processing and pulse briefly, until just combined for deliciously crunchy ice cream treat. (Food Processor/Blender Method only.)

CHOCOLATE PEANUT BUTTER

Makes about 4 cups

Add ½ cup peanut or other nut butter and ½ cup cacao or cocoa powder to the canister with the bananas. (Food Processor/Blender Method only.)

8 *Gingersnaps* (page 288) or
Peanut Butter Cookies
(page 299)

2 cups ice cream (pages 275–
279), slightly softened

ICE CREAM SANDWICHES

After over 5 years of not having an ice cream sandwich, creating this recipe felt life-changing and so normalizing! Have fun experimenting with different combinations of cookies and ice cream flavours. These wonders are nothing less than divine and you'll discover that playdates will never be the same again. *Makes 4*

DIRECTIONS

Spread $\frac{1}{2}$ cup of ice cream each on four of the cookies. Top with another cookie, pressing down gently to create a sandwich. Using a spatula or gloved hands, spread the ice cream evenly around the sides of each sandwich. Place in the freezer in a parchment paper-lined container to freeze fully and have ready to pull out for a great treat on a moment's notice.

Theresa's Tip

If you'd like smaller ice cream sandwich treats, simply reduce the size of the cookies and use less ice cream to fill each delectable sandwich.

INSTANT RASPBERRY SHERBET

I love to create recipes that take less than 5 minutes to prepare. If you knew the kind of schedule we live by in our home, you would understand why! Here's what the test kitchens had to say about this dessert: "It was yummy... With a blender this couldn't be easier. Just put on ice cream setting and it's done..." "Unable to obtain the New Roots stevia so went with a substitute stevia. It turned out fine..." "It was a breeze ... I would make it just prior to serving for dessert... I really liked this recipe. I am vegetarian so the fact that it provides protein was a real plus for me. I also like the simple recipe and short time to prepare." *Serves 2*

INGREDIENTS

¾ cups silken tofu or coconut cream (see page 31 for method)

1 cup frozen raspberries, plus a few more for garnish

2 tbsp lime or lemon juice

1 tsp *Chicory Root Inulin with Stevia* (page 324) or favourite sweetener, or to taste

dash Himalayan salt (optional)

DIRECTIONS

Blend all ingredients together until creamy. You'll have a very soft sherbet using this method. If you would like a firmer dessert and have more time, process in an ice cream maker or use the Freezer-Stir Method (see page 275). Garnish with a few fresh raspberries before serving.

Bev's Bit 🌿
Blessed with a dizzying array of phytonutrients, raspberries are delicious little morsels of anti-inflammatory goodness!

Bee Bite

Have you ever wondered what honey really is?
Honey comes from the nectar that bees have ingested and then regurgitated. To convert the regurgitated substance into honey, bees air-dry it by flapping their wings until the nectar has the desired consistency and becomes honey. It's strange to think of honey as bee vomit! Honey bees collect this golden treasure to feed their community in the hive.

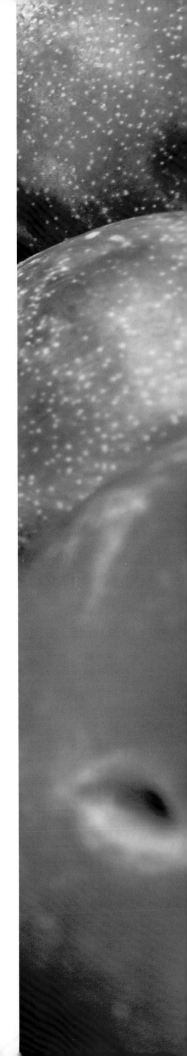

SWEET TREATS
COOKIES, CANDIES
& SWEET SNACKS

GINGERSNAPS

DRY INGREDIENTS

2 cups Bob's Red Mill
or favourite gluten-free
all-purpose flour

1 tsp ground ginger

1 tsp baking powder

¼ tsp baking soda

¼ tsp cinnamon

¼ tsp Himalayan salt

1 cup coconut sugar

WET INGREDIENTS

⅓ cup melted coconut oil

¼ cup maple syrup

3 tbsp blackstrap molasses

2 tbsp water

1 tsp vanilla extract

Whenever I think of gingersnaps, I can't help but think of a very special person who touched my life and the lives of thousands. His name was Donald Bowers (affectionately known as "Mr. B"). He ran the school choir and musical programs, and both he and his beloved wife Bunny LOVED gingersnap cookies. Mr. B was a person who must have walked this planet with a halo and very able wings! He had the most positive attitude about everything... life and people and music and love. His goatee so suited him and added to the effect of his buoyant gait and infectious laugh. Mr. B made each and every student in his Chamber Singers and A Cappella Choir at Alta Loma High School in Southern California feel important, beautiful and worthy of love. You can only imagine what a challenge he had on his hands—to herd up to 100 wild-at-heart teenagers and bring them together to create magical music. So many great memories! Mr. B, wherever you are, this one's for you! *Makes about 2 dozen cookies*

DIRECTIONS

In a medium bowl, whisk together the dry ingredients, except the coconut sugar, then set aside. In a large mixing bowl, cream together the coconut sugar and coconut oil. While continuing to stir, slowly add the remaining wet ingredients, incorporating until well blended. Stir in the flour mixture until just combined.

Scoop out heaping tablespoons of dough and place on a parchment paper-covered cookie sheet or silicone mat, spacing cookies 3–4 inches apart to allow for them to spread. Bake in a preheated 350°F oven for 14–16 minutes, or to desired firmness. Allow to cool before serving.

NOTE If the cookies will be used for *Ice Cream Sandwiches* (page 282), you will want them to be more firm. But if you want a chewier cookie, you can take them out a little sooner.

Theresa's Tip

Spring-handled ice cream scoops, which come in a variety of sizes, are great time-savers when making cookies (and meatballs!). They make evenly measured and shaped results, easy for kids and adults alike.

SNICKERDOODLES

What a fun journey it was to create these cookies that were high on my recipe-development wish list. They are great to make with your kids. The hardest task with these yummy treats is keeping hands of desire away from them right after they are made! (You might want to double this recipe.) *Makes about 2 dozen cookies*

DIRECTIONS

In a medium bowl, whisk together the dry ingredients, except the coconut sugar and set aside. In a large mixing bowl, cream together the coconut sugar and coconut oil. While continuing to stir, slowly add the maple syrup and water, incorporating until well blended. Stir in the flour mixture until just combined. In a separate bowl, stir together the 2 tbsp coconut sugar and cinnamon for rolling.

Form the dough into 1-inch diameter balls and roll each one in the sugar-cinnamon mixture. Place the balls onto a parchment paper-covered cookie sheet or silicone mat, spacing the cookies 2–3 inches apart to allow for them to spread. Bake in a preheated 350°F oven for 12–15 minutes, or to desired firmness. Cool completely before serving.

DRY INGREDIENTS

2 cups Bob's Red Mill or favourite gluten-free all-purpose flour

1 tsp baking powder

¼ tsp cinnamon

¼ tsp baking soda

¼ tsp Himalayan salt

1 cup coconut sugar

WET INGREDIENTS

⅓ cup melted coconut oil

¼ cup maple syrup

2 tbsp water

INGREDIENTS FOR ROLLING

2 tbsp coconut sugar

½ tsp cinnamon

> **Bee Bite**
>
> Did you know that honey bees have a complex social system, with different "chores" assigned to them in the hive? In the honey bee hive household, there are the childcare workers (nurse bees) who take care of the young; the queen's special attendant bees, who bathe and feed her (she really does live like a queen!); guard bees who protect the hive; and construction bees who build the beeswax where the queen can lay her eggs. In addition, there are bees who serve as undertakers, removing the dead bodies from the hive, and the foragers who bring the pollen and nectar to feed the whole community. If they live long enough, most of the worker bees in the hive do the majority of these jobs at different times during their lifetime.

SHORTBREAD COOKIES

DRY INGREDIENTS

2 cups Bob's Red Mill
or favourite gluten-free
all-purpose flour

1 tsp baking powder

¼ tsp baking soda

½–¾ tsp Himalayan salt,
to taste

¼ tsp cardamom

1 cup coconut sugar or xylitol

WET INGREDIENTS

½ cup unmelted coconut oil

½ cup coconut butter

⅓ cup maple syrup

Just when I was about to give up on making shortbread, this is what happened! Whether you enjoy them as they are, cover them with chocolate or decorate the tops with frosting for festive events, these cookies will always be a hit. *Makes about 2 dozen cookies*

DIRECTIONS

In a medium bowl, whisk together the dry ingredients, except the coconut sugar or xylitol, and set aside. With a stand mixer or in a large mixing bowl, cream together the coconut sugar or xylitol, coconut oil and coconut butter. Then with the beaters still going, slowly add the maple syrup and continue to mix until completely blended. Stir in the flour mixture until well combined.

For round shortbread cookies, form the dough into 1-inch diameter balls. Place the balls onto a parchment paper-covered cookie sheet or silicone mat, spacing the cookies 2–3 inches apart to allow for them to spread. Gently press with the palm of your hand to flatten each to about ¼-inch thick. To make shaped cookies, place a cookie cutter on the sheet or mat and firmly press the dough ball inside the form, to about ¼-inch thick, then carefully lift the form away. Bake in a preheated 350°F oven for 10–12 minutes, or to desired firmness. Cool completely before serving or decorating with chocolate or frosting.

> **Theresa's Tip** 🌢
>
> For a beautiful, classic chocolate-dipped shortbread cookie, put the cooled cookies in the freezer for at least 30 minutes. In the top of a double-boiler, slowly melt your favourite dark chocolate. Once melted, dip half of each cookie in the melted chocolate and then set on parchment paper to cool.
>
> Alternatively, you can frost the tops of the cookies with your favourite frosting. You can then add coconut shreds, cacao nibs or other sprinkles on top of the frosting—a fun decorating activity to do with your little ones!

LIGHT LEMON COOKIES

Like many people, any lemon treat is a favourite of mine. However, getting a cookie with the classic chewy, yet delicate texture and lemony flavour was a monumental task. After three years of attempts, I was totally thrilled with this irresistible cookie that is free of grain and starch! Be sure to let them cool before enjoying.

Makes 2–2½ dozen cookies

DIRECTIONS

In a small bowl, soak the psyllium with the lemon juice and zest and set aside for 5–10 minutes. Put the almond meal, shredded coconut, sweetener, baking soda, cardamom, turmeric and salt in a food processor (required tool for this recipe!) and process for about 2 minutes until it is a fine meal (do not over-process), scraping the inside of the vessel a couple of times to ensure even processing. Add the lemon-soaked psyllium, oil and maple syrup and pulse about 10 times just until mixed well—the dough will stick together when pressed between your fingers. Drop heaping teaspoon-sized mounds onto a parchment paper-covered cookie sheet or silicone mat, spacing the cookies 1–2 inches apart to allow for them to spread. You can also form the dough into 1-inch balls (about one heaping teaspoon each) and gently press them to about ⅓-in thick. Bake in a preheated 350°F oven for 13–14 minutes, or until the tops just start to become golden brown. Allow to cool before serving.

INGREDIENTS

¼ cup lemon juice

2 tsp lemon zest, packed

1½ tsp psyllium husk powder

2 cups blanched almond meal

1 cup shredded coconut

1½ tsp *Chicory Root Inulin with Stevia* (page 324) or favourite sweetener

½ tsp baking soda

¼ tsp Himalayan salt

¼ cup unmelted coconut oil

¼ cup maple syrup, to taste

⅛ tsp cardamom

⅛ tsp turmeric

Theresa's Tip
I like both how psyllium husk behaves and its health benefit as a great source of fibre, so it is imy preferred binding agent. Alternatives for those unable to use psyllium husk powder are ground flax or chia seeds, but these are not ideal (see *Funky Ingredients*, page 22).

Bev's Bit
According to some, cardamom is a good remedy for nausea and is also a great aphrodisiac!

OLD-FASHIONED CHOCOLATE CHIP COOKIES

No cookbook is complete without a delicious and chewy chocolate chip cookie recipe! With these delectable cookies, no one will guess that they are completely vegan, as well as gluten- and sugar-free! *Makes 2–3 dozen cookies*

DRY INGREDIENTS

2 cups Bob's Red Mill or favourite gluten-free all-purpose flour

1 tsp baking powder

1 tsp *Chicory Root Inulin with Stevia* (page 324) or favourite sweetener

¼ tsp baking soda

¼ tsp Himalayan salt

1 cup coconut sugar or xylitol

WET INGREDIENTS

½ cup melted coconut oil

⅓ cup maple syrup

¼ cup coconut milk or almond milk or other favourite non-dairy milk

1 tsp vanilla extract

ADD-INS

½ cup cacao nibs

⅔ cup sugar-free chocolate chips, chocolate chunks, or a chocolate kiss for the top of each cookie

1½ cups chopped nuts (optional)

DIRECTIONS

In a medium bowl, whisk together the dry ingredients, except the coconut sugar or xylitol. In a large mixing bowl, cream together the coconut sugar and coconut oil. While continuing to stir, slowly add the remaining wet ingredients, incorporating until well blended. Add the flour mixture and stir until just combined. Once mixed, stir in the add-ins.

Scoop out heaping tablespoons of dough and place on a parchment paper-covered cookie sheet or silicone mat, spacing the cookies 3–4 inches apart to allow for them to spread. Bake in a preheated 350°F oven for 12 minutes, or to desired firmness. If you'd like to add a chocolate kiss on top, gently press one in the top of each cookie while they are still warm. Allow to cool before enjoying—if you can wait!

Theresa's Tip

If making these cookies for *Ice Cream Sandwiches* (page 282) and want a more stable cookie, omit the chocolate chips, chunks or kiss, leaving in only the cacao nibs for the chocolate chip flavour and crunch.

PEANUT BUTTER COOKIES

Inspired by my husband's irrational love of peanut butter cookies...
need I say more? These cookies will rock your world!
Makes about 2 dozen cookies

DIRECTIONS

In a medium bowl, whisk together the dry ingredients, except the coconut
sugar or xylitol. In a large mixing bowl, cream together the coconut sugar or
xylitol and coconut oil. While continuing to stir, slowly add the remaining wet
ingredients, incorporating until well blended. Stir in the flour mixture until
just combined.

Scoop out heaping tablespoons of dough and place on a parchment paper-
covered cookie sheet or silicone mat, spacing the cookies 3–4 inches apart to
allow for them to spread. With a clean fork, press the top of each cookie to
get that familiar peanut butter cookie pattern we know and love. Bake in a
preheated 350°F oven for 13–15 minutes, or to desired firmness. Allow to cool
before serving.

Theresa's Tip

If you are unable to eat peanuts, you might
like to experiment with other nut, seed or soy
butters and see what new taste variations
you can create!

DRY INGREDIENTS

2 cups Bob's Red Mill
or favourite gluten-free
all-purpose flour

1 tsp baking powder

1 tsp *Chicory Root Inulin
with Stevia* (page 324) or
favourite sweetener

¼ tsp baking soda

¼ tsp Himalayan salt

1 cup coconut sugar or xylitol

WET INGREDIENTS

½ cup smooth, unsalted,
unsweetened peanut butter
or other nut/seed butter or
soy (nut-free) nut butter
alternative

⅓ cup melted coconut oil

¼ cup maple syrup

¼ cup almond milk or other
favourite non-dairy milk

1 tsp vanilla extract

PEANUT BUTTER COOKIE SANDWICHES

INGREDIENTS

1 dozen *Peanut Butter Cookies*
(page 299)

1 cup *Peanut Butter
Buttercream Frosting*
(page 273)

Several years ago, a little bakery called "Butter" opened in the Dunbar area of Vancouver that rapidly became the talk of the town, particularly famous for their peanut butter cookie sandwiches. Being so decadent, this was our family's all-time favourite treat for special occasions (like Eric's birthday). Of course, being anything but gluten-free or vegan, this indulgence became only a fond memory after the changes in our diets. After innumerable unsuccessful attempts, I finally created a gluten- and sugar-free, vegan, mind-blowing version, inspired by Butter's invention—pure bliss you'll want to experience! *Makes 6 cookie sandwiches*

DIRECTIONS

Pair the cookies up by size and shape. Spread the frosting evenly about ¼- to ⅓-inch thick on the flat (bottom) side of one cookie in each pair. Place the other cookie on top of the frosting (flat side pressed against the frosting). Serve immediately, refrigerate for a maximum of 3 days or freeze for longer storage. Because of the coconut oil and coconut cream in the frosting, be sure not to leave these cookie sandwiches out of the fridge for any long length of time.

Theresa's Tip

You can use other firm cookies with your favourite frosting to make a variety of delectable cookie sandwiches. Some of the combinations I've found to be really yummy are:

>> *Gingersnaps* (page 288) filled with *Coconut Vanilla Buttercream Frosting* (page 272)
>> *Old-Fashioned Chocolate Chip Cookies* (page 296) filled with *Light Chocolate Buttercream Frosting* (page 273)
>> *Shortbread Cookies* (page 292) filled with *Lemon Buttercream Frosting* (page 272)

Let me know if you come up with any other great cookie sandwich combinations!

PECAN DATE BUTTERBALL RAW COOKIES

I was really excited when I developed this easy recipe, which reminds me of the traditional powdered sugar-covered butterball cookies I enjoyed so much on special occasions while growing up! The combination of Brazil nuts and pecans creates an incredibly buttery taste and mouth-feel, without a smidgen of butter! The dates, *Chicory Root Inulin with Stevia*, almonds and Himalayan salt create a powdered-sugar flavour that never seemed possible without sugar. So easy and so delicious!

Here's some of what the test kitchens had to say about these cookies: "I LOVED this recipe—it was my favourite." "It was delicious eating with a spoon right out of the food processor and I struggled to save some for the dehydrator. Could be eaten right after forming the balls raw without baking or dehydrating—delicious!!" "Love, love, love... delicious... Next time I will double it because it was so delicious I ate most of it myself very quickly!" *Makes about 2 dozen cookies*

DIRECTIONS

Soak the seeds in 1 tbsp of water for 1 minute. Put all the other ingredients in a food processor and pulse for about 1 minute. Add the soaked seeds and continue processing until the dough sticks together when pressed between your fingers, but still has small nutty pieces for crunch (do not overprocess). Form into balls.

Place the cookies on a dehydrator sheet in the dehydrator at 105°F (or use the Oven Dehydration Method, page 233, if you don't have a dehydrator) until the desired texture is achieved (24–48 hours). You can also enjoy and serve these cookie balls without dehydrating. You might want to double the recipe to account for the dough that will disappear before the cookies can be served to your guests!

INGREDIENTS

1 tbsp water

1 tsp chia seeds or flax seeds

½ cup raw Brazil nuts

½ cup raw pecans

½ cup dates, pitted

1 cup almond meal

1½ tsp *Chicory Root Inulin with Stevia* (page 324)

½ tsp Himalayan salt, or to taste

Theresa's Tip

You can also use this recipe as a delicious alternative to *Raw Basic Crust* (page 325) for an even more decadent caramel-flavoured crust. Just make a batch of *Pecan Date Butterball Cookies* and press the dough into the bottom of a pie dish, then fill as desired.

RAW LEMON CAROB TRUFFLES

INGREDIENTS

¾ cup raw walnuts

7 Medjool dates, pitted

¼ cup raw carob powder

¼ tsp Himalayan salt

¼ tsp vanilla powder or extract

zest of ¼ lemon

pinch cayenne pepper (optional)

dried fruit or whole nuts, to fill

OPTIONAL COATINGS

hemp seeds, banana flakes, coconut, cacao powder, chia seeds, poppy seeds, ground walnuts, ground peanuts

Anyone who has ever been on a quest to discover which foods they are sensitive to has likely gone on at least one elimination diet, the gold standard for such an assessment. It was when I was on one such protocol, including the elimination of chocolate, that this masterpiece was created. I had learned how to make classic, filled raw chocolate truffles from Lovena Galyide during her Raw Food Chef Series at the Indigo Food Café and thought it would be great to create something similar using carob. As I developed the recipe, it took a while to find what worked with the distinctive carob flavour. Finally, I came up with the idea of lemon and vanilla to brighten the taste, adding a touch of sour contrast to the sweet carob and date combination. I was thrilled with this creation, as were my friends who are unable to eat chocolate! *Makes about 2 dozen truffles*

DIRECTIONS

Process all the ingredients (except the fillings) in a food processor until fine. Form into truffle-sized balls in the palm of your hand and press a piece of dried fruit or whole nut into the centre, reforming the ball. Then roll each truffle in something fun to coat them before freezing. Best eaten when still firm and cold from the freezer.

Haely's Hint ✿
Walnuts are a great source of omega-3s!

CARAMEL POPCORN BALLS

Creating this recipe was a great victory and very exciting. While certainly not a food for everyday consumption, these popcorn balls are much healthier than conventional versions, with a significantly lower glycemic index, especially when yacon syrup is used. This recipe is a guaranteed hit! *Makes 10–12 balls*

INGREDIENTS

- ⅜ tsp baking soda
- ⅛ tsp Himalayan salt
- 1 cup nuts (optional)
- 10 cups air-popped popcorn
- 2 tbsp coconut oil
- 2 tbsp maple syrup, plus yacon, coconut nectar, maple syrup, brown rice syrup, or other favourite syrup to make up 1 cup in total

DIRECTIONS

Put the baking soda, salt and nuts (if using) into a small bowl and set aside (but keep close at hand). Put the popped popcorn in a very large bowl, with plenty of extra room. Heat the coconut oil and syrup in an oversized saucepan* over high heat, stirring frequently with a straight-edged wooden spoon (or other straight-edged heat-resistant tool) until it begins to boil. Then reduce the heat slightly (to keep the syrup from rising too high) and stir constantly for 8 more minutes as the mixture continues with a rolling boil. Remove from the heat and immediately stir in the baking soda mixture. Working very quickly, pour the mixture over the popcorn and stir rapidly until well coated. (The candy sets *really* fast, so you need to work *very* quickly at this stage.) Tip the popcorn mixture onto a parchment paper-lined baking pan or a silicone baking sheet and, wearing sanitary gloves to reduce the risk of being burned, *very carefully and rapidly* press handfuls of the popcorn mixture into balls. (For safety purposes, this is one job for adults only.) Let cool completely before serving. Best eaten within 2 days.

* **IMPORTANT NOTE** When you stir in the baking soda mixture, the cooked syrup will rise significantly, so it is essential to use a pan that is about 3 times larger than what seems necessary to cook the ingredients.

OTHER CARAMEL POPCORN TREATS

KRACKER JACKS *(Makes 10 cups)*
Create your own home-made version of Kracker Jacks by making the *Caramel Popcorn Balls*, but replace the optional nuts with 2 cups of peanuts along with the baking soda mixture. Instead of forming into balls, spread the mixture onto a parchment paper-lined baking pan or silicone baking sheet to cool. Once cooled completely, break into pieces and store in a sealed container.

CARAMEL POPCORN *(Makes 10 cups)*
To make Caramel Popcorn, omit the nuts and instead of forming the candied popcorn into balls, simply spread the mixture onto a parchment paper-lined baking pan or silicone baking sheet to cool in the same way as for Kracker Jacks.

PEANUT BUTTER COCONUT MELTS

INGREDIENTS

2 cups shredded or desiccated unsweetened coconut

⅔ cup melted coconut oil

⅓–½ cup smooth, unsalted, unsweetened peanut butter or other nut/seed butter or soy (nut-free) nut butter alternative

1 tsp–1 tbsp maple or yacon syrup, to preferred sweetness

1 tsp *Chicory Root Inulin with Stevia* (page 324) or favourite sweetener

½ tsp blackstrap molasses

¼ tsp Himalayan salt

Many of my relatives suffered from diabetes (including my father), so I have seen what a cruel disease it can be and also the extreme lifestyle changes such a diagnosis requires. I have also witnessed how difficult it can be for individuals living with such challenges to follow their medical professionals' recommendations to make dietary and other lifestyle changes, especially limiting sugar consumption. It makes me really happy to be able to offer such a decadent low-GI candy to people who otherwise are unable to enjoy such pleasures. This recipe was inspired by "Delicious Obsessions" (www.delicious-obsessions.com) Maple Coconut Bars with Coconut Oil. With a little experimenting, I was able to transform these bars into a delicious peanut butter candy recipe with a delightful texture and depth of flavour. Even better, you can press these winners into silicone or other candy moulds in minutes, with fresh candy ready and waiting in just an hour. *Makes about 3 dozen candies*

DIRECTIONS

Stir all the ingredients well in a bowl then press into candy moulds, ensuring the oil is evenly distributed to all candies. Refrigerate for 1 hour, or until solid. Store in the refrigerator for several days (if they last that long) and for over 1 month in the freezer in a sealed container.

Chocolate-Covered Peanut Butter Cups

My family is crazy about chocolate-covered peanut butter cups. This simple variation of the melts recipe has all of the tasty goodness of the familiar candies from the store, but without the ingredients that don't agree with our bodies. Dip frozen *Peanut Butter Coconut Candy Melts* in melted sugar-free chocolate, place on a piece of parchment paper and refrigerate until solid (about 15 minutes). If you would like a thicker coat of chocolate, return the candies to the freezer for a few minutes, then dip each back into the melted chocolate, place on the parchment paper and refrigerate until ready to serve. Like the melts, these candies can be stored in the refrigerator for several days or for over 1 month in the freezer in a sealed container. Perfect for unexpected guests or those times when a chocolate craving strikes!

TRUFFLES

A sweet indulgence that doesn't need to be missed. These chocolates are so rich and delicious, you would swear that they must be unhealthy... but they aren't! *Makes 2–3 dozen*

INGREDIENTS

¾ cup coconut butter

⅓ cup coconut cream (see page 31 for method)

¼–⅓ cup cacao or cocoa powder, to taste, plus 2–4 tbsp for rolling

2 tbsp unmelted coconut oil

3 tbsp maple syrup

1 tsp *Chicory Root Inulin with Stevia* (page 324) or favourite sweetener

⅛ tsp Himalayan salt

DIRECTIONS

Pulse all ingredients together in a food processor until very creamy, scraping the edges frequently. Remove from the food processor and refrigerate to allow the mixture to firm up. When firm enough to shape, scoop out teaspoonfuls and form into small balls. Roll each truffle in the extra cacao powder and place on a plate. Refrigerate or freeze in an airtight container to store. To serve, allow to warm to room temperature and enjoy!

FUDGE

What can I say about this recipe, but "Wow!" No cooking, no fussing... just pure heaven!
Makes 2–3 dozen

INGREDIENTS

1 cup coconut butter

½–⅔ cup cacao or cocoa powder, to taste

¼ cup unmelted coconut oil

½ cup coconut cream (see page 31 for method)

⅓–½ cup maple syrup, to taste

2 tsp *Chicory Root Inulin with Stevia* (page 324) or favourite sweetener

⅛–¼ tsp Himalayan salt, to taste

1 cup walnuts, chopped (optional)

DIRECTIONS

Pulse all the ingredients except the walnuts together in a food processor until creamy, scraping the edges very frequently. Stir in the walnuts and press into an 8-inch square glass or silicone baking dish and refrigerate until firm. To serve, cut into 1-inch squares. For longer-term storage, freeze in an airtight container. To serve, allow to warm to room temperature and enjoy!

ESSENTIAL EXTRAS
CONDIMENTS & SAUCES

RAW PARMESAN

In the world of raw food, there are some very creative ideas that I love, and bringing together the fat of nuts and the cheesy flavour of nutritional yeast is one of them! With its savoury and cheesy flavour, this delicious condiment does not actually taste like parmesan, but has a similar mouth-feel and other qualities reminiscent of the cheese. This alternative is terrific on salad, pasta, pizza and other dishes where you might otherwise reach for parmesan. Have fun experimenting with this versatile and flavourful topping! *Makes 2 cups*

INGREDIENTS

1 cup walnuts

⅓ cup Brazil nuts, almonds or more walnuts

⅓ cup sunflower seeds

½ cup nutritional yeast

½ tsp Himalayan salt

1 tsp dried parsley

½ tsp dried rosemary

½ tsp dried oregano

¼ tsp dried thyme

⅛ tsp dried jalapeño (optional)

DIRECTIONS

Pulse all the ingredients in a food processor until they have a granular consistency, like parmesan. This can be stored in an airtight container away from heat, light and moisture for up to 1 month.

NUT-FREE RAW PARMESAN

I wanted to make a nut-free variation of this delicious and important condiment as well. You'll notice the addition of extra cheesiness with more nutritional yeast, as well as very subtle sweetening to balance out the bitterness of the seeds. *Makes 2½ cups*

INGREDIENTS

½ cup hemp seeds

⅔ cups sunflower seeds

1 cup nutritional yeast

½ tsp Himalayan salt

1 tsp dried parsley

½ tsp dried rosemary leaves

½ tsp dried oregano

¼ tsp dried thyme

⅛ tsp dried jalapeño (optional)

⅛ tsp *Chicory Root Inulin with Stevia* (page 324) or favourite sweetener

DIRECTIONS

Pulse all the ingredients in a food processor for about 1 minute until they have a granular consistency, like parmesan. Store in an airtight container away from heat, light and moisture for up to 1 month.

> **Theresa's Tip** 💧
> Because this recipe includes omega-3 rich hemp seeds, this nut-free variation has been designed to be used in recipes that are not cooked, or to be sprinkled on after the dish has been heated.

PLAIN CROUTONS & BREADCRUMBS

With any gluten-free bread, you can make these very useful croutons and breadcrumbs and know exactly what's in them! *Makes 3 cups*

INGREDIENTS

3 cups gluten-free bread (or as much as you want to use), cut into small cubes

DIRECTIONS

Place the cubes on a cookie sheet or other baking dish and bake in a preheated 300°F oven until dry and crisp—about 60 minutes, depending on the moisture content of the bread and the size of the cubes. Use to make stuffing or in any recipes requiring plain croutons. To make breadcrumbs, pulse the croutons in a food processor until they reach desired texture. Store in an airtight container for up to 1 month.

SPICY BREADCRUMBS

This spicy breadcrumb recipe uses dried almond pulp left over from making almond milk.
Makes 1 cup

INGREDIENTS

½ cup plain gluten-free breadcrumbs

½ cup almond meal or flour, or dried almond pulp

2 tsp dried oregano

¼ cup nutritional yeast

1 tsp garlic powder

½ tsp Himalayan salt

dash black pepper

½ tsp cayenne pepper

DIRECTIONS

Stir together and store in an airtight container for up to 1 month.

Bee Bite

Did you know that a worker bee typically only lives for about 3 to 6 weeks and that queen bees can live for up to 5 years? In an entire lifetime of hard work, each worker honey bee only produces about $1/12$ of a teaspoon of honey. For a hive of bees to collect just 1 kilogram of honey, they must fly around 90,000 miles and visit over 4 million flowers. There are no slackers there!

HERBED CROUTONS

For recipes that call for croutons or bread-crumbs that have a savoury herb flavour, here's an easy and delicious version. *Makes 3 cups*

INGREDIENTS

3 cups gluten-free bread, cut into small cubes

½ tsp dried rosemary

¼ tsp dried basil

¼ tsp dried thyme

¼ tsp dried oregano

1 tsp nutritional yeast

¼–½ tsp Himalayan salt, to taste

3 tbsp extra virgin olive oil

DIRECTIONS

In a large bowl, toss together all ingredients until the bread cubes are evenly coated. Place in a single layer on a cookie sheet or other baking dish and bake in a preheated 300°F oven until completely dry and crispy—about 60 minutes, depending on the moisture content of the bread and size of the cubes. Enjoy as a snack, use to make stuffing or sprinkle on top of salads. To make breadcrumbs, pulse in a food processor. Store in an airtight container for up to 1 month.

RAW PESTO

The Raw Parmesan in this recipes makes the taste, texture and mouth-feel of this classic one of my summer favourites!
Makes about 1 cup

INGREDIENTS

½ cup extra virgin olive oil

1 tbsp lemon juice

1 cup chopped basil, firmly packed

½ cup chopped parsley, firmly packed

¼ cup raw cashews, pine nuts or almonds

¼ cup *Raw Parmesan* or *Nut-Free Raw Parmesan* (page 314)

3 garlic cloves

1 tbsp nutritional yeast

Himalayan salt and black pepper, to taste

DIRECTIONS

Put the olive oil and lemon juice in the blender, followed by the basil and parsley and pulse for about 30–60 seconds. Add the remaining ingredients and process until your desired consistency is achieved. Use on any favourite raw vegetable or gluten-free pasta or quinoa. It can also be a pizza sauce base, a spread or a condiment in wraps. Best used immediately, it can be stored in the refrigerator for up to 3 days.

> **Theresa's Tip** ◗
> This pesto is incredible on raw zucchini noodles!

➤ Spiralized raw zucchini pasta noodles with Raw Pesto

CREAMY SUNFLOWER SEED SAUCE

You will fall in love with this sauce! The ever-popular Hollyhock Yeast Dressing was the inspiration for this thicker, sweeter and brighter sauce with allergy-friendly variations. You can make it without the nutritional yeast and it is still delicious. In that case, throw in a few extra seeds to achieve the desired texture. This recipe thickens a bit over time.
Makes about 3½ cups

INGREDIENTS

½ cup nutritional yeast

⅓ cup water

⅓ cup tamari or coconut aminos

⅓ cup apple cider vinegar

2–3 tbsp lemon juice, to taste (with pulp, if desired)

1½ cups extra virgin olive oil

2 tbsp sunflower or sesame seeds

Himalayan salt, to taste (optional)

3 garlic cloves

½ red bell pepper, cut into pieces (optional)

DIRECTIONS

Blend all the ingredients together. Enjoy this versatile dressing on salads, pasta, in wraps, with kale chips... so many uses! Can be stored in a sealed container in the refrigerator for up to 2 weeks.

Haely's Hint ❁
Nutritional yeast is a great source of B vitamins.

RAW HOISIN SAUCE

This healthy and authentic version of the traditional favourite is flavour-balanced to perfection and tastes absolutely divine! Experiment with it in stir-fries or as a condiment with spring rolls or steamed vegetables. It can be added to salads, wraps or rice and quinoa dishes for a special spicy twist. Feel free to make recipe adjustments to meet your personal needs and preferences. This particular blend is outrageously delicious—makes me crazy, it is so good! *Makes 1 cup*

INGREDIENTS

¼ cup tamari or coconut aminos

5 tsp peanut or almond butter

1 tbsp blackstrap molasses

1 tbsp yacon syrup or coconut nectar

2 tsp rice vinegar

1–2 garlic cloves

1 tbsp finely minced onion

2 tsp sesame or peanut oil

1–3 small fresh red hot chili peppers (optional)

½ tsp miso (chickpea or soya), optional

⅛ tsp black pepper

1 tsp *Chicory Root Inulin with Stevia* (page 324) or favourite sweetener

DIRECTIONS

Process all the ingredients in a blender until creamy. Can be stored in a sealed container in the refrigerator for up to 2 weeks.

ITALIAN SEASONING

This is a simple and flavourful condiment that you can create straight from your garden after dehydrating the fresh herbs. Once you see how easy it is to make, you may never want to buy this handy condiment again! *Makes about ½ cup*

INGREDIENTS

2 tbsp dehydrated rosemary bits

2 tbsp dehydrated oregano flakes

2 tbsp dehydrated thyme flakes

2 tbsp dehydrated savory flakes (optional)

2 tsp dehydrated sage flakes

DIRECTIONS

Place all the ingredients in a glass jar and shake until well combined. Store in an airtight glass jar a in a cool, dry place.

TOMATO SAUCE

A simple, fresh and healthy sauce that can be used in a wide range of dishes. *Makes 2 cups*

INGREDIENTS

1 x 6 oz (175 ml) can tomato paste

1–1½ cups fresh diced tomatoes

¾ tsp *Chicory Root Inulin with Stevia* (page 324) or favourite sweetener

¾ tsp white vinegar

¼ cup water

¼ tsp Himalayan salt

DIRECTIONS

Purée all the ingredients in a blender into a beautifully smooth sauce. Use immediately or store in the refrigerator for up to 1 week. Because tomatoes vary so much in terms of water content, start with using less water and add more until you reach the desired consistency.

MARINARA SAUCE

Simple, versatile, fresh and easy.
Makes about 3–3½ cups

INGREDIENTS

4 cups chopped fresh tomatoes

1 x 6 oz (175 ml) can tomato paste (for cooked version) or ¼ cup tomato powder (for raw version)

½ cup diced red bell pepper

¼ cup extra virgin olive oil

1–2 garlic cloves

¾–1 tsp crushed hot red pepper flakes, to taste

1 tsp dried basil

1 tsp salt, or to taste

1 tsp lemon juice (2 tsp for the raw version)

½ tsp dried oregano

½ tsp dried rosemary

½ tsp dried thyme

DIRECTIONS

Pulse all ingredients in a food processor to desired consistency.

RAW VERSION Use as is.

COOKED VERSION Stew the sauce in a medium saucepan for 20–30 minutes, until the desired thickness is achieved.

Feel free to add other favourite sauce additions—such as mushrooms, fresh herbs, roasted garlic or eggplant to craft variations. Can be stored in a sealed container in the refrigerator for up to 3 days.

KETCHUP

Once I created the veggie burger recipe, I knew I had to create delicious burger condiments that weren't loaded with sugar and lots of other ingredients that I couldn't pronounce. It took some time to get the precise flavour combination, but boy, it was a happy moment when the final product was indistinguishable from the most popular ketchup on the market—but this one is actually healthy to eat! *Makes ½ cup*

INGREDIENTS

½ cup *Tomato Sauce* (page 319)

1 tsp onion powder

¼ tsp *Chicory Root Inulin with Stevia* (page 324) or favourite sweetener

⅛ tsp blackstrap molasses

⅛ tsp white vinegar

pinch garlic powder

pinch mustard powder

pinch ground cloves

pinch Himalayan salt

DIRECTIONS

Process all the ingredients in a blender until smooth. This ketchup can be used immediately or stored in a sealed container in the refrigerator for up to 1 week. When chilled, the ketchup can gel up slightly, so simply blend or whisk it again to return it to a creamy texture.

SPICY BARBEQUE SAUCE

Both Eric and I have a special love of spicy food, so this is another favourite of ours, mimicking our all-time favourite barbeque sauce. We love that this recipe is very healthy and free of the junk that is usually present in store-bought products. If you enjoy a spicy, smoky-flavoured barbeque sauce, this recipe is for you!

Makes ½ cup

INGREDIENTS

½ cup *Ketchup* (left)

1½ tsp white vinegar

1½ tsp lemon juice

½ tsp blackstrap molasses

⅛–¼ tsp cayenne pepper, to taste

⅛ tsp chili powder

⅛ tsp paprika

⅛ tsp black pepper

Himalayan salt, to taste

DIRECTIONS

Process all the ingredients in a blender until smooth. Like the *Ketchup*, if stored in a sealed container in the refrigerator (for up to 1 week), it can gel up slightly. Just blend or whisk again to return it to its original creamy texture.

CREAMY HOT MUSTARD

Not for the faint of heart, this mustard packs an awesome punch! Rich in magnesium, selenium, antioxidants and vitamins, it is a wonderful anti-inflammatory condiment for those who enjoy the strong flavour. It's important to note that there are many types of mustard, with varying flavours and colours. I designed this recipe around one of the spicier varieties, but you can experiment with less spicy mustard powders if you prefer a milder taste.

Makes ½–⅔ cup

INGREDIENTS

¼ cup white vinegar

2 tbsp lemon juice

2 tbsp dry mustard powder

2 tsp starch (tapioca, corn, or potato) or arrowroot powder

6–8 raw Brazil nuts

pinch turmeric

Himalayan salt, to taste

DIRECTIONS

Process all the ingredients in a blender until smooth, varying the amount of Brazil nuts to achieve the desired consistency. This can be enjoyed immediately or stored in the refrigerator for up to 1 week.

> **Bev's Bit** 🌱
> Interestingly, mustard seeds contain a goodly amount of antioxidants and omega-3 fatty acids!

CHICORY ROOT INULIN WITH STEVIA

INGREDIENTS

1 cup chicory root inulin powder, such as Purica's Fiberlicious

1 tsp powdered stevia concentrate

Theresa's Tip 🌿
It's great to add a silica gel packet to the mix to help prevent this powder from clumping.

Being committed to creating as many low glycemic index (GI) recipes as possible, I developed a creative way to mimic familiar sweetness in my recipes, without the blood sugar spikes to go with it. I was able to do this after I discovered a product I absolutely love, Stevia Sugar Spoonable by New Roots Herbal (a respected supplement company in Canada), which I combine with other natural sweet foods. While the product has stevia in its name, this is extremely deceiving, since it actually contains very little stevia! Though easily available in Canada, this wonderful product is difficult to find in other countries. Because of this big hurdle, I realized I needed to create an ingredient that anyone, anywhere, could make. So, if you can get New Roots Herbal's Stevia Sugar Spoonable, that's terrific—it's wonderful and very inexpensive. However, if you can't, you can still create the same awesome recipes by making this low-GI blend that is full of prebiotic fibre. Because it is mostly inulin, this condiment doesn't overwhelm or distort the flavour of food as straight stevia does. *Makes 1 cup*

DIRECTIONS

Place both ingredients in a very clean and dry bottle and shake well to combine. Seal the bottle and store in a dry place.

BASIC RAW CRUST

One of the earliest great dessert innovations of the raw food pioneers!
Makes about 2 cups

DIRECTIONS

Place all the ingredients in a food processor and pulse until finely crumbed and the dough begins to stick together when pressed between your fingers, but still has some crunchy texture. Form the crust in the bottom of small spring-form or silicone pans (the number will vary, depending on the size and shape of the crust you are creating). The dough can also be pressed into shaped forms or pressed into 1-inch diameter balls and dehydrated for a super-simple and delicious cookie.

INGREDIENTS

2 cups raw walnuts, pecans, almonds, Brazil nuts and/or favourite raw nuts

1 cup soft dates, pitted

¼ tsp Himalayan salt

ORANGE CRANBERRY SAUCE

According to Alex, it's not Thanksgiving without cranberry sauce. I've always loved this delicious holiday dish, which I also think of as a treat, and there's no reason that it can't be enjoyed year-round. There's something about the orange and the touch of cinnamon that makes this recipe extra special. Who knows, it could become one of your family favourites too! *Makes about 3½ cups*

DIRECTIONS

Peel the orange and purée the sections in a blender. Add enough water to the orange purée to make 2½ cups liquid. Pour into a large saucepan and add all of the remaining ingredients, stir and heat on high until it reaches a rolling boil. Then reduce the heat to medium and boil for another 7 minutes, stirring very frequently to keep the sauce from sticking to the bottom of the pan. Reduce the heat to low and mash the cranberries with a potato masher to your desired consistency. You can serve immediately while hot or refrigerate for a chilled dish later. If you've used the agar agar, you can pour the hot sauce into decorative silicone moulds and chill in the refrigerator for an extra special presentation.

INGREDIENTS

2½ cups cranberries, fresh or frozen

1 orange

water

¼ tsp orange zest, packed

½ cup xylitol, coconut sugar or other favourite sweetener

4 tsp agar agar (optional, for more firm gelling)

¼ tsp cinnamon

⅛ tsp Himalayan salt

Bev's Bit

Cranberries have delicious anti-cancer properties! To reap the most benefit from cranberries, eat them in their whole form, rather than dried or as juice.

Theresa's Tip

This recipe is also really delicious as a topping on your favourite vanilla ice cream.

CARAMEL SAUCE

INGREDIENTS

½ cup coconut nectar

2 tbsp coconut oil

½ cup non-dairy cream or milk

¾ tsp mesquite powder
(optional)

½ tsp vanilla extract

¼–½ tsp Himalayan salt,
to taste

Chocolate Sauce
To make a chocolate
sauce, add ¼ cup
cacao or cocoa powder
before boiling.

My first caramel sauce creation used agave nectar, but when the suspect manufacturing practices were revealed, I had to rework the recipe using other sweeteners, making the necessary flavour adjustments. This was not as straightforward as you might think: the slightly fruity flavour of coconut nectar can vary significantly from brand to brand, but I discovered that adding mesquite powder, with its somewhat smoky, caramel-like quality, gave the sauce the right, familiar flavour. Adding the powder may or may not be necessary, depending on the coconut nectar you use. *Makes about ¾ cup*

DIRECTIONS

Put all the ingredients in a saucepan. Heat over medium-to-high heat, stirring frequently, until the mixture begins to boil. Stir constantly for 4–9 minutes until a caramel-like texture develops. If you are using milk instead of cream, this will take more time. Remove from the heat and either serve immediately as a hot caramel sauce or allow to cool in a glass container for use later. Enjoy this decadent sauce on ice cream or other delicious desserts.

COCONUT WHIPPED CREAM

This important recipe is easy, but does require care. The quality, fat content and other attributes of canned coconut creams vary and are critical to success with this recipe. You must use an organic coconut milk that is very creamy (I like Earth's Choice Premium Coconut Milk). The less creamy ones (likely those made from older coconuts) do not result in the fluffy, smooth and delectable mouth-feel that you want from a whipped cream. *Makes about 1 cup*

DIRECTIONS

Chill the coconut milk in the can overnight or for at least 3–4 hours. Remove the chilled can of coconut milk from the refrigerator (do not shake). Carefully remove the thick cream from the top of the can and place in a bowl (you can save the coconut water below to use in smoothies or other recipes). Some coconut cream has such a high fat content that no additional coconut oil is required in order to create the fluffiness. Others (sometimes by the same company and label) may have a more liquid consistency. In these cases, 1–3 tbsp of additional coconut oil may be needed for optimal results. Add the syrup of your choice to the coconut cream and whip it up on high with a stand mixer if you have one (my preferred method) for about 1–3 minutes, otherwise you can use a hand-held beater, which will likely require a bit more time. Then, with the beaters still whipping the cream, drizzle in the coconut oil (if needed) *extremely slowly*. This is critical, otherwise you will have an undesirable, granular texture. Continue to whip until the desired consistency is achieved. This whipped cream has a luscious thick texture and mouth-feel. Enjoy on desserts, with fruit or in other recipes. Best served immediately or shortly after being made.

INGREDIENTS

1 x 13.5 oz (400 ml) can premium full-fat coconut milk

2 tbsp maple or yacon syrup, or favourite sweetening syrup (optional)

up to 3 tbsp melted coconut oil, if needed

¾ tsp *Chicory Root Inulin with Stevia* (page 324) or favourite sweetener, or to taste (optional)

dash Himalayan salt

SUSTAINABLE KITCHEN TIPS 101
WONDERFUL WAYS TO REDUCE KITCHEN WASTE

IT'S AMAZING HOW EASY IT IS TO FIND WAYS to reduce, reuse and recycle in the kitchen! The hardest part of doing so is changing your way of thinking. A few years ago, my family went on an environmentally friendly, educational whale watching adventure at Telegraph Cove in British Columbia, sponsored by the Vancouver Aquarium. Along the way, we passed a former First Nations settlement. The guide explained how this community had lived in ways that were gentle to the Earth, leaving a minimal footprint in their wake. It was truly inspirational.

We have much to learn from communities such as these to help us rethink our modern-day ways of living. As in other areas of my life, I love to find creative ways to add healthy and sustainable lifestyle practices, rather than focusing on removing negative ones. In this chapter, I'm excited to share fun little tips and tricks I've learned, discovered or created over the years, which are easy and painless to implement in the kitchen—practical changes that help the planet in small, positive ways.

This list is by no means comprehensive, but hopefully will help you shift your mindset and spur your own creativity about finding ways to reduce waste. Making the conscious decision to do a few more generous acts for the environment is amazingly energizing. The bonus is that when you do so, you often also save money and get more back than you put in!

1. FREEZE THE EDIBLE PARTS OF VEGETABLES THAT YOU USUALLY THROW OUT AND USE THEM TO MAKE SOUP BROTH IN THE FUTURE.

There is a great deal of goodness we can get from parts of our food that we often discard! Onion and garlic peels, woody vegetable and herb stems, wilted or otherwise less attractive parts of vegetables, peels from carrots or zucchini or tomatoes or sweet potatoes or... (you get the idea) can be tossed in a zipper bag or other sealed container in the freezer to use later for vegetable stock. Obviously, don't save unhealthy bits of the food, but there are a lot of parts that you'll discover you can save.

To make the broth, just throw all of the scraps into a slow cooker, cover with water and cook with the lid on for several hours. Alternatively, put them into a large stock pot (in a nut-milk bag if you have one) with water and heat on low on the stove for several hours, inviting the flavours to infuse the liquid (adding more water as needed to ensure the vegetables remain covered). When done, allow the stock to cool, then strain to use as a base for soups or as a tasty replacement for some of the water when making rice, lentils, beans or quinoa. Some people like to freeze broth in ice cube trays, then store the cubes in a sealed bag or container. I just store broth in glass containers in the freezer instead (leaving plenty of room at the top of the container and the lid initially ajar, to prevent the glass from breaking). The leftover vegetable scraps can then go back to the earth in the compost bin.

2. ONLY PEEL OR REMOVE SEEDS AND PITH FROM FRUITS AND VEGETABLES WHEN YOU REALLY NEED TO, SINCE THOSE PARTS ARE OFTEN FILLED WITH VALUABLE NUTRIENTS.

For example, if you can get away with not peeling a tomato or removing the seeds and pith from a pepper, do it! If you are using a hot pepper and leaving in the seeds, you can use a little less of the pepper than you otherwise would, since the seeds can be quite a bit hotter than the flesh. Save zucchini peels if making white raw "noodles" to put

I like to infuse the air with parts of lavender plants, cinnamon, thyme, or a variety of other herbs, depending on the day. During cold and flu season, I do make a conscious practice of using herbs thought to have antimicrobial and other healing properties—such as oregano, thyme, sage, mint and cinnamon, as well as ginger and turmeric (placebo effect or not)—choosing different ones based on my mood and what's available. If my sinuses are a bit congested, I also enjoy taking a few moments to stand above the pot and inhale deeply, sometimes with a towel over my head to capture more of the steam. You can save herb stems in the freezer until you want to use them for a pick-me-up or for those times when you begin to feel under the weather.

4. USE STRAINED HERB INFUSIONS FOR BEAUTY AND RELAXATION AS WELL AS HEALTH.

After enjoying the aromatic steam from the herb infusions, strain the bits out and use the luscious scented water in your bath and for your skin and hair. Soaking in a tub with these delightful non-toxic herbs on your skin is pure heaven. If you are a lavender or lemon balm fan like I am, those could become your own home spa relaxation favourites before going to bed.

You can also mix some of the scented liquid in your favourite shampoo as an extra healing bonus for your body, mind and soul (as well as your scalp). I like to mix the rosemary water with apple cider vinegar and apply this mixture to my face and hair. I could swear that my skin and hair have become more vibrant and healthy from these applications, which I leave on for several minutes before washing off. Because of the vinegar scent, I prefer to do this in the evening before bed so that the acid smell can wear off before being out in the world with other people.

5. USE THE INSIDE OF A BANANA PEEL AS A SKIN MOISTURIZER.

Okay, this is a weird one and truly shows how crazy I really can be! You probably know that we "eat" what we put on our skin, absorbing into our bodies whatever is in it. For this reason, I have

into soups, stir-fries or salads. No need to lose all of the awesome goodness!

Bob Sorenson, my beloved Grade 6 teacher, was the first to really get my attention about this. I remember him telling our class one day that when he got sick, he would eat a *whole* orange—seeds, pith, peel and all! Trying to imagine actually *eating* orange peel and seeds seemed pretty crazy to me at the time. However, whenever I use orange zest or make a delightful hot beverage with the orange peel brightening the flavour and aroma, I think fondly of Mr. Sorenson, appreciating his willingness to open my eyes to new possibilities. And whenever a few seeds find their way into a smoothie or on my salad, I make a toast to him and good health!

3. USE THE WOODY STEMS FROM HERBS TO INFUSE YOUR HOME WITH A DELIGHTFUL AROMA, TO HELP CLEAR THE AIR AND YOUR SINUSES WHEN FEELING UNDER THE WEATHER, OR TO CREATE HERB-INFUSED WATER.

Place the stems in a pot of water and simmer, uncovered, on the stove for several hours. The flavoured water can be used as part of a soup base, and you'll enjoy the steam and delightfully healing aromas in your kitchen. (Be sure to keep adding more water as it simmers.) I've heard that rosemary was used in European hospitals years ago for antiseptic purposes. Regardless of the potential benefits, it simply smells wonderful.

become a bit of a zealot about trying to put on my skin only non-toxic ingredients that I could, at least hypothetically, eat.

Banana peels are full of antioxidants and other nutrients, and I have heard that people in some cultures eat them prepared in different ways. I haven't developed any recipes using them, but do use them for my skin. I certainly seem to have fewer wrinkles than previously, but I couldn't say that it was just because of banana peels—I've made many other lifestyle and nutritional changes that have likely been instrumental in this (especially increasing the raw food content in my diet). Whatever the "beauty benefit" may be, I find the banana peel trick to be very soothing and a lot of fun. Massaging my face with a banana peel makes me a bit giddy and it is great to embrace such childlike and harmless pleasures in life. It is also great to do with your kids for a fun night-in! They love to experiment with wild ideas!

6. USE AN AVOCADO PIT AS A SKIN MOISTURIZER.
Full of vitamins A and E, a freshly freed avocado pit feels lovely massaged on the skin and the high fat content provides wonderful moisture. I can see it now, you are chuckling away—first banana peels and now avocado pits? Pretty crazy, I know. For those rare moments when you do have the time and want to create your own healthy home spa experience, it's great to have options at your fingertips that are readily available in your kitchen and that don't cost a penny.

7. DEHYDRATE THE PARTS OF VEGETABLES YOU DON'T TYPICALLY USE TO MAKE CONDIMENTS OR ADD TO OTHER RECIPES.
You know those seeds and pithy parts of peppers, either bell or hot? If you remove them, dehydrate and then pulverize them into flakes or powder, they make a wonderful condiment to sprinkle lightly on salads, pizza, rice or quinoa dishes, and on other vegetable dishes as a natural flavour enhancer. Being a lover of spice, I especially love the hot pepper powder. The seed beds and peels of tomatoes can also be made into "sun-dried" tomato powder—an amazingly delicious condiment.

Let yourself be creative and curious—you'll be amazed by the range of condiments you can create from items that you would otherwise discard. As you discover the flavour profile of each, you'll be able to do your own recipe development, adjusting the taste of your food in ways you previously thought unimaginable.

8. FREEZE OR DEHYDRATE PERISHABLES BEFORE YOU LEAVE ON HOLIDAYS OR WHEN YOU KNOW YOU WON'T BE ABLE TO USE THEM BEFORE THEY EXPIRE.
We've all been there... getting ready to leave for a holiday, knowing that many or all of the fruits and vegetables in the fridge or fruit bowl will go bad before we return. Or, we realize there is more food in the fridge than we can healthfully eat before some of it goes bad. We could give some to friends and neighbours, but others, well... you know, would be kind of strange to offer.

Instead of just tossing out these fruits and vegetables, think about ways you might be able to use them at a later date if they were cut up, ready for use and stored in the freezer. Alternatively, you can cut up and dehydrate food that might otherwise go to waste, to use in a variety of ways.

Dehydrated fruit can be a super-delicious treat or a sweet addition to cereals and granola, as well as a salad topper or in cookies and on ice cream. Some of our favourite dried fruits are bananas, watermelon, pears, apples and papaya. If I am planning on making something into a powder or into flakes, I find it easiest to thinly slice or purée the produce before dehydrating, then finish it off in the blender or pulse it in a food processor to the desired consistency.

Frozen eggplant cubes, peppers, tomatoes, zucchini and mushrooms can be instant, time-saving additions to pasta sauces, soups and chili, making your food preparation much easier for those busy evenings after a long day at work. Berries are an easy freeze for smoothies, pies, ice cream, sorbet, sauces and crisps, but so are other fruits that can be cut up and frozen for the same purpose. You'll be amazed by how little you'll need to throw away. While you're at it, you can

also feel good about reducing your need to purchase packaged frozen fruits and vegetables. The more we can do for ourselves in this way, the less negative impact we'll have on the environment.

9. **FREEZE CITRUS PEELS FOR ZESTING.**

This is a really cool trick that my friend Lynda Hydamaka told me about years ago. You know how tricky it can sometimes be to zest fresh lemons and how awkward it can be when a recipe calls for more zest than the juice that you need? Well, when you freeze the peels, they become really easy to zest or microplane. You can also do the same with orange and lime peels. If you are able to enjoy citrus, you'll be so happy to know this tip. Like the frozen herb stems, these peels can also be lovely in an aromatic infusion, as steam for your face, and as an infused liquid for your bath.

10. **USE WATER FROM STEAMED VEGETABLES FOR SOUP BROTH OR TO REPLACE LIQUID FOR COOKING DRIED GRAINS OR LEGUMES.**

Instead of throwing away the water from steamed vegetables, use the liquid as part of a soup base or to make rice, lentils, beans or quinoa.

11. **AFTER FINISHING FOODS THAT ARE STORED IN MARINADES OR A STRONGLY FLAVOURED LIQUID, SUCH AS GARLIC-STUFFED OLIVES, PEPPERONCINIS AND OTHER PICKLED VEGETABLES, SAVE THE REMAINING JUICE AND BE CREATIVE!**

Use it as a base for salad dressings, marinades and sauces. Pickling liquid, for example, has a salty and acidic base, so by adding some vegetable oil, water and herbs, and giving it all a whirl in the blender with other ingredients of your choice, you have an instant dressing for salad! You can even use this liquid in soups or as a condiment to create new flavour dimensions.

12. **MAKE NATURAL FOOD COLOURING OR DYES.**

It's hard to imagine a better way to colour food and fabric, thread, or yarn than with chemical-free, clean food. Save clean vegetable, fruit and leaf scraps, sorted by colour, in bags in the freezer. I haven't yet done much experimenting with creating colourings from food, but it sounds like a blast. I am excited by my friend Monica Renard,

who is passionate about growing plants in her garden specifically to create dyes that offer beautiful natural colours for spinning yarn for her tapestries. This is certainly a landscape I want to explore in the future.

I sure hope that Monica publishes a book of her discoveries one day, but in the meantime, here are a few ideas for natural dyes: brown/tan (yellow onion peels, coffee grounds, tea leaves, cinnamon); orange (carrots); yellow (turmeric, saffron); green (spinach, parsley); blue (blueberries); purple (purple grapes, red cabbage); and red (beets, raspberries, pomegranate).

13. **WHEN IT IS DIFFICULT TO GET ALL OF THE FOOD OUT OF THE BLENDER, FIND WAYS TO ADD MORE LIQUID TO IT TO MAKE ANOTHER RECIPE THAT WOULD GO WELL WITH THAT FLAVOUR PROFILE.**

One of my favourite examples of this is to use what is left in the blender after making dips, nut cheese, or other thick recipes, such as pudding or frosting. Using the leftover dip in the blender to make salad dressing is just one idea. If you have made a sweet pudding or other thick dessert, add flavoured non-dairy milk to what's left in the blender to make a delicious smoothie or flavoured milk. This means that you don't have to work so hard to clean out the canister—I love that! Not only is this a great way to make kitchen clean-up easier, it also can lead to brilliant new recipe ideas—and indeed already has!

14. **REPURPOSE THE PULP FROM JUICE AND NUT MILKS.**

Since beginning to juice vegetables and fruits, I've wondered about what to do with the leftover pulp. Full of fibre and often many valuable nutrients, it always seemed a shame to just put it in the compost. Another benefit of the natural fibre in most plant-based foods is its prebiotic content, which feeds the friendly bacteria in our digestive tract. While I'm still exploring ways to use pulp, here are just a few ideas to get your (post-) juices flowing.

ALMOND PULP: At the Living Light Culinary Institute, I remember our instructor Chef James Sant saying that fresh (or frozen) almond pulp is "gold." Because I hadn't yet experimented with it

very much and knew that most people just throw it away, I became very curious. Many wonderful raw food creations, especially for grain-free crusts, breads, cakes and cookies rely heavily on the use of almond pulp.

It can be used immediately, stored in the freezer, or dehydrated and ground into almond pulp flour.

A little olive, avocado or almond oil added to almond pulp makes a gently exfoliating, hydrating face mask.

BROCCOLI, KALE AND CELERY PULP: These pulps (alone or in combination) are among my favourite savoury pulps because they are so versatile. The various juicing methods result in different textures and moisture content of the remaining pulp. In moderation, these pulps can be a welcome addition to soups or some stir fries. This pulp can be used immediately or stored in the freezer for later to use in recipes or when creating soup stocks, as described in Tip No.1.

If dehydrated and pulverized into a powder, pulp from these vegetables can also be used as a condiment. I keep a bottle of this powder in a shaker to sprinkle on my salads, soups, rice and quinoa dishes.

APPLE PULP: Because of its naturally high pectin content, apple pulp or pulp powder can be used as a thickener in recipes such as apple pie, fruit crisps and applesauce. Apple pulp is not as sweet as whole apples, and different juicing methods result in different qualities in the leftover pulp. So, when creating recipes using apple pulp, make flavour and texture adjustments as necessary. I have found that replacing or adding a small amount of apple pulp (up to one part pulp to four parts fruit) to an apple crisp or applesauce works well, with few additional adjustments necessary in terms of adding moisture or sweeteners.

Apple pulp can be dehydrated and then ground into a powder for a slightly sweet condiment or powdered flavouring.

GINGER PULP: Dehydrated and pulverized ginger pulp makes a fantastic condiment. Because the dried pulp is milder than fresh ginger, the flavour can be tolerated by more people. It is very versatile and is useful in both sweet and savoury dishes. It is wonderful very lightly sprinkled on cereal, in Asian cuisine, on salads, rice and quinoa dishes, in smoothies and hot chocolate, and even on ice cream.

Whether or not you decide to try any of these ideas (several are integrated in recipes in this collection), I hope that they made you smile and maybe even put a bee in your bonnet about coming up with other possibilities yourself. I am always game to learn more if you ever want to share your ideas via my website, www. yumfoodforliving.com or on my Facebook page (AuthorTheresaNicassio).

GIVING BACK
CHOOSE A CHARITY PROGRAM

MY JOURNEY IN WRITING THIS BOOK HAS BEEN ONE OF healing and discovery that I couldn't have done without the love and support of others. While I hope that the recipes in this book will help individuals and families live a healthier and more delicious life, it is also my vision for *YUM* to serve on a grander scale by helping causes that are committed to making a difference.

With the Choose a Charity Program, a portion of the proceeds from each hard copy of *YUM* sold via www.yumfoodfor-living.com will be donated to charity. Those purchasing books will be able to choose from one of four charities, which will be selected each year through a nomination process. Nominations for future charities may be made at any time.

If you have a cause that you think is congruent with the vision of YUM Living, please let us know. We are seeking charities that support one or more of the following categories and are also philosophically consistent with the spirit of all of these causes:

» health-related organizations, especially those that serve individuals who live with dietary restrictions or are advised to follow special diets due to health concerns
» organizations serving individuals with special needs or challenges
» environmental/sustainability organizations
» humanitarian organizations

Nominations will be reviewed and four charities will be chosen by D&D Publishing. In selecting the charities, we will consider the number of nominations received and the alignment of the charity's vision with the criteria above.

If you have any questions about the nomination guidelines or process, feel free to contact us with your questions at info@danddpublishing.com.

ABOUT THE AUTHOR

DR. THERESA NICASSIO IS A REGISTERED PSYCHOLOGIST (#1541) in Vancouver, Canada. She received her PhD in Counseling Psychology from The Ohio State University in 1991. She then worked in the Counseling Center at the University of Nevada, Las Vegas, until she moved to Canada in 1994 to work at the University of British Columbia. While at UBC, Theresa served in a variety of capacities as the senior psychologist and as the Coordinator of Clinical Services and Training; she also served as an adjunct faculty member for the Department of Counselling Psychology in the Faculty of Education. Both at UNLV and UBC, Theresa served as a committee member for masters and doctoral students' thesis defences and comprehensive exams. She has also enjoyed teaching and supervising at the Adler School of Professional Psychology and at Langara College.

Prompted by personal life experiences, the author sought extensive training in various healing modalities. She became a Certified Integrative Energy Healing Practitioner, a Certified Gourmet Raw Food Chef and Instructor and a Certified Advanced Raw Food Nutrition Educator, and has been an avid student of mind-body therapies such as meditation and osteopathic medicine for over 20 years.

Theresa now focuses her energy providing psychotherapy to clients in her private practice in Vancouver. She is a wife, mother, and a health, environmental and humanitarian activist. In addition to working and spending time with her family, Theresa loves immersing herself in nature, meditating and relishing the precious moments that life has to offer.

GRATITUDE & ACKNOWLEDGEMENTS

THE OLD AFRICAN PROVERB SAYS "IT TAKES A village to raise a child." The same can be said of the evolution of this book. The love, generosity and patience of so many in our wonderful community has been truly humbling, and it would take another book to express my appreciation properly. However, I would like to take this opportunity to thank a handful of some of the beautiful people who have played a central role in this book's becoming.

First, my gratitude goes to my dear friend Rho Tuttle and her loving husband, Richard. Thank you for always giving me words of encouragement, not to mention the delicious, authentic Italian recipes that you offered to share with others in this book.

Thank you also Jenny Chapman and Margaret and Larry Moore, for nurturing beautiful life in your gardens and for sharing them for many of the photographs in this book.

Special thanks go to Lovena Galyide of Vancouver's Indigo Raw Food Café, and to gourmet raw food *grande dame* Cherie Soria and her amazing teaching team at the Living Light International Culinary Institute: Vinnette Thompson, Martine Lussier, James Sant, Roe Robertson and Gina Hudson—your culinary expertise and guidance are deeply appreciated. And Drs. Rick and Karin Dina—thank you for sharing your research-grounded information about raw food nutrition. All of you at Living Light have been pivotal in opening up new horizons of possibilities in the creation of nutritious food and reducing toxicity in food preparation. Thank you for being priceless guides through the world of flavour balancing and the art of texture and design in recipe development. Your nurturing has energized me, and I have tremendous gratitude for your endless enthusiasm for pushing the boundaries of conventional (and often misguided) thinking about food.

I also want to thank Haeley Lindau and Joanne Beverley Edwards-Miller for their informative and delightful nutrition notes about real food, and for their positive approach to living with dietary restrictions.

This list would not be complete without also noting the angels who have directly been a part of the design and production of this collection, which has had many lives. *YUM* never would have taken flight without Colleen Byrum's belief that my notes and recipes were diamonds in the rough, nor without Mari Kim's editorial involvement, test-kitchen organizing and data collection. When the journey to publication took an unexpected turn, Sharon Hanna became *YUM*'s new midwife, introducing the manuscript to the loving hands of garden editor Carol Pope, who helped take the book's garden theme and sustainability message to a new level.

Along the way, other gallant souls joined the journey of Team YUM. Makiko Ara's web design and social media team brought the intimidating world of research and analytics to my fingertips. Incalculable thanks are due to my incredible and beloved editor Kilmeny Jane Denny—you've been amazing beyond comprehension! Thanks, too, to other editorial contributors, Janet Love Morrison, Elaine Jones, Lynn Duncan and Martha Bullen. I also want to thank Jack Canfield and Steve Harrison for the many teachings and guidance around writing and publishing books through the Bestseller Blueprint Program, Publishing and Publicity workshop, and other generous offerings. Words cannot express my gratitude for the endless, heartfelt guidance and love of my friend, Kerry Kilmartin, who has been an inspiration since long before *YUM* was even a twinkle in my eye.

Thank you to my designers: Bill Chung, for creating a beautiful cover, and Mauve Pagé for embracing

the interior design with such joy, competence and vision, handling the many complex bits and pieces fearlessly and with an awesome giggle that always seemed to come at just the right moment. Thanks also to Alejandra Aguirre for her amazing energy during the photo shoots and for helping me learn to stretch into new frontiers of body, mind and spirit. And thank you Amelia Chow, for working by Ali's side to help bring me and the lighting for the photos to new heights, and also Jennifer Little for your magical touch in preparing me for the photos.

Finally, I want to thank the other beings who have touched my life and this project and are threads within the fabric of these pages and my very being— extended family members, friends, plants, animals, the bees and other insects. We are all part of one great whole, reflected in the micro and the macro of all that is. Most importantly, I want to thank my forever loving husband, Eric, and our beautiful daughters, Alex and Angeline. No words can ever express the depth of my love for all of you—you are the wind beneath the wings of *YUM*.

RESOURCES FOR LIVING DELICIOUSLY

WELCOME TO THE YUM COMMUNITY! TOGETHER, we can work on our quest to make a difference and to live vibrantly and healthfully.

In addition to the good stuff in this book, my website, www.yumfoodforliving.com, provides resources, recipes, videos, articles, events, inspiration and health information. It also features free gifts and promotions.

New resources are popping up daily for the products and ingredients mentioned in this book. You can find an up-to-date list of vendor and other links on the "Where to Buy" page of the YUM website.

Let me know if you discover any new resources you'd like to offer others or if you want to share your story or exciting new recipes that you unleash in your own kitchen. Feel free to message me or post your experiences on your favourite social media network. Let's connect!

Website: yumfoodforliving.com
Email: info@yumfoodforliving.com
Facebook: AuthorTheresaNicassio
Twitter: @TheresaNicassio

Once you've had the taste of the good life of living passionately and eating outrageously delicious food that genuinely honours and nourishes your body, there's no turning back. Before you know it, the old way of living will simply become a memory of the past.

OTHER RESOURCES

NUTRITION INFORMATION

If you are interested in calculating the nutrition content of the food you eat or of the recipes in this book, check out the USDA National Nutrient Database. It is a free online resource from the USDA Agricultural Research that is available to anyone 24-7 (ndb.nal.usda.gov).

CLEAN PRODUCE INFORMATION

For information about pesticides in foods, check out the online Environmental Working Group resources (www.ewg.com).

CELIAC DISEASE AND GLUTEN SENSITIVITY INFORMATION

For information about the gluten-free diet, celiac disease and gluten sensitivity, see:

Davis, William, MD. *Wheat Belly: Lose the Wheat, Lose the Weight, and Find Your Path Back To Health.* Emmaus, PA: Rodale Books, 2014.

Fasano, Alessio, MD, with Susie Flaherty. *Gluten Freedom: The Nation's Leading Expert Offers the Essential Guide to a Healthy, Gluten-Free Lifestyle.* Hoboken, NJ: Wiley, 2014.

Perlmutter, David, MD, with Kristin Loberg. *Grain Brain: The Surprising Truth about Wheat, Carbs, and Sugar — Your Brain's Silent Killers.* New York, NY: Little, Brown and Company, 2013.

Shepard, Jules E. Dowler. *The First Year: Celiac Disease & Living Gluten-Free: An Essential Guide for the Newly Diagnosed.* Boston, MA: DaCapo Lifelong Books, 2008

BEES AND THE ENVIRONMENT

Dogterom, Margriet, PhD. *Pollination with Mason Bees: A Gardener's Guide to Managing Mason Bees for Fruit Production.* Coquitlam, BC: Beediverse Publishing, 2009

Hanna, Sharon, and Carol Pope. *The Book of Kale and Friends: 14 Easy-to-Grow Superfoods with 130+ Recipes.* Madeira Park, BC: Douglas & McIntyre, 2014

Von Frisch, Karl and Leigh Chadwick (trans). *The Dance Language and Orientation of Bees.* Cambridge, MA: Harvard University Press, 1967

JOURNALS:

Di Prisco, G. et al. "Neonicotinoid clothianidin adversely affects insect immunity and promotes replication of a viral pathogen in honey bees," *Proceedings of the National Academy of Sciences of the United States of America* 110, No. 46 (2013): 18466

Gill, R. J. et al. "Combined pesticide exposure severely affects individual- and colony-level traits in bees." *Nature* 491 (2012): 105

Hallman, C. A. et al. "Declines in insectivorous birds are associated with high neonicotinoid concentrations." *Nature* 511 (2014): 341

Henry, Mickaël, et al. "A common pesticide decreases foraging success and survival in honey bees." *Science* 336 (2012): 348

Whitehorn, Penelope R. et al. "Neonicotinoid pesticide reduces bumble bee colony growth and queen production." *Science* 336 (2012): 351

Williamson, Sally M., and Geraldine A. Wright. "Exposure to multiple cholinergic pesticides impairs olfactory learning and memory in honeybees." *The Journal of Experimental Biology* 216 (2013): 1799

RECOMMENDED READING

Amen, Daniel G., MD. *Magnificent Mind at Any Age: Natural Ways to Unleash Your Brain's Maximum Potential.* New York, NY: Three Rivers Press, 2009

Boyd, David, PhD. *Dodging the Toxic Bullet: How to Protect Yourself from Everday Environmental Health Hazards.* Vancouver, BC: Greystone Books, 2010

Brach, Tara, PhD. *Radical Acceptance: Embracing Your Life with the Heart of a Buddha.* New York, NY: Bantam, 2004

Bremness, Lesley. *The Complete Book of Herbs: A Practical Guide to Growing and Using Herbs.* New York, NY: Viking Studio Books, 1988

Campbell, T. Colin, PhD, and Thomas Campbell II, MD. *The China Study: The Most Comprehensive Study of Nutrition Ever Conducted and the Startling Implications for Diet, Weight Loss, and Long-term Health.* Dallas, TX: BenBella Books, 2006

Carr, Kris. *Crazy Sexy Diet: Eat Your Veggies, Ignite Your Spark, and Live Like You Mean It.* Guildford, CT: Skirt!, 2011

Carr, Kris. *Crazy Sexy Cancer Tips.* Guildford, CT: Skirt!, 2007

Carr, Kris, with Chef Chad Sarno. *Crazy Sexy Kitchen: 150 Plant-Empowered Recipes to Ignite a Mouthwatering Revolution.* New York, NY: Hay House, 2014

Daniluk, Julie, RHN. *Meals That Heal Inflammation: Embrace Healthy Living and Eliminate Pain, One Meal at a Time*. New York, NY: Hay House, 2012

Dog, Tieraona Low, MD. *Life Is Your Best Medicine: A Woman's Guide to Health, Healing, and Wholeness at Every Age*. Washington, DC: National Geographic, 2014

Fuhrman, Joel, MD. *Eat to Live: The Amazing Nutrient-Rich Program for Fast and Sustained Weight Loss*. New York, NY: Little Brown and Company, 2011

Hanna, Sharon. *The Book of Kale: The Easy-to-Grow Superfood 80+ Recipes*. Madeira Park, BC: Harbour Publishing, 2012

Hansen, Rick, PhD. *Hardwiring Happiness: The New Brain Science of Contentment, Calm, and Confidence*. New York, NY: Harmony, 2013

Hyman, Mark, MD. *The Blood Sugar Solution: The UltraHealthy Program for Losing Weight, Preventing Disease, and Feeling Great Now*. New York, NY: Little, Brown and Company, 2014

Kabat-Zinn, Jon. *Coming to Our Senses: Healing Ourselves and the World Through Mindfulness*. New York, NY: Hyperion, 2005

Lindlahr, Victor H. *You Are What You Eat*. National Nutrition Society, 1940

Lipton, Bruce H., PhD. *The Biology of Belief: Unleashing the Power of Consciousness, Matter, and Miracles*. New York, NY: Hay House, 2007

May, Rollo. *The Courage to Create*. New York, NY: W. W. Norton & Company, 1994

Pipher, Mary. *The Green Boat: Reviving Ourselves in Our Capsized Culture*. New York, NY: Riverhead Books, 2013

Remen, Rachel Naomi, MD. *Kitchen Table Wisdom*. New York, NY: Riverhead Books, 1996

Siegel, Daniel J. *The Mindful Brain: Reflection and Attunement in the Cultivation of Well-Being*. New York, NY: W. W. Norton & Company, 2007

Siegel, Daniel J., MD. *Mindsight: The New Science of Personal Transformation*. New York, NY: Bantam, 2010

Silverstone, Alicia. *The Kind Diet: A Simple Guide to Feeling Great, Losing Weight, and Saving the Planet*. Emmaus, PA: Rodale Books, 2009

Soria, Cherie, Brenda Davis, RD, and Vesanto Melina, MS, RD. *The Raw Food Revolution Diet*. Summertown, TN: Healthy Living Publications, 2008

Stone, Gene (ed). *Fork Over Knives: The Plant-Based Way to Health*. New York, NY: The Experiment, 2011

Turner, Natasha, Dr. *The Hormone Diet: A 3-Step Program to Help You Lose Weight, Gain Strength, and Live Younger Longer*. Emmaus, PA: Rodale Books, 2011

SPECIAL DIET & ALLERGY CHART

RECIPES	PAGE	GLUTEN-FREE	WHEAT-FREE	DAIRY-FREE	EGG-FREE	MEAT-FREE	POTATO-FREE	SUGAR-FREE	NUT-FREE	SEED-FREE	SOY-FREE	CORN-FREE	GRAIN-FREE	CITRUS-FREE	NIGHTSHADE-FREE	CAFFEINE-FREE	BEAN- & LENTIL-FREE	RAW OR MOSTLY RAW	COOKED	RAW-INFUSED
POUR ME A STIFF ONE—HOT & COLD BEVERAGES																				
Angeline's Favourite Hot Chocolate	38	X	X	X	X	X	X		X	X	X	X	X	X	X		X		X	
Alex's Chai Latte	40	X	X	X	X	X	X	X		X	X	X	X	X	X	X	X			
Dandelion Tea	40	X	X	X	X	X	X	X	X	X	X	X	X	X	X	X	X		X	
Mint & Lavender Tea	41	X	X	X	X	X	X	X	X	X	X	X	X	X	X	X	X			
Carrot Blossom Tea	45	X	X	X	X	X	X	X	X	X	X	X	X	X	X	X	X			
Berry Punch Slushy	46	X	X	X	X	X	X	X	X	X	X	X	X		X	X	X	X		
Lemonade	48	X	X	X	X	X	X	X	X	X	X	X	X		X	X	X	X		
Classic Raw Green Juice	49	X	X	X	X	X	X	X	X	X	X	X	X		X	X	X	X		
Milks																				
Raw Nut Milk	50	X	X	X	X	X	X	X		X	X	X	X	X	X	X	X	X		
Raw Hemp Seed Milk	52	X	X	X	X	X	X	X	X		X	X	X	X	X	X	X	X		
Raw Flax Seed Milk	52	X	X	X	X	X	X	X	X		X	X	X	X	X	X	X	X		
Raw Coconut Milk	53	X	X	X	X	X	X	X	X	X	X	X	X	X	X	X	X	X		
Quinoa Milk	53	X	X	X	X	X	X	X	X	X	X	X		X	X	X	X		X	
Sweet Milk Variations	53																			
Vanilla Milk	53	X	X	X	X	X	X	X	X	X	X	X	X	X	X	X	X		X	
Chocolate Milk	53	X	X	X	X	X	X	X	X	X	X	X	X	X	X		X	X	X	
Strawberry Milk	53	X	X	X	X	X	X	X	X	X	X	X	X	X	X	X	X			X
Caramel Milk	53	X	X	X	X	X	X	X	X	X	X	X	X	X	X	X	X		X	
Smoothies																				
Peach Banana Green Smoothie	55	X	X	X	X	X	X	X	X	X	X	X	X	X	X	X	X	X		
Pineapple Banana Hemp Smoothie	55	X	X	X	X	X	X	X	X		X	X	X		X	X	X	X		
Orange Banana Green Smoothie	56	X	X	X	X	X	X	X	X	X	X	X	X		X	X	X	X		

RECIPES	PAGE	GLUTEN-FREE	WHEAT-FREE	DAIRY-FREE	EGG-FREE	MEAT-FREE	POTATO-FREE	SUGAR-FREE	NUT-FREE	SEED-FREE	SOY-FREE	CORN-FREE	GRAIN-FREE	CITRUS-FREE	NIGHTSHADE-FREE	CAFFEINE-FREE	BEAN- & LENTIL-FREE	RAW OR MOSTLY RAW	COOKED	RAW-INFUSED
Chocolate Banana Smoothie	56	X	X	X	X	X	X	X		X	X	X	X	X	X		X	X		
Strawberry Cheesecake Smoothie	57	X	X	X	X	X	X	X		X	X	X	X	X	X	X	X	X		
Sunrise Sensation Omega Smoothie	57	X	X	X	X	X	X	X	X		X	X	X	X	X	X	X	X		
MORNING GRUB																				
Flax & Chia Raw Power Breakfast	60	X	X	X	X	X	X	X	X		X	X	X	X	X	X	X	X		
Superfood Raw Breakfast Cereal	62	X	X	X	X	X	X	X			X	X		X	X	X	X	X		
Apple Cinnamon Granola	63	X	X	X	X	X	X	X		X	X	X		X	X	X	X			X
Mango Banana Granola	66	X	X	X	X	X	X	X		X	X	X		X	X	X	X			X
Granola Bars	66	X	X	X	X	X	X	X		X	X	X		X	X	X	X			X
Kilmeny's Fruity Orange Breakfast Quinoa	67	X	X	X	X	X	X	X	X		X	X			X	X	X		X	
Rise & Shine Instant Hot Breakfast Cereal	69	X	X	X	X	X	X	X			X	X	X	X	X	X	X			X
Savoury Onion Herb Pancakes	70	X	X	X	X	X	X	X	X	X	X	X		X	X	X	X		X	
Old-Fashioned Pancakes	72	X	X	X	X	X	X	X	X	X	X	X		X	X	X	X		X	
Jane's Korean Zucchini Pancakes	73	X	X	X	X	X	X	X	X	X	X	X		X	X	X	X		X	
Herb-Infused Breakfast Sausage	75	X	X	X	X	X	X	X		X	X	X	X		X	X	X	X	X	
Breakfast Scramble	76	X	X	X	X	X	X	X	X	X		X	X	X		X	X		X	
Peach Rhubarb Compote	79	X	X	X	X	X	X	X	X	X	X	X	X	X	X	X	X		X	
Instant Raw Applesauce	80	X	X	X	X	X	X	X	X	X	X	X	X	X	X	X	X	X		

RECIPES	PAGE	GLUTEN-FREE	WHEAT-FREE	DAIRY-FREE	EGG-FREE	MEAT-FREE	POTATO-FREE	SUGAR-FREE	NUT-FREE	SEED-FREE	SOY-FREE	CORN-FREE	GRAIN-FREE	CITRUS-FREE	NIGHTSHADE-FREE	CAFFEINE-FREE	BEAN- & LENTIL-FREE	RAW OR MOSTLY RAW	COOKED	RAW-INFUSED
GETTING FRESH—SALADS & DRESSINGS																				
Raw Kale & Avocado Salad	84	X	X	X	X	X	X	X	X		X	X	X	X	X	X	X	X		
Dandelion Quinoa Salad	87	X	X	X	X	X	X	X	X		X	X				X	X	X		X
Pachamama Salad	88	X	X	X	X	X	X	X	X			X	X	X		X	X	X		
Beet & Cilantro Salad	91	X	X	X	X	X	X	X	X	X	X	X	X			X	X			X
Asian Coleslaw with Kale	92	X	X	X	X	X	X	X			X	X	X	X	X	X	X	X		
Rainbow Quinoa Basil & Pepper Salad	95	X	X	X	X	X	X	X	X	X	X	X				X	X			X
Lentil Salad	97	X	X	X	X	X	X	X	X	X	X	X	X	X		X				X
Tabbouleh with Mint & Cilantro	98	X	X	X	X	X	X	X	X	X	X	X	X			X	X	X		X
Cumin Vinaigrette	102	X	X	X	X	X	X	X	X	X	X	X	X		X	X	X	X		
Spicy Asian Dressing	102	X	X	X	X	X	X	X			X	X	X	X	X	X	X	X		X
Lemonette Dressing	103	X	X	X	X	X	X	X	X	X	X	X	X		X	X	X	X		
Italian Vinaigrette Dressing	103	X	X	X	X	X	X	X	X	X	X	X	X	X	X	X	X	X		
LIFE'S A BOWL OF SOUP!																				
Cheesy Broccoli Soup	106	X	X	X	X	X	X	X												
Creamy Carrot & Ginger Soup	109	X	X	X	X	X	X	X	X	X	X	X	X		X	X	X		X	
Creamy Cucumber & Sorrel Soup	110	X	X	X	X	X	X	X	X	X	X	X	X	X	X	X	X	X		X
Lovage, Leek & Kale Soup	113	X	X	X	X	X	X	X	X	X	X	X	X		X	X	X			X
Rosemary- Infused Cream of Mushroom Soup	114	X	X	X	X	X	X	X	X	X	X	X	X	X	X	X	X			X
Fennel & Tomato Soup	115	X	X	X	X	X	X	X	X	X	X	X	X	X			X	X		X
Roasted Red Pepper & Tomato Cream Soup	116	X	X	X	X	X	X	X	X	X	X	X	X	X			X	X		X

RECIPES	PAGE	GLUTEN-FREE	WHEAT-FREE	DAIRY-FREE	EGG-FREE	MEAT-FREE	POTATO-FREE	SUGAR-FREE	NUT-FREE	SEED-FREE	SOY-FREE	CORN-FREE	GRAIN-FREE	CITRUS-FREE	NIGHTSHADE-FREE	CAFFEINE-FREE	BEAN- & LENTIL-FREE	RAW OR MOSTLY RAW	COOKED	RAW-INFUSED
Spicy Thai Lemongrass Soup	119	X	X	X	X	X	X	X		X	X	X	X			X				X
Italian Wedding Soup	120	X	X	X	X	X	X	X		X	X	X	X		X	X	X		X	
Instant Minestrone Soup Mix	123	X	X	X	X	X	X	X	X	X	X	X	X	X		X	X	X		
LIVING ON THE EDGE—SIDES & APPETIZERS																				
Apricot Basil Appetizer Stacks	126	X	X	X	X	X	X	X	X	X	X	X	X	X	X	X	X			X
Basil-Wrapped Stuffed Dates	129	X	X	X	X	X	X	X	X	X	X	X	X	X	X	X	X	X		
Cheesy Tofu Cubes	130	X	X	X	X	X	X	X	X	X		X	X	X	X				X	
Rho's Giardiniera Pickled Vegetables	132	X	X	X	X	X	X	X	X	X	X	X	X	X	X	X	X		X	
Carrot & Cabbage Probiotic Sauerkraut	135	X	X	X	X	X	X	X	X	X	X	X	X	X	X	X	X	X		
Rho's Garlic-Marinated Mushrooms	136	X	X	X	X	X	X	X	X	X	X	X	X	X	X				X	
Spicy Pickled Okra	138	X	X	X	X	X	X	X	X	X	X	X	X	X		X	X		X	
Spicy Pickled Kale Seed Pods	139	X	X	X	X	X	X	X	X	X	X	X	X	X		X	X		X	
Cheesy Italian Herb Tomatoes	143	X	X	X	X	X	X	X	X	X	X	X	X			X	X	X		
Italian Stuffed Artichokes	144	X	X	X	X	X	X	X		X	X	X	X	X	X		X		X	
Pimento Cheese Stuffed Mushroom Caps	146	X	X	X	X	X	X	X			X	X	X	X		X	X		X	
Italian Zucchini & Onions	149	X	X	X	X	X	X	X	X	X	X	X	X			X	X	X	X	
Cheesy Baked Broccoli & Cauliflower	150	X	X	X	X	X	X	X	X	X	X	X	X	X	X	X	X		X	
Stuffed Grape Leaves (Dolmas)	153	X	X	X	X	X	X	X	X	X	X	X	X			X	X	X	X	
Garlic-Infused Polenta	155	X	X	X	X	X	X	X	X	X	X	X	X		X	X	X		X	

RECIPES	PAGE	GLUTEN-FREE	WHEAT-FREE	DAIRY-FREE	EGG-FREE	MEAT-FREE	POTATO-FREE	SUGAR-FREE	NUT-FREE	SEED-FREE	SOY-FREE	CORN-FREE	GRAIN-FREE	CITRUS-FREE	NIGHTSHADE-FREE	CAFFEINE-FREE	BEAN- & LENTIL-FREE	RAW OR MOSTLY RAW	COOKED	RAW-INFUSED
Portobello Quinoa	156	X	X	X	X	X	X	X	X	X	X	X		X	X	X	X		X	
Mashed No Potatoes	157	X	X	X	X	X	X	X	X	X	X	X	X		X	X			X	
Sweet Potato Fries	158	X	X	X	X	X	X	X	X	X	X	X	X	X	X	X	X		X	
The Ultra-Basics																				
Basic Cooked Quinoa	160	X	X	X	X	X	X	X	X	X	X	X		X	X	X	X		X	
Quinoa Rice	161	X	X	X	X	X	X	X	X	X	X	X		X	X	X	X		X	
Lentils	161	X	X	X	X	X	X	X	X	X	X	X	X	X	X	X			X	
Quick-Cook Lima Beans	162	X	X	X	X	X	X	X	X	X	X	X	X	X	X	X			X	
Roasted Garlic	163	X	X	X	X	X	X	X	X	X	X	X	X	X	X	X	X		X	
Cauliflower Rice	163	X	X	X	X	X	X	X	X	X	X	X	X	X	X	X	X	X		
CHOW TIME! MAIN DISHES																				
Best No-Meat Meat	166	X	X	X	X	X	X	X		X		X	X		X	X	X	X	X	
Meatless Ground	167	X	X	X	X	X	X	X		X	X	X	X		X	X	X	X	X	
Meatless Taco Ground	167	X	X	X	X	X	X	X		X	X	X	X		X	X		X	X	
Best Veggie Burgers	169	X	X	X	X	X	X	X		X	X	X	X		X	X	X	X	X	
Veggie Meatballs	169	X	X	X	X	X	X	X		X	X	X	X		X	X	X	X	X	
Shepherd's Pie	170	X	X	X	X	X	X	X		X	X	X	X			X			X	
Cajun Sausage Jambalaya	172	X	X	X	X	X	X	X		X	X				X	X	X	X	X	
Cajun Spice Mix	174	X	X	X	X	X	X	X	X	X	X	X	X	X		X	X	X		
Spaghetti & Veggie Meatballs	175	X	X	X	X	X	X	X		X	X	X	X		X	X	X		X	X
Raw Zucchini "Pasta" with Creamy Sunflower Seed Sauce	177	X	X	X	X	X	X	X	X		X	X	X		X	X	X	X		X
Mac 'n' Cheese	178	X	X	X	X	X	X	X	X	X	X	X	X		X	X	X		X	
Eggplant Parmesan	181	X	X	X	X	X	X	X	X	X	X	X	X		X	X	X		X	
Curried Cauliflower & Chickpea Stew	182	X	X	X	X	X	X	X	X	X	X	X	X	X		X			X	
Raw Curry Paste	182	X	X	X	X	X	X	X	X	X	X	X	X	X		X	X	X		

RECIPES	PAGE	GLUTEN-FREE	WHEAT-FREE	DAIRY-FREE	EGG-FREE	MEAT-FREE	POTATO-FREE	SUGAR-FREE	NUT-FREE	SEED-FREE	SOY-FREE	CORN-FREE	GRAIN-FREE	CITRUS-FREE	NIGHTSHADE-FREE	CAFFEINE-FREE	BEAN- & LENTIL-FREE	RAW OR MOSTLY RAW	COOKED	RAW-INFUSED
Eric's Famous Chili	184	X	X	X	X	X	X	X	X	X		X	X	X		X			X	
Cabbage Rolls	186	X	X	X	X	X	X	X	X	X	X	X		X		X	X		X	
Classic Margherita Tortilla Pizza	187	X	X	X	X	X	X	X	X	X	X	X		X		X	X		X	
Polenta Pizza	190	X	X	X	X	X	X	X	X	X	X			X	X	X	X		X	
Crustless Cheesy Broccoli Quiche	193	X	X	X	X	X	X	X	X	X		X	X	X	X	X	X		X	
Alex's Tahini Kale with Tofu	194	X	X	X	X	X	X	X	X			X	X	X	X	X	X		X	
Pad Thai	197	X	X	X	X	X	X	X	X	X		X	X			X	X			X
Alex's Tahini Sauce	198	X	X	X	X	X	X	X	X		X	X	X	X	X	X	X	X		
Raw Pad Thai Sauce	199	X	X	X	X	X	X	X	X	X	X	X	X			X	X	X		
Sesame Cabbage Stir-Fry	200	X	X	X	X	X	X	X	X		X	X	X	X	X	X	X		X	
Teriyaki Udon Stir-Fry	203	X	X	X	X	X	X	X	X			X	X	X	X	X	X			X
Spicy Szechuan Eggplant	204	X	X	X	X	X	X	X			X	X	X	X		X	X		X	
Stuffed Portobello Mushrooms	207	X	X	X	X	X	X	X	X	X	X	X	X	X	X	X	X		X	
Raw Corn & Avocado Lettuce Boats	208	X	X	X	X	X	X	X	X	X	X			X	X	X	X	X		
Cheesy Bean & Kale Quesadillas	211	X	X	X	X	X	X	X	X	X	X	X		X	X	X			X	X
Tacos	212	X	X	X	X	X	X	X	X	X	X	X	X	X		X	X			X
Black Bean & Kale Cheesy Enchiladas	213	X	X	X	X	X	X	X	X	X	X	X		X		X			X	X
Enchilada Sauce	213	X	X	X	X	X	X	X	X	X	X	X		X			X			X
Stuffed Bell Peppers	214	X	X	X	X	X	X	X		X	X	X				X	X		X	
Nori Rice Paper Wraps	217	X	X	X	X	X	X	X	X	X	X	X		X	X	X	X	X		X
Collard Wraps	218	X	X	X	X	X	X	X	X	X	X	X	X	X	X	X	X	X		X
Kale & Bean Collard Wrap	218	X	X	X	X	X	X	X			X	X	X		X	X				X

RECIPES	PAGE	GLUTEN-FREE	WHEAT-FREE	DAIRY-FREE	EGG-FREE	MEAT-FREE	POTATO-FREE	SUGAR-FREE	NUT-FREE	SEED-FREE	SOY-FREE	CORN-FREE	GRAIN-FREE	CITRUS-FREE	NIGHTSHADE-FREE	CAFFEINE-FREE	BEAN- & LENTIL-FREE	RAW OR MOSTLY RAW	COOKED	RAW-INFUSED
Vietnamese Spring Rolls	221	X	X	X	X	X	X	X		X	X	X	X	X	X	X	X			X
FOR THE MUNCHIES—CHIPS, DIPS & SAVOURY SNACKS																				
Quick Kale Chips	224	X	X	X	X	X	X	X	X	X	X	X	X	X	X	X	X		X	
Deluxe Kale Chips	225	X	X	X	X	X	X	X	X		X	X	X		X	X	X	X		
Crunchy Chickpeas	228	X	X	X	X	X	X	X	X	X	X	X	X	X	X	X			X	
Baked Eggplant Rounds	231	X	X	X	X	X	X	X	X	X	X	X	X	X		X	X		X	
Vegetable Flax Crackers	232	X	X	X	X	X	X	X	X		X	X			X	X	X	X		
Chia Chips	235	X	X	X	X	X	X	X	X		X	X	X	X		X	X	X		
Nachos	236	X	X	X	X	X	X	X		X	X	X			X	X	X		X	X
Salsa	237	X	X	X	X	X	X	X	X	X	X	X	X			X	X	X		
Guacamole with Cilantro & Basil	238	X	X	X	X	X	X	X	X	X	X	X	X			X	X	X		
Hummus	241	X	X	X	X	X	X	X	X		X	X	X		X	X				X
Cheesy Pimento Dip	242	X	X	X	X	X	X	X		X	X	X	X			X	X	X		
Raw Sweet & Savoury Trail Mix	245	X	X	X	X	X	X	X			X	X	X	X	X	X	X	X		
PURE DECADENCE—DESSERTS																				
Fresh Figs	249	X	X	X	X	X	X	X	X	X	X	X	X	X	X	X	X	X		
Baked Cinnamon Plantains	249	X	X	X	X	X	X	X	X	X	X	X	X	X	X	X	X		X	
Baked Apples with Pecan Crumble Topping	250	X	X	X	X	X	X	X		X	X	X	X	X	X	X	X		X	
Pecan Crumble Topping	250	X	X	X	X	X	X	X		X	X	X	X	X	X	X	X		X	
Blueberry Crumble	253	X	X	X	X	X	X	X	X	X	X	X		X	X	X	X		X	
Juice Jelly	254	X	X	X	X	X	X	X	X	X	X	X	X	X	X	X	X	X		
Strawberry Jelly	257	X	X	X	X	X	X	X	X	X	X	X			X	X	X	X		
No-Bake Pumpkin Pie	258	X	X	X	X	X	X	X	X	X	X	X	X	X	X	X	X		X	
No-Pumpkin Pumpkin Pie	260	X	X	X	X	X	X	X			X	X	X	X	X	X	X			X

RECIPES	PAGE	GLUTEN-FREE	WHEAT-FREE	DAIRY-FREE	EGG-FREE	MEAT-FREE	POTATO-FREE	SUGAR-FREE	NUT-FREE	SEED-FREE	SOY-FREE	CORN-FREE	GRAIN-FREE	CITRUS-FREE	NIGHTSHADE-FREE	CAFFEINE-FREE	BEAN- & LENTIL-FREE	RAW OR MOSTLY RAW	COOKED	RAW-INFUSED
Extra-Creamy Pumpkin Pudding	261	X	X	X	X	X	X	X	X	X	X	X	X	X	X	X	X		X	
Zucchini Carrot Crumb Cake	263	X	X	X	X	X	X	X		X	X	X			X	X	X		X	
Walnut Crumble Topping	263	X	X	X	X	X	X	X		X	X	X	X		X	X	X	X		
Shortbread Pie Crust	264	X	X	X	X	X	X	X	X	X	X	X			X	X	X		X	
Raw Pineapple Banana Dream Pies	265	X	X	X	X	X	X	X		X	X	X	X		X	X	X	X		
Fudge Lava Cake	266	X	X	X	X	X	X	X	X	X	X	X		X	X				X	
Lemon Cupcakes	268	X	X	X	X	X	X	X	X	X	X	X			X	X	X		X	
Chocolate Cupcakes	269	X	X	X	X	X	X	X	X	X	X	X			X	X	X		X	
Buttercream Frostings																				
Coconut Vanilla Buttercream Frosting	272	X	X	X	X	X	X	X	X	X	X	X	X	X	X	X	X			X
Lemon Buttercream Frosting	272	X	X	X	X	X	X	X	X	X	X	X	X		X	X	X			X
Peanut Butter Buttercream Frosting	273	X	X	X	X	X	X	X		X	X	X	X	X	X	X	X			X
Light Chocolate Buttercream Frosting	273	X	X	X	X	X	X	X	X	X	X	X	X	X	X		X			X
Ice Cream																				
Vanilla Coconut Ice Cream	275	X	X	X	X	X	X	X	X	X	X	X	X	X	X	X	X			X
Raw Vanilla Ice Cream	275	X	X	X	X	X	X	X		X	X	X	X	X	X	X	X	X		
Butter Pecan Ice Cream	276	X	X	X	X	X	X	X		X	X	X	X	X	X	X	X	X		
Strawberry Vanilla Ice Cream	276	X	X	X	X	X	X	X	X	X	X	X	X	X	X	X	X	X		X
Salted Caramel Swirl Ice Cream	276	X	X	X	X	X	X	X	X	X	X	X	X	X	X	X	X			X

RECIPES	PAGE	GLUTEN-FREE	WHEAT-FREE	DAIRY-FREE	EGG-FREE	MEAT-FREE	POTATO-FREE	SUGAR-FREE	NUT-FREE	SEED-FREE	SOY-FREE	CORN-FREE	GRAIN-FREE	CITRUS-FREE	NIGHTSHADE-FREE	CAFFEINE-FREE	BEAN- & LENTIL-FREE	RAW OR MOSTLY RAW	COOKED	RAW-INFUSED
Peanut Butter Chocolate Coconut Ice Cream	278	X	X	X	X	X	X	X		X	X	X	X	X	X		X			X
Piña Colada Ice Cream	278	X	X	X	X	X	X	X	X		X	X	X			X	X			X
Chocoholic's Chunky Delight Raw Ice Cream	279	X	X	X	X	X	X	X		X	X	X	X		X		X	X		
Instant Banana Raw Ice Cream	280	X	X	X	X	X	X	X	X	X	X	X	X	X	X	X	X	X		
Instant Banana Ice Cream Variations																				
Fruity-Banana Ice Cream	281	X	X	X	X	X	X	X	X	X	X	X	X	X	X	X				
Chocolate-Banana Ice Cream	281	X	X	X	X	X	X	X	X	X	X	X	X	X	X		X	X		
Nuts & Nibs Banana Ice Cream	281	X	X	X	X	X	X	X		X	X	X	X	X	X		X	X		
Chocolate Peanut Butter Banana Ice Cream	281	X	X	X	X	X	X	X		X	X	X	X	X	X		X	X		
Ice Cream Sandwiches	282	X	X	X	X	X	X	X	X	X	X	X		X	X	X	X		X	X
Instant Raspberry Sherbet	285	X	X	X	X	X	X	X	X	X	X	X	X		X	X	X			X
SWEET TREATS																				
Gingersnaps	288	X	X	X	X	X	X	X	X	X	X	X		X	X	X	X		X	
Snickerdoodles	291	X	X	X	X	X	X	X	X	X	X	X		X	X	X	X		X	
Shortbread Cookies	292	X	X	X	X	X	X	X	X	X	X	X		X	X	X	X		X	
Light Lemon Cookies	295	X	X	X	X	X	X	X		X	X	X	X		X	X	X		X	
Old-Fashioned Chocolate Chip Cookies	296	X	X	X	X	X	X	X	X	X	X	X		X	X		X		X	
Peanut Butter Cookies	299	X	X	X	X	X	X	X		X	X	X		X	X	X	X		X	
Peanut Butter Cookie Sandwiches	300	X	X	X	X	X	X	X		X	X	X		X	X		X		X	X

RECIPES	PAGE	GLUTEN-FREE	WHEAT-FREE	DAIRY-FREE	EGG-FREE	MEAT-FREE	POTATO-FREE	SUGAR-FREE	NUT-FREE	SEED-FREE	SOY-FREE	CORN-FREE	GRAIN-FREE	CITRUS-FREE	NIGHTSHADE-FREE	CAFFEINE-FREE	BEAN- & LENTIL-FREE	RAW OR MOSTLY RAW	COOKED	RAW-INFUSED
Pecan Date Butterball Raw Cookies	303	X	X	X	X	X	X	X			X	X	X	X	X	X	X	X		
Raw Lemon Carob Truffles	304	X	X	X	X	X	X	X		X	X	X	X	X	X	X	X	X		
Caramel Popcorn Balls	307	X	X	X	X	X	X	X	X	X	X			X	X	X	X		X	
Kracker Jacks	307	X	X	X	X	X	X	X		X	X			X	X	X	X		X	
Peanut Butter Coconut Candy Melts	308	X	X	X	X	X	X	X		X	X	X	X	X	X	X	X	X		
Chocolate Covered Peanut Butter Cups	308	X	X	X	X	X	X	X		X	X	X	X	X	X		X	X		
Truffles	311	X	X	X	X	X	X	X	X	X	X	X	X	X	X		X			X
Fudge	311	X	X	X	X	X	X	X		X	X	X	X	X	X		X			X
ESSENTIAL EXTRAS																				
Raw Parmesan	314	X	X	X	X	X	X	X		X	X	X	X	X	X	X	X	X		
Nut-Free Raw Parmesan	314	X	X	X	X	X	X	X	X		X	X	X	X	X	X	X	X		
Plain Croutons & Breadcrumbs	315	X	X	X	X	X	X	X	X	X	X	X		X	X	X	X		X	
Spicy Breadcrumbs	315	X	X	X	X	X	X	X		X	X	X		X		X	X		X	
Herbed Croutons	316	X	X	X	X	X	X	X	X	X	X	X		X	X	X	X		X	
Raw Pesto	316	X	X	X	X	X	X	X			X	X	X		X	X	X	X		
Creamy Sunflower Seed Sauce	318	X	X	X	X	X	X	X	X		X	X	X		X	X	X	X		
Raw Hoisin Sauce	318	X	X	X	X	X	X	X		X	X	X	X	X	X	X	X	X		
Italian Seasoning	319	X	X	X	X	X	X	X	X	X	X	X	X	X	X	X	X	X		
Tomato Sauce	319	X	X	X	X	X	X	X	X	X	X	X	X	X			X			X
Marinara Sauce	322	X	X	X	X	X	X	X	X	X	X	X	X			X	X	X	X	
Ketchup	322	X	X	X	X	X	X	X	X	X	X	X	X	X		X	X			X
Spicy Barbeque Sauce	323	X	X	X	X	X	X	X	X	X	X	X	X	X		X	X			X
Creamy Hot Mustard	323	X	X	X	X	X	X	X		X	X	X	X		X	X	X	X		
Chicory Root Inulin with Stevia	324	X	X	X	X	X	X	X												

RECIPES	PAGE	GLUTEN-FREE	WHEAT-FREE	DAIRY-FREE	EGG-FREE	MEAT-FREE	POTATO-FREE	SUGAR-FREE	NUT-FREE	SEED-FREE	SOY-FREE	CORN-FREE	GRAIN-FREE	CITRUS-FREE	NIGHTSHADE-FREE	CAFFEINE-FREE	BEAN- & LENTIL-FREE	RAW OR MOSTLY RAW	COOKED	RAW-INFUSED
Basic Raw Crust	325	X	X	X	X	X	X	X		X	X	X	X	X	X	X	X	X		
Orange Cranberry Sauce	327	X	X	X	X	X	X	X	X	X	X	X	X		X	X	X		X	
Caramel Sauce	328	X	X	X	X	X	X	X	X	X	X	X	X	X	X		X		X	
Chocolate Sauce	328	X	X	X	X	X	X	X	X	X	X	X	X	X	X		X		X	
Coconut Whipped Cream	329	X	X	X	X	X	X	X	X	X	X	X	X	X	X	X	X			X

CONVERSION CHARTS

VOLUME

¼ tsp	1 mL
½ tsp	2.5 mL
1 tsp	5 mL
1½ tsp	7.5 mL
2 tsp	10 mL
1 Tbsp	15 mL
1½ Tbsp	22.5 mL
2 Tbsp	30 mL
¼ cup	60 mL
⅓ cup	80 mL
½ cup	125 mL
⅔ cup	160 mL
¾ cup	185 mL
1 cup	250 mL
1¼ cups	310 mL
1⅓ cups	330 mL
1½ cups	375 mL
1¾ cups	435 mL

WEIGHT

1 oz	30 g
2 oz	60 g
3 oz	100 g
4 oz	125 g
5 oz	175 g
6 oz	200 g
8 oz	225 g
9 oz	250 g
10 oz	300 g
12 oz	350 g
1 lb	454 g
1½ lb	750 g

LENGTH

¼ inch	6 mm
½ inch	1 cm
1 inch	2.5 cm
2 inches	5 cm
3 inches	8 cm
4 inches	10 cm
6 inches	15 cm
8 inches	20 cm

TEMPERATURE

275°F	140°C
300°F	150°C
325°F	170°C
350°F	180°C
375°F	190°C
400°F	200°C
425°F	220°C
450°F	230°C

INDEX